Gates County North Carolina

Court Minutes

- 1779-1793

(2 Volumes in 1)

By:
Marilyn Poe Laird, Vivian Poe Jackson
& Judith Krause Reid

Southern Historical Press, Inc.
Greenville, South Carolina

This volume was reproduced from
Personal copies located in the
Publisher's private Library

All rights reserved. No part of this publication may be reproduced,
stored in a retrieval system, transmitted in any form, posted
on to the web in any form or by any means without
the prior written permission of the publisher.

Please direct all correspondence and orders to:
www.southernhistoricalpress.com
or
**SOUTHERN HISTORICAL PRESS, Inc.
PO Box 1267
375 West Broad Street
Greenville, SC   29601**
southernhistoricalpress@gmail.com

Originally published: Dolton, IL
ISBN #0-89308-151-5
All rights Reserved.
Printed in the United States of America

Gates County was formed in 1778 from Chowan and Hertford Counties, North Carolina. The County Court Minutes of Gates County start Monday May 3rd. 1779 and are contained in this first volume.

An attempt has been made to include all names and pertinent information contained in these Court Minutes.

The spelling of <u>all</u> words, including names, has been followed as nearly as possible, however, a work such as this is subject to many erros of oversight, omission and mis-spelling.

A Surname Index has been provided, however, a name may appear more than once on a given page which is not indicated in the Index.

In providing this volume of Court Minutes we sincerely hope we have been of some help to those interested in the history of North Carolina, but even more so to those interested in searching for an Ancestor that may have once resided in Gates County.

Marilyn Poe Laird
Vivian Poe Jackson
Judith Krause Reid

KEY

Admr.	-	Administrator
Decd.	-	Deceased
Extr.	-	Executor
Extrx.	-	Executrix
Junr.	-	Junior
Pc.	-	Pence
Pds.	-	Pounds
Senr.	-	Senior
Sh.	-	Shilling
Wts.	-	Witnesses

GATES COUNTY, NORTH CAROLINA

MINUTES OF COUNTY COURT

Feb. 1779 - July 1784

State of North Carolina

Whereas by an act of Assembly passed at Halifax in the State of North Carolina the Twelfth day of February in the Year of Our Lord One Thousand Seven Hundred and Seventy Nine establishing a County by the name of Gates, in which act it is Directed that Courts shall be held in the said County at the House of Kedar Riddicks on the First Monday in May, August, November and February in each and every year, in consequence of which his Excellency Richard Caswell Esqr. Governor and Commander in Chief in and for the said State, issued Commission of Peace and directed to Demsey Sumner, Jesse Eason, James Sumner, Jacob Hunter, Lawrance Baker, Jethro Benton, Luke Sumner, Thomas Hunter, Josiah Granbery, Charles Rountree, Christopher Riddick, William Baker, Jethro Ballard, Joseph Riddick and Isaac Pipkin, Esqrs. appointing them Justices of the Peace for the said County, and pursuant to the said Act and Commission Christopher Riddick, William Baker and Isaac Pipkin Esqrs. did meet at the House of Kedar Riddick's on the First Monday in May in the same Year and Qualified as Justices of the Peace for the said County of Gates.

Monday May 3rd., 1779.

Court Met and adjourned until Tomorrow morning.

Tuesday May 4th.

Court met and adjourned until tomorrow 3 O'Clock P. M.

Wednesday May 5th.

Court met. Present: Christopher Riddick, William Baker, Isaac Pipkin, Justices.

Thomas Hunter and Joseph Riddick, Esqrs. qualified as Justices of the Peace.

William Baker, Esqr. to act as Clerk.

Christopher Riddick, Esqr. to act as Sheriff.

Mordica Perry moved for Administration on the Estate of Amos Perry decd. - Granted. He to give Security in the sum of 6000 pds.

Thursday May 6th.

Mordica Perry moved the Court for leave to sell the perishable Estate of the said decd. - granted.

Isaac Pipkin Esqr. to receive an account of the Taxable property of the Inhabitants within the following Districts viz. Capt. John Bentons, Capt. Jesse Harrell's and Capt. Isaac Pipkins.

Thomas Hunter Esqr. to receive an account of the Taxable property of the Inhabitants in the following District viz. Capt. Christopher Riddick's, Capt. Charles Rountree's and Capt. Thomas Hunters.

Joseph Riddick Esqr. to receive an account of the Taxables property of the Inhabitants in the following Districts viz. Capt. David Rice's and Capt. Jacob Gordons.

William Vann appointed Constable in the District he formerly acted as Constable in and that he warn the Inhabitants in that part of his District that is in Capt. Christopher Riddicks bounds to give an account of their Taxable property to Thomas Hunter Esqr. and that he warn all the rest of the Inhabitants in his District to give an account of their Taxable property to Isaac Pipkin Esqr.

Charles Vann appointed Constable in the District he formerly acted as Constable in and that he warn all the Inhabitants in his District that belongs to Capt. Christopher Riddick's Militia Bounds to return an account of their Taxable property to Thomas Hunter Esqr. and all the rest of the Inhabitants in his Bound to return an account of their Taxable property to Isaac Pipkin Esqr.

Kedar Hill appointed Constable in the District he formerly acted as Constable in and that he warn all the Inhabitants in his district and also all the Inhabitants in Capt. Charles Rountree's Militia Bounds to give an account of their Taxable property to Thomas Hunter Esqr.

Jacob Norfleet appointed Constable in the District he formerly acted as Constable in and also in the District of Capt. Jacob Gordons Company and that he warn all the Inhabitants in said District to give an account of their Taxable property to Joseph Riddick Esqr.

William Harris, James Riddick and Edward Doughty appointed to assess the Taxable property in the District of William Vann Constable.

George Dunn, Jesse Vann and Philip Lewis appointed to assess the Taxable property in the District of Charles Vann Constable.

Demsey Bond, Amos Trotman and Henry Walton appointed to assess the Taxable property in the District that Kedar Hill warns the Inhabitants to give a list of their Taxable property.

Docton Riddick, James Norfleet and William Arnell appointed to assess the Taxable property in the District of Jacob Norfleet.

Jurors summoned: Francis Saunders, Stephen Eure, William Doughtie, Jeremiah Speight, Thomas Hurdle, John Riddick, James Costen, James Freeman, Jesse Barnes, Charles Eure, Samuel Baker, Wright Hays, Abraham Eason, James Knight, Timothy Lassiter, Mordica Perry, Lewis Braddy, Moor Carter, William Walters, Kedar Riddick, John Powell, Aaron Lassiter, Junr., George Outlaw and Demsey Trotman.

First Monday in August 1779 - at the House of Kedar Riddick-

Present: Joseph Riddick and Isaac Pipkin, Justices.

Jesse Eason, James Sumner, Jacob Hunter and Lawrence Baker Esqrs. appointed in the Commission of the Peace - qualified as Justices of the Peace.

Deed of Sale from Hardy Jones to Isaac Langston proved by the oath of Jesse Vann.

Deed of Sale John Alston to Robert Parker proved by the oath of James Brown.

Deed of Sale Jonathan Williams to James Browne proved by the oath of Robert Parker.

Deed of Sale John Riddick and Mary his Wife to Micajah Riddick proved by the oath of Edward Doughtie.

On Motion of John Brickell Atto. at Law in behalf of Joseph Speight praying leave to turn the road leading through his Mill Pond, from the foot of his Mill Path below his Mill unto the Meherin road to the fork - Granted and ordered that the following persons lay out the same agreeable to Law viz. Isaac Pipkin, George Dunn, Francis Parker, Jesse Saunders, Francis Saunders, Thomas Brown (?) William Odom, Demsey Barnes, Philip Lewis, Jesse Barnes, John Odom, Jesse Vann, Seprian Cross, David Watson, Henry King and Jonathan Boyce.

Deed of Gift Aaron Blanshard Senr. to Demsey Blanshard proved by the oath of Aaron Blanchard, Junr. and Elizabeth Blanshard.

Last Will of Aaron Blanshard decd. exhibited by Elizabeth Blanshard and Demsey Blanshard Extr. and proved by the oaths of Absolom Blanshard and Amerias Blanshard.

Deed of Sale Solomon Alphin and James Alphin to Presillia Lassiter proved by the oath of Demsey Blanshard.

Deed of Sale Prescilla Lassiter to Solomon Alphin proved by the oath of Demsey Blanshard.

James Sumner to be exempt from the payment of Public Tax for the following Negroes to Wit: Hannah and Lucy.

Demsey Bond brought into Court one Negro Boy named Abram belonging to the Estate of Aaron Blanshard decd. praying the Courts judgment whither or not he is liable to Taxable property under the law - - opinion Negative.

Samuel Harrell appointed Constable in the room of Jacob Norfleet.

Tuesday Morning

Present: Jesse Eason, Lawrence Baker, Isaac Pipkin, Thomas Hunter, Justices.

Jethro Benton qualified as Justice of the Peace.

Deed of Sale Richard Parker to Jacob Sumner proved by the oath of Israel Beeman.

Deed of sale Josiah Granberry to Jonathan Nichols proved by the oath of Jacob Norfleet.

Mariah Bird orphan of Darkis Green about the age of 4 years bound as an apprentice to James Hodges and Wife to be taught the business of spinning and weaving.

Deed of sale James Garott, Senr. to Jethro Meltear proved by the oath of George Williams.

William Baker, Esqr. qualified as Justice of the Peace.

William Baker resigned as Clerk of the Court whereupon Lawrence Baker was appointed who gave for Securities Elisha Hunter and Seth Riddick.

Last Will of Joseph Tugwell decd. exhibited by William Baker Extr. and proved by the oath of James Brady witness.

Inventory of the Goods & etc. of the Estate of Joseph Tugwell decd. exhibited on oath of William Baker Extr.

Jacob Powell Extr. of the Last Will of Robert Powell decd. moved the court to appoint persons to divide the Estate of the decd.

Ordered Elisha Hunter, Jacob Hunter, Jethro Ballard and James Norfleet or any three of them divide the same.

John Miller Atto. at Law appointed Atto. for the State.

Account of the Sales of the Estate of Amos Perry decd. exhibited by Mordica Perry.

Deed of Sale Anthony Matthews to Isaac Walters proved by the oath of Micajah Riddick.

Deed of Sale Seasbrook Wilson to James Garrott, Senr. proved by the oath of George Williams.

Grand Jurors appointed: James Costen (Foreman), Francis Saunders Lewis Brady, Samuel Baker, Jeremiah Speight, Kedar Riddick, Thomas Hurdle, Abram Eason, John Riddick, James Knight, Timothy Lassiter, George Outlaw, James Freeman, Mordica Perry, Demsey Trotman.

Jesse Vann, George Dunn and Philip Lewis made return of the Valuation of the Taxable property in their Districts.

William Harris, James Riddick and Edward Doughtie made return of the Valuation of the Taxable property in their District.

Docton Riddick, James Norfleet and William Arnell made return of the Valuation of the Taxable property in their District.

James Riddick informed the Court of his having a Negro Boy Cary who is subject to fits, asked judgment whether or not he is taxable property - opinion Negative.

Neebs a Negro man the property of Jesse Eason Esqr. being subject to fits and much burnt the Court is of the opinion that he be exempt from paying tax.

Samuel Eure appointed Overseer of the road in the room of Peter Harrell

Grand Jury Discharged.

Milley a Negro Woman of the Estate of Joseph Tugwell decd. being much subject to Fits and much burnt she to be exempt from paying Tax.

John Shepherd to pay only a Single Tax on the following Negroes and Cattle belonging to the Estate of William Copeland decd. (to wit) Sam, Back, Miler, Sam, Poll and three Head of Cattle and one other Negro belonging to the Estate of Kedar Best decd. (to wit) Jim.

The Clerk to be allowed the sum of 20 pds. for extra Service.

Mordica Perry appointed Guardian to Susanna Zelf and Samuel Hobbs orphans of John Hobbs decd. He to give Security in the sum of 2000 pds each. Securities: James Freeman and Kedar Hill.

Demsey Bond, Amos Trotman and Henry Walton made a return of the Valuation of the Taxable property in their District.

Richard Richardson a Base Born Child of 16 years of age bound an apprentice to James Knight to learn the business of a House Carpenter.

George Dunn, Jesse Vann and Philip Lewis allowed 40 pds. each for their Services assessing the property in their District.

Demsey Bond, Amos Trotman and Henry Walton allowed 20 pds. each for their service in assessing the property in their District.

William Harris, James Riddick and Edward Doughtie allowed 24 pds. each for their services in assessing the property in their District.

Docton Riddick, William Arnel and James Norfleet allowed 24 pds. each for their services in assessing the property in their District.

Wednesday Aug. 4th, 1779.

Present: Jacob Hunter, Thomas Hunter, Jethro Benton and William Baker, Justices.

Following persons to be continued Overseers of the different roads in the County. James Freeman the main road that leads by Capt. James Summers to Freemans Ferry and that George Outlaw, William Freeman, Demsey Freeman, Jacob Outlaw, James Baccus, Henry Hill, Jesse Ward, Jonas Taylor, Jacob Taylor and Nathaniel Taylor with their Hands work on the same.

William Spivey Overseer of the road from the Main road leading by Capt. James Sumners to Old Town Landing and that James Sumner, Henry Moore, and James Woodward work on the same.

Timothy Lassiter Overseer of the road from the Watry Swamp to Costens Chappel.

Absolom Blanshard Overseer of the road from the Swamp by Henry Waltons to the Bennets Creek road.

Thomas Rountree Overseer of the road that Simon Stallings was Overseer of and that the Hands that worked under the said Stallings do work under the said Rountree.

Thomas Hurdle Overseer of the road from the Quarter Old Field to Speights Race Paths.

Joseph Riddick Overseer of the road from the Sandy Ridge road to the Virginia road by Matthew Smalls.

Thomas Walton Overseer of the road from the Pipeing Branch to Major Jacob Hunters Mill.

Isaac Harrell Overseer of the road from Major Hunters Mill to the Folly.

Jacob Norfleet Overseer of the road he was formerly Overseer of.

Demsey Bond Overseer of the road he was formerly Overseer of.

Jethro Meltear Overseer of the road he was formerly Overseer of.

Amos Lassiter Overseer of the road in the room of Maxamilion Minshew.

William Hinton Overseer of the road he was formerly Overseer of.

John Dardin Overseer of the road he was formerly Overseer of.

James Knight Overseer of the road he formerly was Overseer of.

James Norfleet Overseer of the road he formerly was Overseer of.

William Harris Overseer of the road from the Honey Potts road across the Creek to William Speights and that the hands of William Speight and Docton Riddick work on the same.

James Pruden Overseer of the road he formerly was Overseer of.

James Riddick Overseer of the road he formerly was Overseer of.

George Williams Overseer of the road he formerly was Overseer of.

Moses Ketherell Overseer of the road he formerly was Overseer of.

John Benton Overseer of the road he formerly was Overseer of.

Demsey Odom Overseer of the road he formerly was Overseer of.

William Warren Overseer of the road he formerly was Overseer of.

Jesse Saunders Overseer of the road he formerly was Overseer of.

Francis Parker Overseer of the road he formerly was Overseer of.

Demsey Barnes Overseer of the road he formerly was Overseer of.

Charles Vann Overseer of the road he formerly was Overseer of.

Philip Lewis Overseer of the road he formerly was Overseer of.

Job Umfleet Overseer of the road he formerly was Overseer of.

Jacob Gordon Overseer of the road he formerly was Overseer of.

William Baker Overseer of the road he formerly was Overseer of.

William Odom Overseer of the road he formerly was Overseer of.

Isaac Hunter, Junr. appointed Public Register.

Joseph Riddick Esqr. appointed Surveyor.

William Harris appointed Public Entry Taker.

The following persons appointed to serve as Jurors at the next Superior Court to be held for the District of Edenton at Edenton on the 1st. Monday in November next. James Sumner, Esqr., James Knight, James Garrott and Solomon King.

The following persons appointed to serve as Petit and Grand Jurors the next Inferior Court of Pleas: Moses Kitherell, John Benton, William Daughtie, John Both____, Demsey Odom, Jesse Harrell, Charles Eure, George Williams, Robert Parker, Senr., Francis Parker, Jesse Saunders, Abram Morgan, Micajah Riddick, James Pruden, Seth Riddick, Abraham Sumner, John Powell, Moses Hill, Simon Stallings, Thomas Rountree, Absolom Blanshard, Aaron Blanshard, Solomon Briggs, John Darden, Moses Davis, Caleb Polson, Moses Hare, Junr., Thomas Parker, Junr., Moses Briggs and Guy Hobbs.

12 pds. to be allowed Kedar Hill Constable for his services.

Samuel Harrell to be allowed 12 pds. for his services.

Charles Vann and William Vann allowed 12 pds. each for their services.

Samuel Smith appointed Constable in the room of William Vann.

2 sh. to be levied on each Hundred pounds Taxable property and the Sheriff collect the same.

Inventory of the Goods & etc. of the Estate of Aaron Blanshard decd. exhibited in Court on oath of Demsey Blanshard Extr.

Jacob Gordon appointed as Standard Keeper for the County and he procure Weights and Measures and be allowed for the same.

James Sumner Esqr. to run the dividing line between the Counties of Chowan, Perquimans and Gates.

William Draper allowed the sum of 16 pds. for the use of his house for to hold this and the last Court and for making four benches and etc..

1st. Monday in November, 1779 - at the House of Kedar Riddick.

Present: Jethro Benton, Isaac Pipkin, William Baker, Justices.

Last Will of Demsey Sumner decd. exhibited by Martha Sumner Extrx. and Jethro Sumner Extr. and proved by the oath of Jesse Benton one of the witnesses.

Inventory of the goods & etc. of the Estate of Demsey Sumner decd. exhibited by the Extrx. and Extr. Martha & Jethro Sumner.

Joseph Riddick Esqr., Thos. Rountree, William King and David Rice or any three of them to devide the Estate of Demsey Eason decd. and make report.

Deed of land John Duke, Junr. to William Walters proved by the oath of Wm. Daughtie.

Deed of land Hardy Cross to Demsey Odom proved by the oath of John Bethey, Junr.

Jury appointed to lay out a road leading below Joseph Speights Mill made report - Agreeable - Ordered that it be a public road and that Demsey Barnes Overseer work on the same with the hands that formerly worked on the road under him.

Deed of Gift of land Thomas Hare to Demsey Sumner proved by the oath of Jesse Saunders.

Deed of land from Seasbrook Wilson to James Garrott proved by the oaths of Christopher Riddick and Jonathan Nichols.

Thomas Vann records his Ear Mark a Cross & Slit in the left ear and a Cross in the Right Ear.

The Sheriff returned for Grand Jury the following persons: Moses Witherill (Foreman), John Benton, Wm. Daughtie, John Bethey, Jesse Harrell, Charles Eure, Robert Parker, Jesse Saunders, Abram Morgan, Micajah Riddick, Seth Riddick, Moses Hill, Thomas Rountree, Absolom Blanshard, Aaron Blanshard, Moses Davis, Moses Briggs, Thomas Parker, Junr., Solomon Briggs, John Darden and Caleb Polson.

Deed of land John Powell to Docton Riddick proved by the oath of Abraham Sumner.

Deed of land Everand Garrett to James Garrett proved by the oath of John Elliss.

Benjamin Robins Indian about 14 years of age bound as an apprentice to James Garrett, Senr. to learn the art of Plantation business.

Penelope Byrd daughter of Mary Byrd about 5 years old, a Base Born Child bound as an apprentice to James Riddick (Honey Potts) to learn

House business.

George Hargrove records his Ear Mark a Swallow Fork in each Ear and a half moon under each Ear.

Martha Sumner Extrx. and Jethro Sumner Extr. of the last Will of Demsey Sumner decd. moved that persons be appointed to make a division of the Estate of the decd. - Granted - Ordered William Baker, Jacob Hunter, Jethro Benton and Saml. Baker or any three of them divide the same.

Jesse Barnes records his Ear Mark a Cross Square under the Right Ear and a half moon under the Left Ear.

Philip Lewis records his Ear Mark a Cross Square under the Right Ear and a Cross and half moon under the left Ear.

Thomas Smith records his Ear Mark a Swallow Fork in each Ear and a half moon under the left Ear.

William Harriss records his Ear Mark a Under Square in each Ear and a Cross off the Right Ear.

John Morgan, son of Olive Morgan, a Base Born Child about the age of 16 years bound as an apprentice to William Baker Esqr. to learn Plantation business.

Tuesday Nov. 2nd., 1779.

Present: William Baker, Isaac Pipkin, Jethro Benton, Justices.

Deed of land Henry Hill to Robert Taylor proved by the oath of Henry Hill, Junr.

Present: Thomas Hunter, Esqr.

Grand Jury Discharged.

Present: Joseph Riddick Esqr.

Deed of land Kedar Odom to John Harrell proved by the oath of William Ellis.

Ordered that the road leading from the Knotty Pine Chappel to Maney's Ferry be turned from Mills's Swamp a short course into the said road on the East side of the Plantation of Isaac Pipkin Esqr. and that the said Isaac Pipkin Esqr. do clear the said road and put it in good order at his own expense.

Suit of Jesse Barnes vs. Sarah Boyce for Slander. Defndt. Sarah made such consessions as was satisfactory to the Plantiff.

William Hinton (Indian Neck) appointed in room of Demsey Bond as Overseer of the road and that the said William Hinton keep the Bridge over Major Waltons Mill Swamp in good order.

The road leading from the Edenton road against Capt. Thomas Hunters to the Sandy Ridge road be turned to go along the swamp side on the

West side of Jacob Bagleys Plantation and that the said Jacob Bagley do clear out the said road and put the same in good order at his own expence.

Deed of sale William Arnell to Edward Arnell proved by the oath of Thomas Parker.

Charity Gatling produced John Bathey and Jesse Saunders as Securities to indemnafy the County of Gates for the Maintenance of an Eligitimate Child begotten on her Body (in the sum of 1000 pds.)

Deed of land William Hurdle to Shadrick _____ (page torn) proved by the oath of Joseph Riddick.

Deed of sale of land John Roberts to Jacob Eason proved by the oath of Joseph Riddick.

Deed of land William Hurdle to John Roberts proved by the oath of Joseph Riddick.

Moore Carter produced Robert Parker and John Green Senr. as Securities who were approved of to Indemnify the County of Gates (for the Maintainance of an Eligitimate Child begotten on the Body of Sarah Eure) and laid so the charge of the said More Carter in the sum of 2000 pds.

Jesse Vann records his Ear Mark a Cross in Eech Ear and a half moon under the Left.

Sheriff to summons the following persons to serve as Grand and Petit Jurors: James Freeman, William Freeman, Demsey Bond, Guy Hill, Guy Hobbs, George Outlaw, Simon Stallings, Moses Hare, Junr., Jacob Norfleet, Jethro Ballard, Docton Riddick, John Powell, John Riddick, William Harriss, James Pruden, Jeremiah Speight, Wm. Cleaves, Jethro Sumner, Demsey Costen, James Riddick, Joseph Figg, Kedar Riddick, James Bathey, James Lang, Henry King, Lott Rogers, Joel Goodman, Thomas Walton, Henry Walton and James Costen.

John Harrell a Base Born Boy about the age of 11 years bound as an apprentice to Kedar Hill to learn the business of a Shoe Maker.

1st. Monday in February, 1780.

Present: Jethro Benton, William Baker and Isaac Pipkin, Justices.

Deed of land James Eure to Lewis Sparkman proved by the oath of Jesse Barnes.

James Sumner and Henry Riddick moved for Administration on the Estate of Luke Sumner decd. - Granted - They to give security in the sum of 200,000 pds. Thomas Rountree and Christopher Riddick Securities.

Wills Cowper appointed guardian to Willis Cowper. He to give security in the sum of 100,000 pds. - William Baker and James Sumner Securities.

Lawrance Baker, William Baker, David Rice and Jethro Ballard or any three of them to divide the estate of Luke Sumner decd.

Josiah Sumner appointed guardian to William Sumner orphen of Davia. He to give security in the sum of 100,000. pds.-James Sumner and Christopher Riddick Securities.

The Sheriff returned for the Grand Jurors the following persons who were duly qualified. Jethro Ballard, James Freeman, Demsey Bond, Guy Hill, Guy Hobbs, George Outlaw, Simon Stallings, Jacob Norfleet, Docton Riddick, John Powell, John Riddick, William Harriss, James Pruden, Jeremiah Speight and William Cleaves.

Last Will of Robert Lassiter decd. exhibited by Job Riddick Extr. and proved by the oath of Demsey Costen a Witness.

Deed of land John Bethey to Jesse Vann.

Deed of Gift Thomas Langston to his Wife and Children proved by the oath of Jesse Vann.

Inventory of the goods & etc. of the Estate of Robert Lassiter decd. exhibited by Job Riddick Extr.

Solomon Green records his Ear Mark a Cross in each Ear and a Half Moon over the Right.

Persons appointed of this Court at last sitting to divide the estate of Demsey Eason decd. made report.

Febeby (?) Hamilton to give Security in the sum of 5000 pds. Thomas Hamilton and Andrew Hambleton appeared as securities to keep Levena Hamilton a Base Born Child from becoming chargable to the County of Gates.

Demsey Barnes appeared in Court charged with Begetting a Base Born Child on the body of Elizabeth Curle - He to give Security in the sum of 5000 pds. William Warren Security - to keep Delitha Curle from becoming chargeable to this County.

Deed of land Henry Hobbs to William Cally proved by the oath of William Felton.

Deed of land Jacob Eason to Edward Perryman.

Deed of land from Elisha Hunter to Jacob Pierce.

Deed of land Jesse Worrell to Jesse Harrell proved by the oath of Lemuel Harrell.

Deed of land Rachal Davis to John Miller proved by the oath of John Davis.

Deed of land Henry Hobbs to John Roberts proved by the oath of Guy Hobbs.

Deed of land John Tommas to Noah Felton proved by the oath of William Felton.

Mr. Thomas Voil Atto. at Law came into Court and produced his Lisince and qualified as a practicing Attorney in this Court.

Tuesday morning February 8, 1780.

Present: Jesse Eason, Thomas Hunter, Isaac Pipkin, William Baker, Justices.

Capt. Isaac Pipkin, Capt. Thomas Hunter, Capt. Christopher Riddick, and Mr. Seth Riddick or any three of them to agree with some person or persons to build a Bridge across the swamp below Saml. Baker's Mill at or near the place where it formerly was.

Lisence granted to Thomas Brickell for keeping a Public House. William Harriss and Docton Riddick Securities.

The following persons appointed as Petit Jurors: Jethro Sumner, James Land, Joel Goodman, Demsey Costen, Kedar Riddick, Thomas Walton, Philip Lewis, James Riddick, James Bethey, Lott Rogers, James Costen and Thomas Vann.

Deed of Gift Thomas Garrott to Kedar Riddick proved by the oath of James Garrott Senr.

Deed of land Thomas Garrott to James Garrott Senr.

Deed of Gift William Goodman Senr. to William Goodman Junr. proved by the oath of John Bethey.

In a Dispute of Entry between Joseph Speight and George Dunn ordered that the Sheriff summon a Jury.

Josiah Granbery, James Gregory, Jethro Ballard and Docton Riddick or any three of them audit and settle the accounts of David Rice and Josiah Riddick Extrs. of Miles Riddick decd. and make report.

Grand Jury discharged.

An additional Inventory of the Estate of Colo. Demsey Sumner was exhibited by Jethro Sumner Extr.

Elisha Ellis records his Ear Mark a Half Moon under each Ear.

Jeremiah Speight records his Ear Mark a Cross off of the Right Ear and a Half Moon under the Left.

Sheriff to summon the following persons to serve as Jurors at the next Superior Court at Edenton the 1st. Monday in May: Joshua Small, Thomas Rountree, John Odom and John Benton.

In a Dispute of Entry between James Brady and John Gatling ordered that the Sheriff summon a Jury.

Sheriff to summon the following persons to serve as Grand Jurors and Petit Jurors: William Goodman, Junr., David Lewis, Jesse Saunders, James Smith, Jesse Harrell, Jesse Barnes, John Gatling, George Dunn, John Miller, Abram Morgan, Jethro Harrell, Jesse Vann, Joseph Hurdle, Abraham Sumner, Isaac Harrell, John Briggs, John Miller, Moses Briggs, Isaac Benton, Moses Hare, William Arnold, David Jones, Jacob Gordon, Abraham Eason, William King, Isaac Miller, Joseph Brinkley, Joseph Warren, Amos Trotman and Jonathan Williams.

Sheriff to pay Mr. John Miller State Atto. for this County the sum of 75 pds. for his services three courts.

Seth Riddick appointed Public Inspector of Beef, Pork and Etc. for this County.

Wednesday Feb. 9th., 1780.

Present: William Baker, Isaac Pipkin, Joseph Riddick, Justices.

In the matter of Dispute concerning the Entry of some land between Joseph Speight and George Dun ordered that the Entry Taker issue his warrent to the Surveyor to run out Fifty Acres the Quanity of land first entered by said Speight and first and then his warrent to the said Surveyor to run out the Quantity of land entered by the said George Dun.

On Motion of Mr. Iredell, ordered that he have leave to file a Petition as of this term, during the Nov., Dec. and the next, _____ Thomas Burgess, Thomas Vann and his Wife, and Others, against Thomas Hare who acts as Extr. of a paper purporting to be the last Will and Testament of Edward Hare Case (?) of this County (then part of Hertford County) decd. and others who claim under the said purported Will, as are interested in extablishing or setting it aside.

James Costen appointed Stray Master in this County.

First Monday in May, 1780. At the House of Kedar Riddick

Present: Jesse Eason, Thomas Hunter, Isaac Pipkin, Justices.

Then the Court adjourned to the Court House on the Plantation of James Garrott on the North Side of Bennets Creek at Two O'Clock this Evening.

Plantation of James Garrott May 1st., 1780 - Two O'Clock.

Present: Jesse Eason, Isaac Pipkin, Thomas Hunter, William Baker, Joseph Riddick, Justices.

Thomas Caspey orphan of William Caspey about the age of 12 years bound as an Apprentice to Thomas Parker to learn the business of a Cooper.

Hardy Wills appeared in Court charged with begetting a Base Born Child on the body of Charity Gatling. Ordered that the said Hardy Wills give Bond and Security in the sum of 500 pds. THIS ENTRY MARKED OUT.

Harvy Gatling a Base Born Child Son of Charity Gatling about the age of 6 years bound an Apprentice to Elisha Cross to learn the business of a Leather Dresser.

The Sheriff returned the following Persons as Grand Jurors: William Goodman, Junr., Foreman, James Smith, Jesse Harrell, Jesse Barnes, George Dunn, John Miller, Abraham Mortan, Joseph Hurdle, Abraham Sumner, Isaac Harrell, Isaac Benton, Moses Hare, William Arnold, William King and Isaac Miller.

Jethro Meltear appointed Constable in the room of Kedar Hill, resigned.

Selah Smith came into Court and offered Anthony Matthews and Kedar Odom as Securities to Indemnify this County for the maintainance of Levi Smith a Base Born Child. Ordered that she give Bond in the sum of 5000 pds.

Deed of land Sarah Odom and Charles King to Moor Carter proved by the oath of William Fryer.

Negro Grace a Woman formerly the property of Nathan Parker of the County of Northampton in this State to be sold to the Highest Bidder for Ready Money.

Negro Man Luke formerly the property of Thomas Nichols of Perquimons County of this State to be sold to the Highest Bidder for Ready Money.

Thomas Hurdle guardian to Christian Rountree presented his account.

James Jones Overseer of the Thickett Road in room of Jacob Norfleet.

Ezekial Trotman Overseer of the road in the room of Joseph Riddick, resigned, and that Ezekiel Trotman and William Hunters Hands work on the same.

Hands of Abraham Sumner work on the road under Thomas Hurdle, Overseer.

William Crafford, Demsey Harrell, John Harrell, James Parker, Benjamin Parker, Samuel Thomas, Richard Stallings and their Hands work on the road under Charles Vann Overseer.

Josiah Harrell, Isaac Fryer, Levi Lee, Elisha Ellis, Daniel Ellis and John Carter and their Hands work on the Road under Benjamin Blyth, Overseer.

Deed of land James Hinton to Isaac Harrell proved by the oath of Moses Hare, Junr.

Tuesday Morning May 2nd., 1780.

Present: William Baker, Thomas Hunter, Isaac Pipkin, Joseph Riddick, Justices.

Sheriff returned the Virdick of a Jury in a Dispute of Entry relative to lands - George Dunn against Joseph Speight - Determined that Joseph Speight holds the Entry of the said Land Disputed - signed by Joel Goodman.

Deed of land George Outlaw to William Freeman.

County Treasurer pay Lawrence Baker the sum of 1000 pds. for building a Bridge over the Swamp below the said Bakers Mill.

William Baker records his Ear Mark a Square under the Left Year with a Slit in the Right Ear and Half Moon under the Right Ear.

Deed of Gift Sarah Hunter to Riddick Hunter proved by the oath of Thomas Walton.

Christopher Riddick exhibited his list of property that is not liable to be taxed in this County for the year 1779.

James Sumner not liable to the Tax on	1400 pds.
Thomas Hare living out of this County	8880 "
Demsey Baker moved out of said County	375 "
Elizabeth Trotman by mistake of Assessors	6300 "
Elisha Copeland denys his having property that is assesed to him	1020 "
Thomas Cotten out of this County	600 "
Benj. Wynns " " " "	300 "
James Wright " " " "	500 "
Joseph Dickinson Insolvent	8880 "
John Ellis inhabitant of Chowan	150 "
James Hinton inhabitant of Cumberland	1150 "

Amarias Blanshard moved for Administration on the Estate of Amos Blanshard decd. - Granted - He to give Security in the sum of 8000 pds. Demsey Bond and Guy Hill Securities.

Inventory of the Goods & etc. of the Estate of Amos Blanshard decd. exhibited by Amarias Blanshard Adm.

Amarias Blanshard Adm. of Amos Blanshard decd. moved leave to sell part of the Estate of the said decd. to pay debts. - Granted - same to be sold at Public sale the First Saturday in June next.

Capt. Thomas Hunter, Joseph Riddick, Demsey Bond and Demsey Costin or any three of them divide the Estate of Amos Blanshard decd. and make report.

James Gregory, Jethro Ballard and Docton Riddick appointed to audit and settle the accounts of David Rice and Jonah Riddick Extrs. of Mills Riddick decd. made report.

Sheriff to pay John Miller State Atto. the sum of 25 pds. for his services.

Grand Jury discharged - Petit Jury discharged - Court adjourned.

Wednesday May 3rd., 1780.

Present: Thomas Hunter, William Baker, Joseph Riddick, Justices.

Deed of Gift Andrew Matthews to William Matthews proved by the oath of Richard Ashberry McKee.

William Baker to act as Sheriff. James Gregory and Christopher Riddick Securities.

Christopher Riddick Esqr. qualified as Justice of the Peace.

The Sheriff to summons the following persons as Petit and Grand Jurors: Jacob Bagley, Marios Perry, Amos Trotman, Job Riddick, Timothy Lassiter, Simon Stallings, George Outlaw, Demsey Costin, Moses Briggs, John Briggs, Jacob Powell, David Rice, Docton Riddick, Charles Eure, Stephen Eure, Stephen Rogers, Solomon Green, Lewis Sparkman, James Landing, Moor Carter, Henry King (Capt.) William Odom, Jeremiah Speight, William Harriss, Demsey Odom, William Walters, Elisha Parker, Moves Boyce, William Matthews and Philip Rogers.

Isaac Pipkin Esqr. to receive an account of the Taxable property of the Inhabitants in the District where Charles Vann is Constable.

Christopher Riddick Esqr. to receive an account of the Taxable property of the Inhabitants in the District where Samuel Smith is Constable.

Thomas Hunter Esqr. to receive an account of the Taxable property in the District whithin Capt. Thomas Hunters Muster Bounds.

Jesse Eason Esqr. to receive a list of the Taxable property of the Inhabitants in the District within Capt. Jethro Sumners Muster Bounds.

Charles Vann Constable to summon the Inhabitants of his District to give a list of their Taxable property to Isaac Pipkin Esqr.

Samuel Smith to warn the Inhabitants of his District to give a list of their Taxable property to Christopher Riddick Esqr.

Jethro Meltear Constable to warn the Inhabitants within Capt. Thomas Hunters Muster Bounds to give a list of their Taxable property to Thomas Hunter Esqr.

Samuel Harrell Constable to warn the Inhabitants within Capt. Joseph Riddicks Muster Bounds to give a list of their Taxable property to Joseph Riddick, Esqr.

William Arnold appointed Constable in Capt. Jethro Sumners Muster Bounds.

William Arnold to summons the Inhabitants within Capt. Jethro Sumners Muster Bounds to give a list of their Taxable property to Jesse Eason Esqr.

Joseph Speight, John Odom and Joel Goodman to assess the property in the bounds where Charles Vann is Constable.

Seth Riddick, Elisha Parker and John Benton, Junr. to assess the property in the bounds where Samuel Smith is Constable.

Demsey Bond, Abraham Eason and Thomas Walton to assess the property in Capt. Thomas Hunters and Capt Joseph Riddicks Districts or Muster Bounds.

Jethro Ballard, John Powell and John Riddick to assess the property in Capt. Jethro Sumners District or Muster Bounds.

John Ball orphan of Richard Ball about 14 years of age bound an apprentice to Edward Doughtie to learn the business of a Cooper.

Third Monday in Aug., 1780.

At the Court House on Bennets Creek on the Plantation of James Garrott.

Present: Jacob Hunter, Isaac Pipkin, Christopher Riddick, Justices.

Deed of land Nathaniel Spivey to Charles Rountree proved by the oath of Jacob Bagley.

Deed of Gift of land Champon Spivey to Nathaniel Spivey proved by the oath of Moses Hill.

Deed of land Aaron Ohdom to Henry Lee proved by the oath of John Bathey.

Deed of land William Goodman, Senr. to Henry Goodman proved by the oath of John Bathey.

Deed of land Garrott Davis and Hester Davis to Joseph Parker.

Moses Hill moved by Mr. John Miller Atto. for administration on the Estate of Abraham Hill decd. - Granted - He to give Security in the sum of 30,000 pds. Thomas Trotman and Charles Rountree Securities.

Inventory of the Goods & etc. of the Estate of Abraham Hill decd. exhibited by Moses Hill Adm.

License granted to James Garrott for keeping a Publick House - Charles Rountree and James Freeman Securities.

Capt. Charles Rountree, Thomas Rountree, Thomas Trotman and Amos Trotman or any three of them to divide the Estate of Abraham Hill and make report.

Deed of land William Green to Uriah Eure proved by the oath of Solomon Green.

Third Monday in Aug., 1780.

Deed of land James Garott to the Commissioners and the Justices - - - agreeing with workmen to erect a Court House.

Deed of sale John Walton to William Hinton proved by the oath of Elisha Hunter.

Deed of land James Parker to William Parker proved by the oath of William Arnold.

Deed of Gift Charity Watson to David Watson proved by the oath of Joseph Speight.

Persons appointed to divide the Estate of Amos Blanshard decd. made report.

Seth Riddick, Michajah Riddick and Elisha Parker made return of the Taxable property in the Districts they were appointed in.

Joesph Speight, John Odom and Joel Goodman made return of the Taxable property in their District.

4 sh. to be levied on each Hundred Pounds Taxable Property and that the Tax Geatherars collect the same.

Deed of land David Watson to Isaac Pipkin proved by the oath of Joseph Speight.

Demsey Bond, Thomas Walton and Abraham Eason made return of the Taxable Property in their District.

Sheriff returned the following persons as Grand Jurymen: David Rice, Foreman, Jacob Bagley, Mordica Perry, Amos Trotman, Job Riddick, Timothy Lassiter, George Outlaw, Demsey Costen, John Briggs, Docton Riddick, Charles Eure, Stephen Eure and Stephen Rogers.

<u>Tuesday morning Aug. 22, 1780.</u>

Present: Jesse Eason, Jacob Hunter, Thomas Hunter, Isaac Pipkin, Christopher Riddick, Joseph Riddick, Justices.

Deed of sale Thomas Norris to Peter Harrell proved by the oath of Jesse Harrell.

Deed of land John Miller to Daniel Ellis proved by the oath of Stephen Eure.

David Small to Court for begetting a Bastard Child on the body of Rachel Davis. He to give bond in the sum of 10,000 pds. Joshua Small and Damuel Harrell Securities.

Sheriff returned for Petty Jury the following persons: William Harriss, Solomon Green, Lewis Sparkman, Moor Carter, Henry King, William Odom, Jeremiah Speight, Demsey Odom, William Walters, Moses Boyce, William Matthews and Robert Parker.

Elisha Parker and Philip Rogers failed to appear as Jurors.

Deed of land James Garrott to Jonathan Roberts proved by the oath of Absolom Blanshard.

Grand Jury Discharged.

Last Will of Jacob Norfleet, decd. exhibited by Elizabeth Norfleet Extrx. and proved by the oath of Willis Wiggins a witness.

Inventory of the Goods & etc. of the Estate of Jacob Norfleet, decd. exhibited in Court by Elizabeth Norfleet Extrx.

Persons appointed at Aug. Court 1779 to divide the Estate of Robert Powell, decd. made report.

Jethro Ballard, James Norfleet, William Arnall and Edward Arnall or any three of them to divide the Estate of Jacob Norfleet, decd.

Disputed Entry between James Costen and William Harriss. The Sheriff to summon a Jury.

Henry Goodman appointed Taxgeatherer in the District where Charles Vann is Constable.

Moses Kitherell appointed Taxgeatherer in the District where Samuel Smith is Constable.

Thomas Hunter appointed Taxgeatherer in the District where Jethro Meltear and Samuel Harrell are Constables.

Jethro Benton, Junr., appointed Taxgeatherer in the District that William Arnell is Constable.

Elizabeth Norfleet, EMtrx. of Jacob Norfleet decd. to sell part of the Perishable Estate of the said decd. as will pay debts.

Anna Morgan orphan of Joseph Morgan 11 years of age bound as an apprentice to Aaron Blanshard to learn House Business.

The Sheriff to summons the following persons to serve as Petty and Grand Jury: Henry Goodman, George Dunn, Francis Parker, Philip Lewis, John Gatlin, George Williams, James Garrott, William Gatling, Isaac Walters, Demsey Parker, Joseph Figg, James Riddick, William Boyce, Philip Rogers, Elisha Cross, Josiah Granbery, James Gregory, William Cowper, Thomas Trotman, Ezekiel Trotman, Demsey Trotman, Joseph Hurdle, Henry Booth, Joseph Parker, Moses Briggs, Jacob Gordon, Richard Briggs, Joshua Small, Jonathan Lassiter and Demsey Blanshard.

The Sheriff to summons the following persons to serve as Jurors at the next Superior Court: Simon Stallings, Isaac Harrell, William Goodman, Junr, and William Walters.

Abraham Morgan orphan of Hardy Morgan about the age of 15 years bound until he is 20 years of age to Edward Arnell to learn the Business of a Leather Dresser and Leather Briches Maker.

Joseph Speight appointed Overseer of the road in room of William Warren and only in the absence of the said Warren.

On Motion of Mr. Iredell - - he have leave to file a Petition as of this term - - Thomas Burgas, Thomas Vann and his Wife and others against Thomas Hare who acts as Extr. of a paper purporting to be the Last Will and Testament of Edward Hare (late of this County then part of Hertford County) decd.

Lewis Sparkman appointed Overseer of the road in the room of Benjamin Blythe.

Third Monday in Nov., 1780.

Present: Christopher Riddick, Justice - Court adjourned.

Tuesday morning Nov. 25, 1780.

Present: Jesse Eason, Christopher Riddick, Isaac Pipkin, Justices.

William Daniel orphan of William Daniel decd. about the age of 12 years bound as an apprentice to Abel Martin to learn the Business of a Cooper.

Deed of Gift Joseph Griffin to Ephraim Griffin proved by the oath of Kedar Hill.

Motion of John Brickell Esqr. Atto. at Law in behalf of Thomas Hare - - a Commission to take the deposition of Mary Hare, Solomon King and William Gatling, Junr. in a suit brought by Thomas Burges, Thomas Vann and his Wife and Others against the said Thomas Hare.

Motion that Josiah Benton have a Commission to take the deposition of George Polson in his suit against Henry Raby.

Jury of Last Court who failed to return their verdict in a Suit David Lewis against William Gatling - They be discharged and a new Jury summoned.

The persons appointed to make a division of the Estate of Abraham Hill decd. made report.

The assessors of the property be allowed the sum of $50.00 for each and every day they were in the service assessing.

Isaac Pipkin, Christopher Riddick, Esqrs. and Mr. Seth Riddick and Mr. Micajah Riddick or any three of them make a division of the Estate of John Kitherell decd. and report.

Moses Hill Admr. to the Estate of Abraham Hill decd. sell the perishable Estate belonging to the orphans of the said decd.

Each Constable to be allowed the sum of $50.00 for each and every day they were warning the Inhabitants.

Samuel Smith allowed the sum of $10.00 for four days service in the Court as Constable.

David Lewis gave Security in the sum of 10,000 pds.- Thomas Vann and Lewis Walters Securities. - - to keep Blake and _____ (left blank) Base Born Children of Fereby Giles from becoming chargeable to this County.

The Sheriff summons the following persons to serve as Grand and Petty Jury: Demsey Trotman, George Outlaw, James Freeman, Jacob Bagley, Lewis Jones, John Randell Wilkinson, Josiah Granbery, William Cowper, Abraham Eason, Demsey Costen, Jacob Spivey, Thomas Hurdle, John Only, Ostin Nixon, William Eason, Demsey Odom, James Riddick, William Matthews, William Boyce, Seth Riddick, Joseph Figg, Micajah Riddick, John Powell, James Norfleet, Joel Goodman, James Bethey, John Thomas, Charles Eure, Stephen Eure and William Harriss.

County Treasurer pay Lawrence Baker the sum of 2,500 pds. for one year extra service as Clerk of the Court.

Thomas Rountree Overseer of the road that leads across Warwick

Swamp do as much work as they formerly did (with the Hands that works under him) before Thos. Hunter Built a Grist Mill below the said road on the said Swamp and that he keep a good foot way across the said Swamp as far as the dividing line of this and Chowan County.

Third Monday in Feb., 1781.

Present: Jesse Eason, Joseph Riddick, Isaac Pipkin, Justices.

Last Will of William Gwinn decd. exhibited by John Slavin and Daniel Gwinn, Extrs. and proved by the oath of Josiah Granbery a Witness.

Inventory of the Goods & etc. of the Estate of William Gwinn decd. exhibited by John Slavin and Daniel Gwinn Extrs.

Last Will of Mary Brinkley decd. exhibited by John Brinkley Extr. and proved by the oath of Lewis Jones and John Riddick, Witnesses.

Inventory of the Goods & etc. of the Estate of Mary Brinkley exhibited by John Brinkley Extr.

James Arline moved for Administration in the Estate of his son Jeremiah Arline decd. - Granted - He to give Security in the sum of 50,000 pds. Demsey Odom and Robert Parker Securities.

Elizabeth Riddick moved by John Brickell Esqr. Atto. at Law for Administration on the Estate of Docton Riddick decd. - Granted - She to give Security in the sum of "Three Million Pounds" - Jethro Sumner, Seth Riddick and William Powell, Junr. Securities.

Inventory of the Goods & etc. of the Estate of Docton Riddick decd. exhibited by Elizabeth Riddick Admr.

Elizabeth Riddick Admr. of the Estate of Docton Riddick decd. moved for leave to sell the perishable part of the Estate. - Granted.

Last Will of Elijah Spivey exhibited by Champion Spivey Extr. and proved by the oath of Jacob Spivey a Witness.

Last Will of Aaron Lassiter decd. exhibited by Aaron Lassiter one of the Extr. and proved by the oath of David Rice a Witness.

Inventory of the Goods & etc. of the Estate of Aaron Lassiter decd. exhibited by Aaron Lassiter Extr.

Inventory of the Goods & etc. of the Estate of Elijah Spivey decd. exhibited by Champion Spivey Extr.

Last Will of Henry Hill decd. exhibited by Henry Hill one of the Extrs. and proved by the oath of Robert Taylor that he heard the said Henry Hill request Thomas Hunter to sign the said Will and saw the said Hill seal publish and declare the said Will to be his Last Will and Testament.

Disputed Entry between Demsey Odom and Thomas Smith. Sheriff to summons a Jury.

Last Will of Elizabeth Trotman exhibited by Amos Trotman Extr. and proved by the oath of Jacob Bagley a Witness.

Inventory of the Goods & etc. of the Estate of Elizabeth Trotman decd. exhibited by Amos Trotman Extr.

License granted to John Courtney for keeping a Publick House. William Harriss Security in the sum of 1000 pds.

Simon Stallings appointed Guardian to James Walton orphan of Richard Walton decd. He to give Security in the sum of 20,000 pds. Thomas Rountree and Joseph Riddick Esqr. Securities.

Edward Doughtie appointed Overseer of the Road in the room of Capt. John Benton.

Elizabeth Norfleet appointed Guardian to Easter Norfleet and Mourning Norfleet orphans of Jacob Norfleet decd. She to give Security in the sum of 15,000 pds. James Norfleet and Jacob Gordon Securities.

William Arnell appointed Guardian to Elizabeth, Kinchen and Pleasant Lawrence Norfleet, orphans of Jacob Norfleet decd. He to give Security in the sum of 20,000 pds. Elisha Parker and Joshua Small Securities.

Jacob Bagley appointed Overseer of the road in the room of Thomas Rountree resigned.

John Powell, James Norfleet, James Sumner and Jethro Ballard or any three of them to make division and settle the estate of Mary Brinkley decd. and make report.

Demsey Barnes Overseer of the road keep the road in good repair leading below Joseph Speights Mill but the road across the Swamp the said Speight is to keep in good repair.

William Arnell Guardian of Elizabeth, Kinchen, Pleasant and Lawrence Norfleet orphans of Jacob Norfleet decd. moved to sell the perishable part of the Estate of the said orphans. Granted.

Deed of land Edward Arnold to Elizabeth Norfleet.

Deed of land Jesse Benton to John Benton, Junr. proved by the oath of Jethro Sumner.

Deed of land Jethro Benton, <u>Junr.</u> to Jethro Benton, <u>Junr</u>. proved by the oath of Jethro Sumner.

Deed of land Thomas Garrott Senr. to Thomas Hoffler proved by the oath of James Freeman.

Deed of land John Freeman, Junr. to Jacob Outlaw proved by the oath of James Freeman.

Deed of land Isaac Benton to Moses Benton proved by the oath of Jethro Benton.

Deed of land Aaron Harrell and Anna Harrell, his Wife, to Samuel Browne proved by the oath of Thomas Hambleton.

Deed of Gift Charity Watson to John Harrell proved by the oath of James Landing.

Deed of land John Gatling to John Shepherd proved by the oath of Moore Carter.

Deed of sale Solomon Alphin to James Gregory proved by the oath of Elisha Hunter.

Thomas Rountree produced his account as Guardian to James Watton.

Additional Inventory of the Estate of Abraham Hill exhibited by Moses Hill Admr.

Feb. 10, 1781.

Present: Christopher Riddick, Isaac Pipkin, Joseph Riddick, Jesse Eason, Justices.

Deed of Gift Andrew Matthews to Henry Smith proved by the oath of Samuel Smith.

Inventory of the Goods & etc. of the Estate of Henry Hill decd. exhibited by Henry Hill Extr.

The Sheriff returned the account of Sales of the Goods & etc. of the Estate of Abraham Hill decd.

Last Will of William Eason decd. exhibited by Mordica Perry one of the Extrs. and proved by the oaths of William King and Samuel Green that they heard the said William Eason acknowledge the said Will which was first read to him and raised up in his bead to sign it but decd. before he could do it.

Inventory of the Goods & etc. of the Estate of William Eason decd. exhibited by Mordica Perry Extr.

Mordica Perry Extr. of the Last Will of William Eason decd. moved that persons be appointed to make division of the Estate of the said decd. -Granted.

Joseph Riddick Esqr., David Rice, Charles Rountree and William King or any three of them divide the said Estate.

Disputed Entry between James Costen and William Harriss. The Sheriff to summon a Jury.

Disputed Entry between Stephen Bure and John Green. The Sheriff to summon a Jury.

Deed of land Elisha Hunter to Samuel Green.

Following persons appointed Jurymen to serve next Superior Court: James Norfleet, David Rice, Jesse Barnes and William Harriss.

Frederick Lassiter appointed Guardian to James Walton orphan of William Walton. He to give Security in the sum of 50,000 pds. Jeremiah Speight and William Harriss Securities.

Josiah Bennet an Indian Boy about 12 years of age bound as an apprentice to Edward Briscow to learn the business of a Shoemaker.

George Bennet an Indian Boy about the age of 13 years bound as an apprentice to Henry Booth to learn the business of a Cooper.

Sheriff summons the following persons to serve as Petty and Grand Jury: William Arnold, Jethro Ballard, Joshua Small, John Miller (Folly), Isaac Miller, George Williams, William Goodman, Junr., Henry Goodman, George Dunn, Francis Speight, Jeremiah Speight, Moor Carter, David Umfleet, Micajah Riddick, Edward Doughtie, Samuel Baker, Seth Riddick, Thomas Smith, William Powell, Senr., James Phelps, Wm. Boyce, James Garrott, Mordica Perry, William King, William Berryman, William Hurdle, Amos Trotman, Thomas Walton, John Riddick and Joseph Figg.

Joseph Riddick resigned his appointment as County Surveyor.

John Polson, Junr., appointed Constable in the room of Samuel Smith resigned.

Elizabeth Norfleet Guardian of Easter and Mouring Norfleet orphans of Jacob Norfleet decd. moved for leave to sell the perishable part of the Estate. Granted.

Third Monday in May- May 25, 1781.

Present: Jesse Eason, Thomas Hunter, Isaac Pipkin and Christopher Riddick, Justices.

Deed of land Abel Martin and Elizabeth Martin to Thomas Brickell proved by the oath of Henry Booth. Elizabeth relinquished her right of Dower.

Deed of land Alexander Eason to Joshua Small proved by the oath of Jesse Eason.

Last Will of Thomas Rountree decd. exhibited by Thomas Hunter, Charles Rountree and James Freeman, Estrs. and proved by the oath of Simon Stallings, Witness.

Inventory of the Goods & etc. of the Estate of Thos. Rountree decd. exhibited by Charles Rountree, Extr.

Willis Riddick, Junr. moved for Administration on the Estate of James Riddick decd. - Granted - He to give Security in the sum of 300,000 pds. Willis Riddick and Christopher Riddick Securities.

John Norfleet Extr. of John Norfleet decd. to sell the personal Estate of said decd. and make report.

Jethro Ballard, James Norfleet, David Rice and James Sumner or any three of them to make division of the Estate of John Norfleet decd.

Deed of land Kedar Odom to John Odom proved by the oath of Abraham Brayshar.

Lawrence Baker, George Williams, Seth Riddick and James Riddick or any three of them to make division of the Estate of Wm. Brooks decd. and make report.

The Sheriff returned verdict of Jury. Dispute of Entry between Stephen Eure and John Green. John Green relinquishes all pretentions to the above land in question. Signed by Jesse Harrell Foreman.

Extrs. of Thomas Rountree decd. to sell the perishable Estate and make report.

Ann Speight and Jeremiah Speight moved for Administration on the Estate of William Speight decd. - Granted - They to give Security in the sum of 100,000 pd. William Harriss and Samuel Smith Securities.

Inventory of the Goods & etc. of the Estate of William Speight exhibited by Ann Speight and Jeremiah Speight, Admrs.

Deed of land James Browne to Willis Browne proved by the oath of Thomas Garrott, Junr. Witness.

Deed of land Robert Parker and Wife to Jonathan Trader proved by the oath of Thomas Garrott.

Last Will of Daniel Parker decd. exhibited by Demsey Parker, Isaac Parker and Robert Parker Extrs. and proved by the oath of Jacob Sumner a Witness.

Inventory of the Goods & etc. of the Estate of Daniel Parker decd. exhibited by Demsey Parker one of the Extrs.

The Sheriff returned the verdict of Jury in the Dispute of Land by William Harriss against James Costen - - 360 Acres should be laid off to William Harris joining the land sold to said Harris by the Heirs of Revd. John Rice, decd. and the vacant land, if any, joining said 360 Acres to James Costen. Seth Riddick Foreman.

Sheriff returned the verdict of Jury in Dispute of land between Demsey Odom against Thomas Smith - - land in question is the property of the said Demsey Odom and that the said Thomas Smith's Entry should be void and of none effect. George Williams and the rest of the Jury.

Robert Riddick appointed Guardian to Mary Riddick orphan of Docton Riddick decd. He to give Security in the sum of 300,000 pds. William Harriss and Christopher Riddick Securities.

The Sheriff returned the account of the Sale of part of the Estate of Docton Riddick decd.

William Brooks appointed Guardian to Lodowick Brooks orphan of William Brooks decd. He to give Security in the sum of 50,000 pds. William Baker and James Bristow Securities.

Thomas Hunter Esqr. appointed Sheriff. William Baker and James Sumner Securities.

Last Will of James Garrott, Senr., exhibited by Thomas Garrott, Junr. one of the Extrs. and proved by the oath of Robert Parker a Witness.

Inventory of the Goods & etc. of the Estate of James Garrott, Junr. was exhibited by Thos. Garrott one of the Extrs.

Henry Booth moved for Administration on the Estate of Abel Martin decd. - Granted. He to give Security in the sum of 50,000 pds. Thomas Brickell and Jonathan Roberts Securities.

Benjamin Robins an Indian Boy about 17 years of age bound as an apprentice to Jethro Meltear.

Elisha Robins an Indian Boy about 11 Years of age bound as an apprentice to Jethro Meltear.

The Admr. and Admrx. of the Estate of William Speight decd. to sell the perishable part of the Estate to pay debts.

Deed of land Thomas Smith to Saml. Smith.

Deed of Land Mills Wilkinson to Luke Sumner proved by the oath of John Wilkinson.

Deed of land to Mills Wilkinson to Luke Sumner proved by the oath of Jno. Wilkinson.

The sum of 2,500 pds. be allowed William Baker Sheriff for his extra services as Sheriff for the last year.

Tuesday May 22, 1781.

Present: Jesse Eason, James Sumner, Christopher Riddick, Justices.

Joseph Rooks produced a Negro Man named Cupet and Jenny a Woman and were judged by the Court the Man Cupit to be Forty Years of age and Jenny to be Forty Five Years of age.

Additional Inventory of the Estate of William Eason decd. exhibited by Mordica Perry one of the Extrs.

Persons appointed to make division of the Estate of William Eason decd. made return.

Inventory of the Estate of Abel Martin decd. exhibited by Henry Booth Admr.

Motion that John Robins, Thomas Brickell, Jonah Roberts and Robert Parker or any three of them make division of the Estate of Abel Martin decd.

William Baker Extr. of the Last Will and Testament of Joseph Tugwell decd. sell such part of the Estate of the said decd. as he shall think most to the advantage of the orphans of the above decd.

David Small appointed Constable in the room of Samuel Harrell.

Mordica Perry to have leave to sell the perishable part of the Estate of the orphans of William Eason decd.

George Bowin about 13 years of age orphan of William Bowin decd. bound as an apprentice to Jacob Bagley to learn the business of a Shoemaker.

Moses Hill appointed Guardian to Henry Hill and Miles Hill orphans of Abraham Hill decd. He to give Security in the sum of 15,000 pds. Jacob Bagley and Mordica Perry Securities.

Following persons appointed as Jurymen: Samuel Eure, Stephen Eure, David Watson, Moses Kitrell, Isaac Walters, Jesse Barnes, Jesse Vann, Abraham Sumner, Jacob Gordon, James Norfleet, Moses Hare, Junr., Thomas Parker, John Dardin, John Only, Henry Booth, William Hinton, John Robins, Timothy Lassiter, John Briggs, William Brooks, Thomas Trotman, Amos Trotman, Moses Hill, Willian Odom, Moses Blanshard, Stephen Rogers, Demsey Odom, Joel Goodman, Henry Goodman and Abraham Eason.

License granted to Ruth Garrott to keep Public House. Thomas Garrott and George Williams Securities.

Third Monday of Aug. - Aug. 20, 1781.

Present: Jesse Eason, Joseph Riddick, Isaac Pipkin, Christopher Riddick, Justices.

Deed of land Henry Walton to Demsey Trotman proved by the oath of Thomas Trotman.

Deed of land Demsey Trotman to Henry Walton proved by the oath of Thos. Trotman.

Deed of land Zadock Hinton to James Gregory proved by the oath of Thos. Brickell.

John Robbins, Thomas Brickell and Robt. Parker made a report of their division of the Estate of Abel Martin decd. and was exhibited by Henry Booth Admr.

The Sheriff returned the following persons as Grand Jurors: John Robins, Stephen Eure, David Watson, Jesse Barnes, Jesse Vann, Abraham Sumner, Moses Hare, Junr., John Briggs, William Brooks, Thomas Trotman, Amos Trotman, Moses Blanshard, Stephen Rogers, Joel Goodman, Abraham Eason, Ephraim Griffin, Robert Taylor and Henry Hill.

Last Will of Alec Hunter exhibited by Thomas Walton one of the Extrs. and proved by the oath of Elisha Hunter a Witness.

Inventory of the Goods & etc. of the Estate of Alec Hunter decd. exhibited by Thomas Walton Extr.

William Daniel orphan of William Daniel decd. about the age of 13 Years bound as an apprentice to Thomas Brickell to learn the business of a Taylor.

George Williams, George Piland and Robert Parker to lay out a road from Troy Plantation into the Bennets Creek Road between Bennets Creek Bridge and the Halfway Run and that Abraham Cowper open and clear the same and after being cleared and opened the same to be deemed a Publick Way.

Levi Lee appointed Overseer of the road in the room of Lewis Sparkman resigned.

County Treasurer to pay John Brickell the sum of 3,225 pds. for one years Sallary as Attorney for the State.

Deed of Gift Mary Ronals to James Crafford proved by the oath of John Harrell, Junr.

Last Will and Testament of William Freeman decd. was exhibited by James Freeman and William Freeman Extrs. and proved by the oath of Samuel Taylor a Witness.

John Riddick appointed Overseer of the road in the room of William Hinton resigned.

Seth Riddick, Jethro Sumner and David Rice Esqrs. Gentlemen, appointed a Commission of the Peace - Qualified as Justices of the Peace.

Tuesday Aug. 21, 1781.

Present: Christopher Riddick, Joseph Riddick, Jethro Sumner, Jesse Eason, Justices.

Joshua Small appointed Overseer of the road in the room of James Norfleet resigned.

Deed of land John Miller to Alexander Eason proved by the oath of Jesse Eason.

Deed of land Samuel Taylor to Richard Briggs proved by the oath of Moses Davis.

Thomas Garrott, Junr., appointed Guardian to Nancy Garrett orphan of James Garrett decd. He to give Security in the sum of 4000 pds. Thomas Hunter and John Gatling Securities.

Deed of land Joseph Norfleet to Jonah Stallings proved by the oath of Demsey Barnes.

Account of Sale of the Estate of Thomas Rountree returned on oath of Thomas Hunter.

Joseph Riddick Esqr. appointed to take a list of the Taxable property in the Muster Bounds of Capt. Joseph Riddick and Capt. Jonathan Roberts.

Jethro Sumner Esqr. to take a list of the Taxable property in the District or Muster Bounds of Capt. Jethro Sumner and Capt. James Arline.

Isaac Pipkin Esqr. to take a list of the Taxable property in the District or Muster Bounds of Capt. William Goodman.

Seth Riddick Esqr. to take a list of the Taxable property in the District or Muster Bounds of Capt. Charles Eure.

Christopher Riddick Esqr. to take a list of the Taxable property in the District or Muster Bounds of Capt. Christopher Riddick.

George Outlaw, Jacob Bagley, and Jonathan Roberts appointed Assessors of the property in the District or Muster Bounds of Capt. Joseph Riddick and Capt. Jonathan Roberts.

Thomas Parker, Edward Arnell and Isaac Walters appointed Assessors of the property in the District or Muster Bounds of Capt. Jethro Sumner and Capt. James Arline.

Solomon King, William Goodman and William Warren appointed Assessors of the property in the District or Muster Bounds of Capt. William Goodman.

Stephen Eure, Jesse Harrell and Moor Carter appointed Assessors for the property in the District or Muster Bounds of Capt. Charles Eure.

Joseph Figg, Isaac Miller and Anthony Matthews appointed Assessors for the property in the District or Capt. Christopher Riddick.

Willis Browne appointed Overseer of the road in the room of the George Williams resigned

Lawrence Baker, Seth Riddick and George Willisms made return of the division of the Estate of William Brooks decd.

The Sheriff returned for Petty Jury the following persons: William Hinton, Junr., Demsey Odom, William Hinton, Senr., William Gatlin, John Miller, Moses Davis, Jonathon Roberts, Jacob Bagley, Timothy Lassiter, Jesse Saunders, Thos. Walton and Ezekiel Trotman.

Part of the Estate of Alec Hunter decd. to be sold at Publick Sale by Thos. Walton Extr.

David Rice, Esqr., Charles Rountree, Thomas Trotman and Simon Stallings or any three of them to make division of the Estate of Alec Hunter decd.

Following persons to be summoned by the Sheriff to serve as Jurymen: Jacob Pierce, Aaron Lassiter, Abraham Harrell, Benjn.

Goodman, John Powell, John Darden, Charles Rountree, Thos. Spivey, Joshua Small, Wm. Vann, James Brady, Wm. Warren, Isaac Parker, Demsey Parker, Jas. Riddick, William Walters, Isaac Walters, Moses Boyce, Francis Parker, Joseph Speight, Robert Parker, James Knight, William Doughtie, Lewis Walters, James Piland, Saml. Eure, James Landing, Thos. Barnes, John Parker, Junr., and Job Umfleet.

George Dunn, William Harriss, Josiah Granbery and William Cowper to attend the next meeting of Superior Court to be held at Edenton.

Jethro Meltear to warn the Inhabitants of Capt. Jonah Roberts District or Muster Bounds to give a list of Taxable property to Joseph Riddick Esqr. before the 15th. of August next.

William Arnell Constable to warn the Inhabitants of Capt. Jethro Sumners District or Muster Bounds to give a list of Taxable property to Capt. Jethro Sumner on or before the 15th. Aug. next.

Charles Vann Constable to warn the Inhabitants of Capt. Charles Eures and Capt. Wm. Goodmans Districts or Muster Bounds to give a list of their Taxable property to Seth Riddick Esqr. on or before the 15th. of Aug. next.

John Polson Constable to warn the Inhabitants of Capt. Christopher Riddicks District or Muster Bounds to give a list of their Taxable property to Christopher Riddick Esqr. and that he warn the Inhabitants of Capt. James Arlines Company to give a list of their Taxable property to Jethro Sumner, Esqr., on or before the 15th. of Aug. next.

Ephraim Griffin appointed Constable in the room of David Small.

Ephraim Griffin Constable to warn the Inhabitants of the District or Muster Bounds of Capt. Joseph Riddick to give a list of their Taxable property to Joseph Riddick, Esqr., on or before the 15th. of Aug. next.

Aaron Lassiter appointed Overseer of the road in the room of Isaac Harrell.

Lawrence Baker, Clerk, of this Court, be allowed the sum of 7,500 pds. for services at May Court last.

Third Monday in Nov., 1781.

Present: Jacob Hunter, Christopher Riddick, William Baker, David Rice, Seth Riddick, Isaac Pipkin, Justices.

Last Will and Testament of John Benton decd. exhibited by Elizabeth Benton Extrx. and Jesse Benton Extr. and proved by the oath of Jethro Sumner, Esqr., a Witness.

Inventory of the Goods & etc. of the Estate of John Benton decd. exhibited by Elizabeth Benton Extrx. and Jesse Benton Extr.

The Sheriff returned for Grand Jurymen the following persons: Chas. Rountree, (Foreman), Abraham Harrell, William Harris (?),

William Walters, Isaac Walters, Moses Boyce, Francis Parker, Joseph Speight, Robert Parker, James Knight, James Piland, Saml. Eure, James Landing, Thomas Barnes, John Parker, Job Umfleet, Joshua Small, Wm. Vann and Jas. Brady.

Inventory of the Goods & etc. of the Estate of William Freeman exhibited by James Freeman and William Freeman, Extrs.

Deed of Gift Trusanah Raby to James Jones proved by the oath of David Jones.

Deed of land Richard Green and Selah Green to Jonathan Collins (?) Cullins (?) proved by the oath of Jesse Harrell.

Deed of land Jesse Harrell to Hezekiah Jones proved by the oath of Moses Jones.

James Sumner, Esqr., appointed Overseer of the road from the Orepeak to the Virginia Line and that the hands of John R. Wilkinson, John Brinkley, Lewis Jones, William Matthias, Josiah Frank and the Negroes of Joseph Jno. Sumner work on the said road under him.

Bond from Josiah Granbery, William Hinton and David Rice Ackd. by David Rice and Josiah Granbery and proved by the oath of Isaac Hunter.

Deed of land William Walton and Rachal Small to James Gregory proved by the oath of John Branbery.

Robert Parker appointed Overseer of the road in the room of Seth Riddick resigned.

Inventory of the Goods & etc. of the Estate of James Riddick exhibited by Willis Riddick, Admr.

Mr. Jethro Sumner, Robert Riddick, Christopher Riddick and Lawrence Baker or any three of them audit and settle the accounts of Elizabeth Riddick, Admrx. of Docton Riddick decd.

William Goodman, William Warren and Stephen Rogers made return of assessment of property in the District that they were appointed.

Deed of land Henry Booth to Joseph Browne, Junr. proved by the oath of Jesse Browne.

John Warren appeared for begetting a Bastard Child on the Body of Ann Curle. He to give Security in the sum of 50 pds. in Gold or Silver. Jesse Barnes and Charles Vann Securities.

Mrs. Elizabeth Riddick appointed Guardian to Saml. Riddick orphan minor of Docton Riddick decd. She to give Security in the sum of 3000 pds. Jethro Sumner and Robert Riddick Securities.

Amerias Blanshard appointed Overseer of the road in the room of William Hinton resigned.

Inventory of the Estate of Thomas Rountree decd. exhibited by Charles Rountree Extr.

Joseph Riddick, Esqr., Simon Stallings, Thomas Trotman and George Outlaw or any three of them to make division of the Estate of Thomas Rountree decd.

Isaac Miller and Anthony Matthews made return of the assessment of the property in the District that they were appointed.

Edward Arnold and Richard Arnold, Joseph Hare, Cadar Benton and Amos Parker work on the road under James Knight Overseer of the road that leads from Bennets Creek to Willis Wiggons.

The Extrx. and Extr. of the Estate of John Benton decd. to sell part of the perishable Estate of the said decd. to pay debts.

Tuesday Nov. 20, 1781.

Present: Jacob Hunter, William Baker, Joseph Riddick, David Rice, Seth Riddick, Justices.

Jeremiah Speight Admr. of William Speight decd. made return of the Sales of the said Estate.

Deed of land William Cleaves to George Williams proved by the oath of Demsey Parker.

Deed of land Kedar Riddick to George Williams, Junr., proved by the oath of Demsey Parker.

Jacob Pierce (?), Aaron Lassiter, Benjamin Gordon, John Powell and Lewis Walters to be summoned to appear at the next Court to show Cause as to why they did not appear as Jurymen.

The Sheriff returned for Petty Jury the following persons: Demsey Parker, Thomas Spivey, James Riddick, Jacob Bagley, Demsey Bond, William Odom, Stephen Rogers, Amos Trotman, Demsey Odom, Joel Goodman, Jeremiah Speight and Abraham Morgan.

Mary Smith moved for Administration on the Estate of James Smith decd. - Granted. She to give Security in the sum of 1500 pds. James Braddy and Samuel Eure Securities.

Inventory of the Goods & etc. of the Estate of James Smith decd. exhibited by Mary Smith, Admr.

Jonathan Roberts, George Outlaw and Jacob Bagley Assessors made return.

Ordered that the Publick House Keepers in this County receive the following rates (to wit) Breakfast 2 pds. or 200 dolls. Dinner 4 pds. or 400 dolls. Supper 2 pds. or 200 dolls. Lodging 1 pd. or 100 dolls. Corn _____ 8 pds. or 68 dolls. Fodder 2 per bundle or 16 2/3 dolls. Pasturage for a Hourse a Knight or day 4 or 3/4 dolls. Rum or Brandy 1 pd. per Gill or 100 dolls. Spirits pr. Gill made in Toddy 1/4 or 133 dolls.

The County Treasurer to pay George Dunn the sum of 325 pds. per day for eight days service attending the Superior Court at Edenton as a Juror.

Edward Arnold, Isaac Walters and Thos. Parker made return of the Assessment of the property in the Districts they were appointed.

Wednesday Nov. 21, 1781.

Present: Jacob Hunter, Joseph Riddick, Christopher Riddick, Isaac Pipkin, David Rice, Jethro Sumner, William Baker, Justices.

Isaac Miller to be allowed for five days services Assessing the property in the District that he was appointed and that Anthony Matthews be allowed for four days services.

Following persons summoned by the Sheriff to serve as Jurors: Joseph Hurdle, Saml. Harrell, Henry Walton, Edward Berriman, John Bethey, James Lang, Charles Eure, Moor Carter, Kedar Hill, Thomas Trotman, William King, Guy Hobbs, Stephen Eure, Jesse Harrell, Jesse Browne, George Williams, Isaac Harrell, John Riddick, Jacob Gordon, David Jones, Senr., Jonathan Williams, Edward Doughtie, Francis Saunders, Jesse Benton, John Odom, Jesse Barnes, Philip Lewis, Henry Lee, Micajah Riddick and James Pruden.

The Assessors to be allowed the sum of 300 dollars for each and every day they were employed assessing the Taxable property.

The sum of 25 Shillings to be levied on each Hundred Pounds Taxable property for the present year.

Jacob Hunter, Esqr., to collect the Publick and County Tax in the District that Jonathan Roberts, George Outlaw and Jacob Bagley were appointed Assessors. He to give Security in the sum of 300,000 pds. Seth Riddick and Christopher Riddick Securities.

Jethro Sumner, Esqr., to collect the Publick and County Tax in the District that Thomas Parker, Edward Arnold and Isaac Walters were Assessors. He to give Security in the sum of 300,000 pds. Mr. George Dunn and Mr. William Walters Securities.

George Dunn to collect the Publick and County Tax in the District that William Goodman, William Warren and Solomon King were appointed Assessors. He to give Security in the sum of 300,000 pds. William Walters and Francis Speight Securities.

Christopher Riddick, Esqr., to collect the Publick and County Tax in the District that Isaac Miller, Anthony Matthews and Joseph Figg were appointed Assessors. He to give Security in the sum of 300,000 pds. Jacob Hunter and Isaac Pipkin, Esqr., Securities.

James Bray Walters to collect the Publick and County Tax in the District that Moor Carter, Stephen Eure and Jesse Harrell were appointed Assessors. He to give Security in the sum of 300,000 pds. Jethro Sumner, Esqr. and Mr. George Dunn Securities.

Moor Carter, Jesse Harrell and Stephen Eure made return of the Assessment of the property in the District they were appointed.

Joseph Riddick, Esqr. appointed Commissioner for this County.

Third Monday in Feb. - Feb. 18, 1782.

Present: Jacob Hunter, Christopher Riddick, David Rice, Jethro Sumner, Isaac Pipkin, Justices.

Mary Riddick appointed Guardian to Henry Riddick, Miles Riddick, Nathaniel Riddick, Elizabeth Riddick and David Riddick orphan minors of Mills Riddick decd. She to give Security in the sum of 200 pds. Jacob Hunter, Esqr. and Christopher Riddick, Esqr. Securities.

Deed of land Samuel Browne to William Vann proved by the oath of Charles Eure.

Deed of land James Gregory to Robert Taylor proved by the oath of Himbrick Hill.

Deed of Gift John Green to Matthias Green proved by the oath of Jesse Harrell.

The County Treasurer to pay William Harriss 320 pds. for eight days attendance as a Juryman at the Superior Court at Edenton in Nov. last.

Deed of land William Cleaves to Arthor (?) Williams proved by the oath of George Williams.

William Crafford moved for Administration on the Estate of James Wallis decd. - Granted - He to give Security in the sum of 200 pds. Joseph Speight and John Thomas Securities.

Inventory of the Goods & etc. of the Estate of James Wallis decd. exhibited by William Crafford Admr.

Simon Stallings Guardian to James Walton made return of his accounts.

Elizabeth Harrell moved for Administration on the Estate of Samuel Harrell decd. - Granted - She to give Security in the sum of 150 pds. Charles Eure and Lewis Sparkman Securities.

Inventory of the Goods & etc. of the Estate of Samuel Harrell decd. exhibited by Elizabeth Harrell, Admrx.

Deed of land James Winborne and Easter Winborne to Jethro Ballard proved by the oath of Kedar Ballard.

Deed of land James Sumner to John Powell proved by the oath of William Ellis.

Thomas Smith orphan of James Smith decd. about the age of 15 years the 15th. day of Oct. last, bound as an apprentice to

Cyprian Cross to learn the business of a Taylor.

Thomas Walton, Extr. of Alec. Hunter Decd. returned an account of the sales of part of the Estate of the said Decd.

David Rice, Charles Rountree, Thomas Trotman and Simon Stallings who were appointed to make division of the Estate of Alec Hunter decd. made report.

John Polson Constable to be allowed 300 dollars per day for three and half days service warning the Inhabitants to give a list of their Taxable property.

James Brady, George Williams, Charles Eure and Stephen Eure to make a division of the Estate of James Smith decd.

Mary Smith appointed Guardian to Thomas Smith orphan minor of James Smith decd. - She to give Security in the sum of 200 pds. Philip Lewis and Jesse Harrell Securities.

James Gregory, James Costen, David Rice and John Gordon or any three of them to audit and settle the accounts of Thomas Walton Extr. of Alec Hunter decd.

Stephen Eure appointed Guardian to Milley (?) Smith orphan of James Smith decd. He to give Security in the sum of 200 pds. Samuel Smith and Israel Beeman Securities.

Joseph Riddick, Simon Stallings, Thomas Trotman and George Outlaw appointed to make division of the Estate of Thomas Rountree, decd.

Edward Arnold, Jethro Ballard and James Norfleet appointed to make division of the Estate of Jacob Norfleet decd.

Deed of land John Twine and Pleasant Twine to Elisha Norfleet proved by the oath of Jacob Gordon.

John Powell and Lewis Walters to pay the sum of 10 pds. for not attending this Court as Jurymen.

Tuesday Morning.

Present: Jacob Hunter, Joseph Riddick, Jethro Sumner, Justices.

James Gregory, Jethro Ballard, William Goodman, Junr. and Moses Kitrell to be summoned to attend the Superior Court as Jurymen to be held at Edenton the 1st. of of May next.

Jacob Powell, Robert Taylor, Kedar Hinton, Moses Davis, Solomon Briggs, Timothy Lassiter, Ruben Lassiter, John Darden, Lewis Jones, James Costen, Jethro Meltear, Edward Brisco, Moses Benton, Thomas Parker, Edward Arnold, Thomas Smith, William Harriss, Jeremiah Speight, Elisha Parker, Joel Goodman, Henry Goodman, Thomas Vann, Thomas Burges, James Landing, Demsey Barnes, Joseph Figg, Wright Hayes, Peter Harrell, William Doughtie and Samuel Eure to be summoned to next Court as Jurymen.

Amos Lassiter appointed Guardian to Meremiah Menya (?). He to give Security in the sum of 50 pds. James Costen and Samuel Smith Securities.

Demsey Trotman appointed Guardian to John Hunter. He to give Security in the sum of 300 pds. Thomas Trotman and Thomas Walton Securities.

Thomas Walton appointed Guardian to Theopholis Hunter orphan minor of John Hunter decd. He to give Security in the sum of 400 pds. Demsey Trotman and Thomas Hunter Securities.

Thomas Brickell to have a license to keep a Public House. He to give Security in the sum of 10,000 pds. Jonathan Roberts and Demsey Bond Securities.

Thomas Hunter made return of his Guardianship of John Banbury Walton.

Thomas Hunter made return of his account with Timothy Walton orphan of Timothy Walton decd.

Deed of land Robert Parker to John Polson.

John Odom appeared being charged by Ann Rooks for begetting a Bastard Child on her Body. He to give Security in the sum of 100 pds. Philip Lewis and Jesse Barnes Securities.

Josiah Parker came into Court - for his begetting a Bastard Child on the Body of Naomi Williams. He to give Security in the sum of 100 pds. Moor Carter and Thomas Vann Securities.

Last Will of William Powell, Junr., exhibited by Kedar Powell and Isaac Powell, Extrs. and proved by the oath of William Powell, Senr. a Witness.

Thomas Walton Guardian to Theopholis Hunter to sell the perishable part of the Estate of John Hunter.

The sum of 240 pds. to be deducted out of the sum that Moses Kitrell, Tax Geatherer, is bound to pay to the County Treasurer over charged him for the Taxes on the Estate of William Sumner orphan of David Sumner.

Thomas Trotman appointed Overseer of the road where Henry Walton was formerly Overseer.

Joseph Riddick, Esqr. appointed Commissioner for this County. Securities Jonathan Roberts and Seth Riddick.

Mary Smith to sell the perishable part of the Estate of Joseph Smith and Nanny Smith orphans of James Smith decd.

<u>Third Monday in May - May 20, 1782.</u>

Present: Isaac Pipkin, Jethro Sumner and David Rice, Justices.

Deed of Gift Joseph Parker to Garrett Davis and Hester Davis proved by the oath of James Freeman.

Last Will of Garrett Davis exhibited by Thomas Mansfield an Extr. and proved by the oath of James Freman a Witness.

Deed of land Demsey Parker to Elisha Cross.

William Crafford, Admr. of the Estate of James Wallis decd. returned an account of the sales of the Estate.

Deed of land John Varnel to James Curle proved by the oath of James Landing.

John Wallis orphan of James Wallis decd. bound as an apprentice to William Crafford to learn the business of a Cooper.

Deed of land Seasbrook Wilson to John Baker proved by the oath of Robert Parker,

Thomas Walton Guardian to Theopholis Hunter made return of the sales of the perishable part of the Estate of the said orphan.

Demsey Trotman Guardian to John Hunter made return of the sales of the perishable part of the Estate of the said orphan.

Moses Hill Guardian to Henry Hill orphan of Abraham Hill decd. made return of the sales of part of the Estate of the said orphan.

Deed of land Andrew Hambleton to Thomas Harris proved by the oath of Thos. Hambleton.

Deed of land Thomas Norris to Andrew Hambleton proved by the oath of Thomas Hambleton.

The Sheriff returned the following persons as Grand Jury: James Costen, Foreman, Jacob Powell, Robert Taylor, Kedar Hinton, Moses Davis, Reubin Lassiter, John Darden, Edward Buses (?), Thomas Parker, Moses Benton, Edward Arnold, William Harriss, Jeremiah Speight, Elisha Parker, Joel Goodman, Henry Goodman, Demsey Barnes and Joseph Figg.

Deed of land Henry Booth and Margaret Booth to Jeremiah Jordon proved by the oath of Thomas Brickell.

Inventory of the Goods & etc. of the Estate of William Powell, Junr., decd. exhibited by Isaac Powell an Extr.

Deed of Gift William Powell to Isaac Powell proved by the oath of John Casey.

Jacob, Sam, Hardy and Cajah, Negroes, the property of William Powell to work on the road under William Harriss, Overseer.

Deed of sale of Land Stephen Eure to Samuel K_____. ackd.

Deed of land Henry Hill to James Gregory ackd.

Complaint of William Arnold against Daniel Ellis for a Forceable

Entry - - - "Found that the said Ellis did detain by force who gave up the possession to the said William Arnold".

Last Will of Sarah Blanshard exhibited by Absolom Blanshard and William Hinton, Extrs. and proved by the oath of Jacob Hunter, Esqr.

Inventory of the Goods & etc. of the Estate of Sarah Blanshard decd. exhibited by William Hinton and Absolom Blanshard, Extrs.

Inventory of part of the Estate of Benjamin Blanshard decd. was exhibited by William Hinton, Extr.

Jacob Hunter, James Sumner, Thomas Hunter and David Rice or any three of them to make a division of the Estate of Benjamin Blanshard, decd.

Stephen Eure, Charles Eure, Moor Carter and William Baker or any three of them to make division of the Estate of Samuel Harrell, decd.

Joseph Smith orphan of James Smith decd. about the age of 13 years (on the 4th. day of Jan. in the present year), be bound as an apprentice to Cyprian Cross to learn the business of a Taylor.

Cyprian Cross appointed Guardian to Joseph Smith orphan of James Smith. He to give Security in the sum of 100 pds. Demsey Barnes and George Williams Securities.

Last Will of William Goodman decd. exhibited by John Brickell Atto. at Law and proved by the oath of William Hughes a Witness. - - - William Goodman and Henry Goodman Extrs.

Inventory of the Goods & etc. of the Estate of William Goodman decd. was exhibited by the Extrs.

Subscribers to a Petition to clear out and keep open Bennets Creek from Bennets Creek Bridge to Benjamin Sumners Landing.

Deed of Gift John Goodman to William Goodman.

<u>Tuesday Morning 21st. April, 1782.</u>

Present: Jacob Hunter, Christopher Riddick, William Baker, Seth Riddick, David Rice, Isaac Pipkin, Justices.

The sum of 10 pds. to be allowed Thomas Hunter Esqr. for one year extra services.

The sum of 5 pds. 8 sh. to be allowed Moses Kitrell for his attendance at the Superior Court as a Juryman.

James Bristow appointed Guardian to Fanny Bristow orphan of William Bristow decd. He to give Security in the sum of 150 pds. Isaac Pipkin and Moses Kitrell Securities.

Jethro Sumner, Esqr. appointed Sheriff for the ensueing year. He to give Bond. William Baker and Christopher Riddick, Esqrs. Securities.

Isaac Miller, William Vann and William Arnold to assess the property in this County.

William Baker Esqr. to take the list of the Taxable property in the Muster Bounds of Capt. Charles Eure and Capt. James Arline.

Seth Riddick Esqr. to take the list of the Taxable property in the Muster Bounds of Capt. Christopher Riddick. Isaac Pipkin Esqr. to take the list of the Taxable property in the Muster Bounds of Capt. William Goodman. Capt. Rice to take a list of the Taxable property in the Muster Bounds of Capt. Jethro Sumner. Thomas Hunter Esqr. to take a list of the Taxable property in the Muster Bounds of Capt. Jonathan Roberts. Colo. Jacob Hunter to take a list of the Taxable property in the Muster Bounds of Capt. Joseph Riddick.

Richard Freeman to pay a Tax on the sum of 1,701 pds. instead of a Tax on 8,760 pds. for the year 1780 - it appearing as a mistake by the Assessor.

Charles Vann to warn the Inhabitants of the District in the Muster Bounds of Capt. William Goodman to give a list of their property to Isaac Pipkin, Esqr. and to warn the Inhabitants of Capt. Charles Eure's District to give a list of their Taxable property to William Baker Esqr. and he likewise to warn the Inhabitants of Capt. Arline's Company to give a list of their property to William Baker Esqr. - - William Arnold to warn the Inhabitants of Capt. Sumners District to give a list of their property to David Rice Esqr. and that Jethro Meltear, Constable, to warn the Inhabitants of the District of Capt. Jonathan Roberts to give a list of their property to Thomas Hunter Esqr. Ephraim Griffin, Constable, to warn the Inhabitants of Capt. Joseph Riddick's District to give a list of their property to Jacob Hunter, Esqr. John Polson, Constable, to warn the Inhabitants of the District of Capt. Christopher Riddick to give a list of their property to Seth Riddick, Esqr.

The Sheriff to summon the following persons to appear at the next Court as Jurymen: Joshua Small, David Small, Benjn. Gordon, Jacob Gordon, Richard Briggs, Moses Hare, Aron Lassiter, Abraham Harrell, Jacob Pearce, Abraham Eason, Charles Rountree, Simon Stallings, Jonathan Roberts, Jethro Benton, Junr., Edward Doughtie, William Harriss, Anthony Matthews, Kedar Riddick, James Pruden, Micajah Riddick, William Walters, Isaac Walters, Demsey Odom, John Catlin, William Warren, Stephen Rogers, John Odom, Demsey Barnes, Charles Eure and Jesse Harrell.

George Williams, James Brady, Stephen Eure and Charles Eure made report of the Division of the Estate of James Smith decd.

Wednesday Morning 10 O'Clock.

Present: Christopher Riddick, William Baker, Seth Riddick, Justices.

(Top of page - August 19th. 1782)

Third Monday in May, 1792

Present: Jesse Eason, James Sumner, Isaac Pipkin, David Rice, William Baker, Justices.

Deed of land Henry Hill to Thomas Hoffler proved by the oath of James Freeman.

Deed of land Henry Hill to James Robbins, Benjamin Robbins, Patience Robbins, Sarah Robbins, Nanny Robbins, Elizabeth Robbins, Darkus Robbins and Christian Robbins proved by the oath of Thomas Hoffler.

Deed of land Peter Piland to Josiah Jordan proved by the oath of Thos. Brickell.

A Bond - Josiah Benton to Katherine Benton proved by the oath of Joseph Speight.

Inventory of the Goods & etc. of the Estate of Garrett Davis decd. exhibited by Thomas Mansfield, Extr.

Deed of Gift Rebecca Lassiter to Reuben Lassiter proved by the oath of Aaron Blanshard.

Last Will of Samuel Green decd. exhibited by William Berreman one of the Extrs. and proved by the oath of Abraham Hurdle a Witness.

Inventory of the Goods & etc. of the Estate of Samuel Green decd. exhibited by William Berreman Extr.

William Bereman to sell part of the Estate of Samuel Green decd. to pay debts.

Joseph Hurdle, Thomas Hurdle, Colo. Jacob Hunter and James Gregory to make a division of the Estate of Samuel Green decd.

Inventory of the Goods & etc. of the Estate of Garrett Davis decd. exhibited by Thomas Mansfield and Extr. (ALL THIS CROSSED OUT)

Deed of land Samuel Harrell to Jacob Hunter proved by the oath of Isaac Hunter.

Deed of land Jacob Hunter to John Rice proved by the oath of Isaac Hunter.

Deed of land Jacob Hunter to Samuel Harrell proved by the oath of Isaac Hunter.

Christopher Riddick, Seth Riddick and James Riddick made return of the division of the Estate of Edward Clark, decd.

Account of the sales of the Estate of Samuel Harrell, decd. was exhibited by Lewis Sparkman, Admr. in behalf of his Wife ___esradria.

Last Will of Thomas Barnes exhibited by Benjamin Barnes and Jesse Barnes the Extrs. and proved by the oath of Edward Warren and Jesse Van, Witnesses.

Jacob, Sam, Hardy and Cajah, Negroes, the property of William Powell to work on the road under James Pruden.

John Duke and Hands to work on the road under William Harriss,, Overseer.

Thomas Garrett granted a License to keep a Public House.

John Russell orphan of William Russell decd. about the age of 10 years bound to Jeremiah Jordan to learn the business of a House Carpenter.

Jethro Meltear to have a License to keep a Public House. Jonathan Roberts and Jacob Gordon Securities.

Jethro Sumner, Moses Kitrell, William Walters and Edwd. Doughtie to audit state and settle the accounts of Jesse Benton and Elizabeth Benton Extr. and Extrx. of Capt. John Benton decd. and make report.

To Colo. Henry Riddick
A Commission Issue to the County of Nansemond in the State of Virginia to take the Deposition of Michal Ellis and Martha Jones for Elenor Frankling in a suit brought by her against Lewis Jones.

Deed of land Demsey Parker to Demsey Odom Ackd.

Tuesday August 20.

Present: Jacob Hunter, William Baker, Isaac Pipkin, Justices.

Account of the sales of the Estate of James Riddick exhibited by Willis Riddick, Admr.

William Goodman allowed the sum of 5 pds. 8 sh. for his services attending the Superior Court for the District of Edenton as a Juryman.

Inventory of the Goods & etc. of the Estate of Thomas Barnes decd. exhibited by Benjamin Barnes and Jesse Barnes, Extrs.

Christopher Riddick, Micajah Riddick and Seth Riddick made report of the division of the Estate of John Kitrell decd.

Deed of land William Walters to James Bray Walters Ackd.

County Treasurer to pay John Brickell Esqr. Atto. at Law 13 pds. 6 sh. 8 pc. for one years service as Attorney for the State.

Justices of the Peace who were appointed to take a list of the Taxable property at the Court at last sitting to take a further list of the Inhabitants owning Negroes on or before the 20th. Sept. next.

Capt. Jesse Eason ordered that a Jury be summoned by the Sheriff to lay off a road either above or below his Mill.

William Baker, Christopher Riddick and Seth Riddick to assess the property in this County on the North Side of Bennetts Creek,

Capt. David Rice, Capt. Jonathan Roberts and William Arnold to assess the property on the South Side of Bennets Creek.

Thomas Garrett, Extr. of James Garrett decd. made teturn of the sales of the Estate.

Benjamin Barnes, and Jesse Barnes Extrs. of Thomas Barnes decd. to sell so much of the Estate of the decd. to pay Debts and Legacies.

Deed of Gift Mary Smith to Thomas Smith, Joseph Smith and Mary Smith.

William Baker, William Goodman, Cyprian Cross and Jesse Warner (?) to make a division of the Estate of Thomas Barnes decd. and make report.

Frederick Eason orphan of Moses Eason decd. about the age of 14 years bound as an Apprentice to Moses Briggs to learn the business of a Shoemaker.

Hardy Eason orphan of William Eason decd. about the age of 12 years bound as an Apprentice to John Duke, Junr. to learn the business of a Blacksmith.

Solomon Eason orphan of William Eason decd. about the age of 10 years bound as an Apprentice to Aaron Lassiter to learn the business of a Cooper.

Samuel Harrell appointed Constable in the room of Ephraim Griffin resigned.

Lawrence Baker Clerk of this Court to be allowed the sum of 20 pds. for one years extra services.

Account of the sales of part of the Estate of the orphans of James Smith decd. exhibited by Saml. Smith Sheriff.

The Sheriff to summon the following persons to serve as Jurymen: Abraham Sumner, Ezekial Trotman, Thomas Trotman, Henry Walton, Thomas Spivey, William Spivey, Jonah Lassiter, Amos Hobbs, Jacob Bagley, Aron Hobbs, Seth Stallings, Demsey Bond, William Hinton, Amos Lassiter, Thomas Walton, William Ellis, Abraham Morgan, James Riddick, William Vann, Thomas Vann, James Braddy, Jonathan Williams, Israel Beeman, Moor Carter, Peter Harrell, Geo. Williams, Jesse Browne, Joseph Speight and James Hayes.

George Outlaw, John Powell, Philip Lewis and Francis Speight to be summoned to serve as Jurymen at the Superior Court.

18 November, 1782.

Present: Christopher Riddick, William Baker, Jesse Eason, Seth Riddick, Justices.

Commission Issue to Colo. Henry Riddick of the County of Nansemond and State of Virginia to take the Deposition of John Brinkley and others for Solomon Hiate in a suit brought by him against Mills Odom.

Commission Issue to Capt. James Sumner of this County to take the Depostion of Priscilla Jones an Infirm person in a suit brought by

43

Noah Wiggins against James Jones.

Last Will of Henry King decd. exhibited by Mary King Admrx. therein appointed and proved by the oaths of George Dunn and Francis Speight, Witness.

Inventory of the Goods & etc. of the Estate of Henry King, decd. exhibited by Mary King Extrx.

Deed of Gift Mary King to Charlotte King Ackd.

Deed of land Jacob Outlaw to Lewis Outlaw proved by the oath of James Freeman.

Last Will of Demsey Costen decd. exhibited by James Costen and David Rice Extrs. therein appointed and proved by the oath of Job Riddick a Witness.

Inventory of the Goods & etc. of the Estate of Demsey Costen exhibited by David Rice Extr.

Deed of land John Robbins and Margaret Robbins to John Hase proved by the oath of Moses Hare.

Account of sales of part of the Estate of Samuel Green decd. exhibited by William Berreman Extr.

Deed of Sale from John Thomas and Elizabeth Thomas to Cyprian Cross proved by the oath of Elisha Brinkley.

Deed of land John Shepherd to James Braddy Ackd.

Account of the sales of the Estate of William Gwinn decd. was exhibited by John Slavin one of the Extrs.

Thomas Spivey appointed Overseer of the road in the room of Jacob Bagley resigned.

Moses Boyce appointed Overseer of the road in the room of Edward Doughtie resigned.

John Shepherd chosed Guardian to Elizabeth Copeland orphan of William Copeland decd. (THIS CROSSED OUT)

George Williams, Isaac Pipkin, Christopher Riddick, and Cyprian Cross or any three of them to audit and settle the Estate of William Copeland decd.

William Baker, Lawrence Baker, David Rice and George Williams or any three of them Commissioners for letting the Building of Bennets Creek Bridge.

Deed of land Thomas Fullington to Alexander Eason proved by the oath of David Small.

David Rice, James Gregory and John Gordon who were appointed to audit and settle the accounts of Thomas Walton Extr. of Wm. Eason decd. proved by the oath of Elisha Hunter.

Moses Hobbs, Henry Hobbs, Jacob Eason, John Roberts, William Hurdle, David Kelly and Jacob Hobbs to work on the road under Thos. Trotman instead of Jacob Bagley.

Philip Lewis allowed the sum of 8 pds. 8 sh. for his attendance as a Juryman at the Superior Court.

So much of the Estate of Docton Riddick decd. to be sold at Publick sale as will pay debts.

Francis Speight to be allowed the sum of 8 pds. 8 sh. for attendance at the Superior Court at Edenton.

Tuesday Morning 10 O'Clock.

Present: David Rice, Christopher Riddick, Joseph Riddick, Thomas Hunter, Jacob Hunter, Seth Riddick, Justices.

Colo. Jacob Hunter, James Gregory and Thomas Hurdle made return of their division of the Estate of Samuel Green decd.

The Sheriff to summon the following persons to serve as Jurymen: Charles Rountree, Jacob Spivey, William Freeman, Henry Hill, Simon Stallings, James Freeman, Demsey Trotman, Thomas Parker, James Knight, Edward Arnold, Daniel Gwinn, Moses Hare, Lewis Jones, James Norfleet, Jacob Gordon, William Harriss, Cador Riddick, William Cleaves, William Boyce, Jonah Benton, Jesse Benton, Samuel Baker, Moses Kitrell, John Bethey, Henry Goodman, John Gatlin, Jesse Vann, John Odom, Saumel Eure and Jesse Harrell.

David Rice Esqr. to collect the Public and County Tax in the district of Capt. Jethro Sumner and that he give Bond in the sum of 200 pds. Jonathan Roberts and Demsey Bond Securities.

Jonathan Roberts to collect the Public and County Tax in the district of Capt. Jonathan Roberts and that he give Bond in the sum of 200 pds. David Rice and Demsey Bond Securities.

Demsey Bond to collect the Public and County Tax in the district of Capt. Joseph Riddick and that he give Bond in the sum of 200 pds. Jonathan Roberts and Thomas Hunter Securities.

Seth Riddick to collect the Public and County Tax for the present year and that he give Bond in the sum of 200 pds. Colo. Jacob Hunter and Major Thomas Hunter Securities.

Moses Kitrell to collect the Public and County Tax for the district of Capt. Jas. Arline and that he give bond in the sum of 200 pds. Christopher Riddick and Seth Riddick Securities.

Francis Speight to collect the Public and County Tax in the district of Capt. Wm. Goodman and Capt. Eure and to give bond in the sum of 200 pds. Isaac Pipkin and Joseph Speight Securities.

Priscilla Martin about the age of 13 years bound as an Apprentice to Elizabeth Mingard (?) Minyard (?) to learn the business of a Spinner.

Christopher Riddick, Seth Riddick and James Riddick made return of the assessment of property in the bounds they were appointed.

David Rice, William Arnold and Jonathan Roberts made return of their assessment.

Abraham Sumner summoned to appear at this Court at next sitting to show cause why he did not appear as a Juryman.

Moor Carter appointed Guardian to Nancy Smith. He to give Security in the sum of 100 pds. George Williams and Saml. Smith Securities.

Samuel Smith appointed Commissioner for this County in the stead of Joseph Riddick resigned. He to give Bond in the sum of 2000 pds. Jethro Sumner, Charles Eure, Anthony Matthews and Moor Carter Securities.

The Assessors of the Taxable property to be allowed 8 sh. for each days service assessing the property.

The sum of 2 sh. and 4 pc. to be levied on each 100 pds. of Taxable property.

William Arnold to be allowed the sum of 25 sh. for five days attendance as Constable at this Court.

Timothy Lassiter allowed the sum of 15 pds. for repairing Benets Creek Bridge.

Feb. 17, 1783

Present: Christopher Riddick, William Baker, Isaac Pipkin, Justices.

Deed of land Daniel Spivey to Moses Spivey proved by the oath of Willis Browne.

Mary King appointed Guardian to William King, John King, Elizabeth King, Mary King, Sarah King and Charlotte King orphans of Henry King decd. She to give Security in the sum of 3000 pds. William Goodman, Henry Goodman and Joseph Speight Securities.

Deed of sale James Gregory and James Gregory to John Walton proved by the oath of Robert Taylor.

Deed of land Moses Blanshard to Jacob Bagley proved by the oath of Joseph Riddick.

Timothy Lassiter allowed the sum of 20 pds. in full for repairing Bennetts Creek Bridge.

Deed of land James Gregory and James Gregory to John Walton proved by the oath of Thomas Hoffler.

Timothy Lassiter allowed the sum of 59 pds. 5 sh. for building Bennetts Creek Bridge and that the County Treasurer pay him the sum of 20 pds. out of the Tax collected for the year 1782.

John Parker moved for Administration on the Estate of John Parker decd. - Granted. He to give Security in the sum of 200 pds. Stephen Eure and Jesse Harrell Securities.

Inventory of the Goods & etc. of the Estate of John Parker decd. exhibited by John Parker, Admr.

Deed of land Henry Booth and Margaret Booth to John Robbins proved by the oath of Thomas Travis.

Deed of land John Robbins to Demsey Jones Ackd.

Deed of land John Robbins to Thomas Travis Ackd.

Each Constable employed in warning the Inhabitants to return a list of their Taxable property to be allowed one Dollar a day.

Benjamin Gordon appointed Overseer of the road in the room of Joshua Small resigned.

Deed of land Seasbrook Wilson to John Baker proved by the oath of James Braddy.

William Baker, George Williams, Jesse Harrell and Seth Riddick or any three of them to make division of the Estate of John Parker decd.

The Sheriff to summon Moses Hill, Thomas Trotman, Thomas Hoffler, Abraham Eason, John Rice, John Briggs, David Harrell, Jacob Bagley, Thomas Hurdle, Samuel Green, Mordica Perry, William King, Isaac Harrell, Reuben Lassiter, Kedar Hill, Stephen Eure, James Landing, Samuel Taylor, Demsey Barnes, Robert Parker, Stephen Rogers, Josiah Parker, David Lewis, Isaac Powell, Abraham Morgan, William Odom, James Brown, William Brooks, Peter Parker and Isaac Walters to appear at this Court as Jurymen in May next.

Jacob Hunter, Seth Riddick and Christ. Riddick Esqrs. and Lawrence Baker or any three of them to make division on the Estate of Mary Baker decd.

Jethro Sumner appointed trustee for this County for the present year.

Court adjourned until Court in Course.

Third Monday in May, 1783.

Present: Christopher Riddick, Isaac Pipkin, Thomas Hunter, Justices.

Deed of land Thomas Tynes to Solomon King proved by the oath of George Dunn.

Deed of land Henry Holland to John Wallis proved by the oath of John Parker.

Thomas Walton Guardian to Theopolis Hunter returned his account.

Moses Hill Guardian to Henry Hill orphan of Abraham Hill decd. returned his account.

Moses Hill Guardian to Miles Hill orphan of Abraham Hill decd. returned his account.

Deed of Gift of land Henry Dilday to Jesse Dilday proved by the oath of William Gatling.

Deed of land Jesse Harrell to William Crafford proved by the oath of Isaac Fryor.

Last Will of Henry Goodman decd. exhibited by Joel Goodman Extr. therein appointed and proved by the oath of William Goodman a Witness.

Inventory of the Goods & etc. of the Estate of Henry Goodman decd. exhibited by Joel Goodman Extr.

Simon Stallings Guardian to James Walton orphan of Richard Walton decd. returned his account.

Demsey Trotman Guardian to John Hunter orphan returned his account.

Deed of land Peter Piland to Edward Piland proved by the oath of David Umfleet.

Deed of land Henry Booth to William Booth proved by the oath of Thomas Travis.

Deed of land Jethro Meltear to Even Murphry proved by the oath of Lawrence Baker.

James Arline appeared for begetting a Bastard Child on the Body of Sarah Collins - - Lewis Brady and Hardy Wills Securities.

May 20, 1783

Present: Christopher Riddick, Thomas Hunter, David Rice, Justices

Thomas Hunter Guardian to Elizabeth Walton orphan of Timothy Walton decd. returned his account.

Demsey Barnes allowed the sum of 4 pds. 16 sh. for his attendance as a Juryman at the Superior Court at Edenton in the year 1778.

Thomas Hunter Esqr. to take a list of the Taxable property in the Bounds of Capt. Jonathan Roberts. Joseph Riddick Esqr. in the District of Capt. Joseph Riddick. James Sumner in the District of Capt. Jethro Sumner. Christopher Riddick in the Bounds where he is Capt. Seth Riddick in Capt. James Arlines District, Major William Baker in Capt. Charles Eures District. Isaac Pipkin Esqr. in the District of Capt. Goodman.

Christopher Riddick, Seth Riddick and James Riddick to assess the property on the North Side of Bennetts Creek.

David Rice, Jonathan Roberts and William Arnold to assess the property on the South Side of Bennetts Creek.

William Gatling to be Exempted from paying a Tax on a Negro Man named (left blank).

William Harriss to be exempted from paying a Tax on a Negro Woman named Cloe.

Jethro Meltear to summons the Inhabitants in the District of Capt. Jonathan Roberts to give a list of their property to Thomas Hunter Esqr. Samuel Harrell in the District of Capt. Joseph Riddick to give list to Joseph Riddick, Esqr. Wm. Arnold the District of Capt. Jethro Sumner to give list to Jas. Sumner Esqr. and also the District of Capt. Wm. Goodman to give list to Isaac Pipkin Esqr. John Polson in the District of Capt. Christo. Riddick to give list to Christo. Riddick Esqr. and also the District of Capt. James Arline to give list to Seth Riddick Esqr.

Wright Hayes, William Cleaves, Jesse Beacon, Wm. Walters, Wm. Doughty, James B. Walters, George Williams, George Dunn, Joseph Speight, Anthony Matthews, Thomas Smith, John Miller, Pency (?) Woods, Jesse Saunders, John Riddick, Henry Goodman, James Riddick, Richard Briggs, Abraham Harrell, Aaron Lassiter, Thomas Walton, Jacob Pierce, Kedar Hill and George Outlaw to be summoned by the Sheriff as Jurymen.

John Duke, Junr. appointed Overseer of the road in the room of William Harriss resigned.

Cyprian Cross exempted from paying a Tax on a Negro Woman named (left blank).

Jethro Sumner Esqr. to be continued as Sheriff. William Baker, and Christopher Riddick Esqrs. Securities.

Wednesday Morning 9 O'Clock

Present: Thomas Hunter, Christo. Riddick, Seth Riddick, Justices.

The County Trustee to pay Timothy Lassiter 10 pds. for carrying on the Building of the Jail in this County.

Elisha Hunter to be paid the sum of 30 pds. by the County Treasurer for carrying on the Building of the Court House of this County.

Third Monday - Aug. 11, 1783

Present: Joseph Riddick, William Baker, Thomas Hunter, Seth Riddick, David Rice, Justices.

Deed of land John Roberts to Charles Rountree proved by the oath of Nathaniel Spivey.

Deed of Gift Christian Lassiter to Aaron Lassiter proved by the oath of David Rice.

Deed of land William Booth to John Robbins proved by the oath of John Robbins, Junr.

Deed of land Edward Howell to David Cross proved by the oath of

David Howell and Michael Howell.

Thomas Fryor by John Brickell Esqr. Atto. at Law moved for Administration on the Estate of Richard Parker decd. - Granted. He to give Security in the sum of 500 pds. James Braddy and Israle Beeman Securities.

Charles Eure allowed the sum of 4 pds. 4 sh. for his attendance as a Juryman at the Superior Court in May last.

Deed of land Jacob Sumner and Sarah Sumner to Willis Parker Ackd.

Deed of land Samuel Smith to James Knight proved by the oath of William Harriss.

Deed of land Henry Hill to Henry Griffin Ackd.

Joseph Brinkley to be exempted from paying a Tax on a Negro Man Jack who is subject to fits.

Deed of land John Robberts to John Barnett proved by the oath of Levi Eason.

Seth Riddick Esqr., James Riddick and William Vann to make assessment of the Taxable property on the North Side of Bennetts Creek.

Edward Doughtie allowed the sum of 5 pds. 1 sh. 5 pc. for his attendance as a Juryman at the Superior Court at Edenton in May last.

Jethro Ballard, James Gregory Esqrs., two of the Gentlemen who where in the Commission of the Peace came into Court and Qualified themselves by taking and Subscribing the State Oath.

William Goodman and Cyprian Cross two appointed to make division of the Estate of Thomas Barnes decd. made report.

Deed of land Thomas Norris to Benjamin Eure Ackd.

James Arline to pay Sarah Collins the sum of 50 pds. for a month until Nov. Court next for the maintenance of the said Sarah Collins and Child.

Luke Langston to be exempt from paying a Tax for the year 1783 he being a very infirm person.

Deed of land Samuel Smith to William Hinton Ackd.

Elisha Hunter, Joseph Riddick and David Rice or any two of them to make division of the Estate of John Hunter decd.

Thomas Walton discharged from his attendance as a Juryman at this Court.

Tuesday Aug. 19.

Present: Isaac Pipkin, Joseph Riddick, James Gregory, Justices.

Samuel Thomas appointed Overseer of the road from the Widdow Elizabeth Odom's to Muddy Creek and that the Hands on the East side of the Hinton Road to the Fork and then down the Bennetts Creek Road to the Cypress Swamp at Ellis's then down the Cypress Swamp to Thos. Sparkman's and from thence to the River Pocoson work on the said road under him.

John Brickell Esqr. Atto. for this County to be allowed the sum of 32 pds. for his services for one year as Attorney for the State.

John Brickell appointed Attorney for the County and he allowed the sum of 8 pds. for each Court he may attend.

Nancy Walton and Selah Walton made choice of Timothy Walton as their Guardian. He to give Security in the sum of 300 pds. Joseph Riddick and Demsey Bond Securities.

Jethro Sumner Esqr. Sheriff appointed as Commissioner to take in possession the Public Property in this County. Securities Jethro Ballard and George Dunn.

Wednesday Morning Aug. 23.

Present: Jacob Hunter, Jethro Ballard, Seth Riddick, David Rice, Joseph Riddick, Isaac Pipkin, Justices.

Deed of land William Booth to Thomas Brickell Ackd.

A Caviat obtained by William Walton from His Excellency the Governor against Demsey Costen for a piece of land lying in this County containing about 480 acres near the Meheren Swamping joining the land of William Cowper, James Costants, Job Riddick and Abraham Spivey, it is ordered that the Sheriff summons a Jury to go on the said land and proceed agreeable to law.

Wright Hayes records his Ear Mark. A Swallow Fork in each Ear.

The Sheriff summons Demsey Trotman, James Riddick, Henry Goodman and James Freeman to attend at the Superior Court at Edenton on the 1st. day in Nov. next.

The Sheriff to summon Absolom Blanshard, Abnor Blanshard, Jonathan Lassiter, Robert Parker, Israel Beeman, William Harriss, Jeremiah Speight, Abraham Eason, Simon Stallings, Mordicai Perry, John Bethey, James Lang, William Gatling, Josiah Parker, Elisha Norfleet, Alexander Eason, James Norfleet, John Powell, Isaac Carter, Job Umfleet, William Crafford, Peter Harrell, Timothy Lassiter, Moses Hill, Guy Hill, James Arline, James Bray Walters, Amos Trotman, Kedar Riddick and Zadock Hinton as Jurymen.

Three Shillings assessed on each 100 pds. Taxable property in this County.

Lawrence Baker the Clerk of this Court allowed the sum of 20 pds. for extra services.

Jethro Sumner Esqr. appointed as County Trustee for the year. He to give Bond for the faithful discharge of the trust. 400 pds.

Jethro Ballard and Thomas Hunter Esqrs. Securities.

Jonathan Roberts appointed to collect the Public and County Tax in his own District or Muster Bounds. He to give Bond in the sum of 500 pds. Thomas Hunter and Joseph Riddick Esqrs. Securities.

Moses Kittrell appointed to collect the Public and County Tax in the District of Capt. James Arline. He to give Bond in the sum of 500 pds. Seth Riddick and Isaac Pipkin Esqrs. Securities.

Isaac Hunter appointed to collect the Public and County Tax in the District of Capt. Joseph Riddick. He to give Bond in the sum of 500 pds. Isaac Hunter and Seth Riddick Esqrs. Securities.

John Pipkin to collect the Public and County Tax in the District of Capt. William Goodman. He to give Bond in the sum of 500 pds. Isaac Pipkin Esqr. and Moses Kitrell Securities.

Edward Sumner to collect the Public and County Tax in the District of Capt. Jethro Sumner. He to give Bond in the sum of 500 pds. Jethro Ballard and Jethro Sumner Esqrs. Securities.

Capt. Thomas Brickell to have his License for Keeping a Public House Continued.

The Public House Keepers in this County to receive the following rates and no more for provisions, Liquours, Lodging & etc.

Dinner 1/8 Supper 1/4 Breakfast 1/. Brandy and Rum a Quill 4 a Quart Bowl of Toddy made out of Good Rum or Brandy 1/8 a pint of ditto of /10 Lodging /6 Corn per gallon 1/. Good Cyder a Quart o/4 Fodder per Bundel the Common Size o/2

Joseph Riddick, Thomas Walton and Jacob Bagley appointed as Patrolls for the District of Capt. Joseph Riddick.

Jacob Gordon, Benjamin Gordon and David Small appointed Pattirolls in the District of Capt. Jethro Sumner.

Simon Stallings, Demsey Bond and Kedar Hill appointed Pattirolls for the District of Capt. Jonathan Roberts.

Willis Parker, Willis Browne and Jonathan Smith appointed Pattirolls in the District of Capt. Christopher Riddick.

Henry Goodman, William Warren and John Bethey appointed as Pattirolls in the District of Capt. William Goodman.

Isaac Carter, Isaac Langston and James Carter appointed as Pattirolls in the District of Capt. Chas. Eure.

Peter Parker, Jas. Bray Walters and Edward Doughtie appointed as Pattirolls in the District of Capt. Jas. Arline.

Reubin Riddick appointed as Entry Taker in this County. He to give Bond agreeable to Law. Seth Riddick, David Rice and Joseph Riddick Esqrs. Securities.

Nov. 17, 1783. - Third Monday in Nov.

Present: Jacob Hunter, Isaac Pipkin, Seth Riddick, David Rice, Justices.

Solomon Alphin exempted from paying a Tax for the year 1783.

Deed of land Daniel Gwinn to Moses Hare proved by the oath of Benjamin Gordon.

Prissilla Rogers moved for Administration on the Estate of Stephen Rogers decd. - Granted. She to give Security in the sum of 4000 pds. Isaac Pipkin and John Gatling Securities.

Inventory of the Goods & etc. of the Estate of Stephen Rogers decd. exhibited by Prissilla Rogers Admrx.

Jacob Gordon moved by Samuel Johnston Esqr. Atto. at Law for Administration on the Estate of Elizabeth Norfleet decd. - Granted. He to give Security in the sum of 1000 pds. James Gregory and John Riddick Securities.

Deed of sale of land Francis Saunders to Henry Speight proved by the oath of Joseph Speight.

Deed of sale of land Sarah Saunders and Benjamin Saunders to Henry Speight proved by the oath of Joseph Speight.

Deed of sale of land John Miller to Joseph Speight proved by the oath of Hy. Speight.

Deed of Gift Joseph Speight to Joseph Freeman, Francis Freeman, John Freeman and David Freeman and Anna Freeman Ackd.

Deed of sale of land Jethro Rogers to Solomon Hiate proved by the oath of Joel Goodman.

Moor Carter appointed Overseer of the road in the stead of Samuel Eure resigned.

Milley Harrell exempt from paying a Tax on a Negro Woman Pegg for the present year.

Deed of sale of land Abner Blanshard to Demsey Blanshard proved by the oath of Timothy Lassiter.

Deed of sale of land James Thompson to James Bristow Ackd.

Edward Davis moved for Administration on the Estate of Evin Murfree decd. He to give Security in the sum of 200 pds. Thomas Brickell and Charles Lawrence Securities.

Deed of Gift Sarah Boyce to William Boyce proved by the oath of Robert Mayner (?) Magner (?).

Inventory of the Goods & etc. of the Estate of Evin Murfree decd. exhibited by Edward Davis, Admr.

Deed of land Elisha Hunter to Demsey Bond proved by the oath of Jonathan Roberts.

Deed of land Elisha Hunter to Demsey Bond proved by the oath of Jonathan Roberts.

Samuel Eure moved by Samuel Johnston Esqr. Atto. at Law for Administration on the Estate of Samuel Eure decd. - Granted. He to give Security in the sum of 300 pds. Caleb Savage and Stephen Piland Securities.

Samuel Eure moved by Samuel Johnston Esqr. Atto. at Law for Administration on the Estate of Charity Eure decd. - Granted. He to give Security in the sum of 500 pds. Caleb Savage and Stephen Piland Securities.

Deed of land Demsey Odom to Henry Lee Ackd.

Deed of land William Pierce to George Lassiter proved by the oath of Jonathan Lassiter.

Inventory of the Goods & etc. of the Estate of Richard Parker decd. exhibited by Thomas Fryer Admr.

The Sheriff returned the virdict of a Jury - Land in Dispute - William Walton against Demsey Costen. - found for the Plaintiff - Jury: William Hinton, Joseph Hurdle, Jacob Bagley, Kedar Hill, Ephraim Griffin, Max Minshew, James Matthews, William Harriss, Wm. Matthews, William Boyce, Lewis Walters, Richd. Briggs, Edward Arnold, Thos. Parker, Moses Hare, Thoms. Smith, Wm. Freeman, Moses Davis, Isaac Powell and Seth Sumner.

William Crafford appointed Guardian to John Wallis orphan of (left blank) Wallis decd. He to give Security in the sum of 200 pds. Joseph Speight and Henry Speight Securities.

Petition of Charles Rountree to Build a Public Water Grist Mill across Katherin Creek the land one side belonging to the Petitioner and on the other side to Thomas Hurdle. Granted.

Tuesday Morning.

Present: Jacob Hunter, Jethro Ballard, David Rice, William Baker, Isaac Pipkin, Justices.

George Hargroves moved for Administration on the Estate of William Hargroves, decd. - Granted. He to give Security in the sum of 200 pds. Lewis Sparkman and Charles Eure Securities.

Inventory of the Goods & etc. of the Estate of William Hargroves exhibited by George Hargroves Admr.

Deed of land William Harris to Samuel Smith proved by the oath of Seth Riddick.

Deed of land Jeremiah Speight to Samuel Smith proved by the oath of William Harris.

Deed of land Jeremiah Speight to William Harris proved by the oath of Sam'l. Smith.

Ordered that George Hargrove Admr. of William Hargrove decd. sell the perishable part of the Estate of the said Deceased.

Inventory of the Goods & etc. of the Estate of Charity Eure decd. was exhibited into Court by Samuel Eure Admr.

Ordered that Cyprian Cross, Jesse Vann, John Odom and James Landing or any three make division of the Estate of William Hargrove decd.

Deed of sale Robert Parker, Senr. to Robert Parker, Junr. Ackd.

Deed of land Robert Parker to Willis Parker Ackd.

Stephen Euri, Charles Euri, Jesse Harrell and Seth Riddick, Esqr. or any three of them to make division of the Estate of Sam'l. Euri decd.

Samuel Robbins about 10 years of age bound as an apprentice to Richard Freeman to learn the business of a Cooper.

George Williams, Senr. to be exempt from paying a Tax for the present year.

Wednesday Morning 10 O'Clock.

Present: Thomas Hunter, William Baker, David Rice, Seth Riddick, Justices.

Thomas Garrett came into Court and moved by Samuel Johnston, Esqr. Atto. at Law for Administration on the Estate of Benjamin Sumner decd. - Granted. He to give Security in the sum of 100 pds. Spiece. James Freeman and Jacob Outlaw Securities.

Jethro Sumner, Esqr. appointed County Trustee presented his Account Current for the year 1783. Allowed the sum of 8 pds. 9 sh. for his services.

Seth Riddick allowed the sum of 3 pds. 12 sh. for his services assessing the property in the District he was appointed. William Vann and James Riddick allowed the sum of 56 sh. for assessing property & etc.

David Rice allowed the sum of 56 sh. for his services assessing the property in his District. Jonathan Roberts allowed the sum of 48 sh. for his services in assessing the property in his District.

George William appointed to collect the Public, County and Parish Tax for the year 1783, in the District of Capt. Christopher Riddick and Capt. Charles Euri. He to give Bond in the sum of 2000 pds. Wm. Baker and Seth Riddick Securities.

Wm. Henry Bell about the age of 16 years bound to Jesse Eason to learn the business of a Shoemaker.

Sheriff to summon the following persons as Jurymen: Jacob Bagley,

James Freeman, Jonathan Roberts, Thomas Trotman, Aaron Hobbs, Abram Harrell, Isaac Harrell, Jacob Powell, Seth Eason, Richard Briggs, Jacob Gordon, Edward Arnold, John Riddick, Jesse Saunders, Demsey Barnes, John Odom, Jesse Vann, Demsey Williams (cask), Joel Goodman, William Goodman, Isaac Powell, Abram Morgan, John Gatling, Philip Lewis, William Warren, William Brooks, James Bristow, Edwin Sumner, Willis Parker and John Darden.

County Trustee to pay Mr. Elisha Hunter the sum of 40 pds. in part for Building the Court House.

Colo. Jesse Eason to put the road in Good order with a Good Hollow Bridge and from the said Bridge to the High Land over Basses Swamp on the North side thereof and that Jacob Gordon Overseer of the road that leads over the said Swamp put the said grounds from the Hollow Bridge to the High Land on the South side in good order.

Third Monday in Feb., 1784.

Present: William Baker, Thomas Hunter, Isaac Pipkin, Justices.

Moses Benson appointed Overseer of the road in the room of John Darden, resigned.

Last Will of Jethro Harrell decd. exhibited by Ann Harrell and George Hargrove two of the Executors therein appointed and was proved by the oath of James Skinner one of the Witnesses.

Inventory of the Goods & etc. of the Estate of Jethro Harrell decd. was exhibited by Ann Harrell and George Hargrove.

Cyprian Cross Guardian to Thomas Smith orphan of Jas. Smith decd. returned his Account.

Cyprian Cross Guardian to Joseph Smith orphan of Jas. Smith decd. returned his Account.

Deed of land William Wallis to Moses Jones Ackd.

Deed of land Samuel Green to Jonathan Lassiter proved by the oath of Jonathan Nichols.

Deed of land Amos Lassiter to James Lassiter Ackd.

Deed of land Ann Minard to James Lassiter proved by the oath of Amos Lassiter.

Demsey Trotman Guardian to John Hunter orphan of John Hunter decd. made return of his Account.

County Trustee to pay Timothy Lassiter the sum of 39 pds. 5 sh. for building Bennetts Creek Bridge.

Thomas Walton Guardian to Theopholes Hunter orphan of John Hunter decd. returned his Account.

John Polson, Constable, allowed the sum of 20 sh. for warning the

Inhabitants of Capt. Riddicks and Capt. Arlines Districts to give a list of their Taxable property.

Simon Stallings Guardian to James Walton orphan of Richd. Walton decd. returned his Account.

Zadock Hinton to be exempt from paying a Tax on two Negroes one of them in the highest class and the other in the lowest in all One Hundred Pounds.

James Brown exempt from paying a Tax on a Negro Man in the Class at 80 pds. Simon (perhaps Stallings-page torn) having enlisted and paid the Tax on the said Negro.

James Jones appointed Guardian to Sally Rogers and that he give Security in the sum of 200 pds. Jethro Sumner and Kedar Bassard Securities.

John Rice summoned to appear at this Court at next sitting to show cause why John Gregory an Apprentice to the said Rice should not be reinso__ed (?).

Jethro Sumner, Moses Kitrell and Demsey Williams appointed to make a division of the Estate of Eliz. Rogers decd.

Mary Eason to be exempt from paying a Tax for the year 1783.

Sam'l. Euri Admr. of Charity Euri decd. to sell the Estate of the said decd. at Public Sale.

Deed of land John Felton and Elizabeth Felton to Jonathan Collins proved by the oath of William Felton.

Deed of sale Mathias Green and Jerueah Green to John Felton proved by the oath of Thomas Felton.

William Arnold allowed the sum of 48 sh. for assessing the Taxable property in the District of Capt. Jethro Sumner, and that he be allowed the sum of 1 pd. 4 sh. for warning the Inhabitants of the said District to give a list of their Taxable property.

Kedar Ballard appeared for begetting a Bastard Child on the Body of Easter Copeland. It was then and there ordered that he give Security in the sum of 200 pds. William Baker Security.

Tuesday Feb. 17, 1784.

Present: Joseph Riddick, William Baker, Isaac Pipkin, Seth Riddick, Justices.

Deed of land James Skinner to John Odom proved by the oath of Jesse Vann.

Deed of land John Barrett to George Eason proved by the oath of Levi Eason.

Cyprian Cross appointed Overseer of the road in the room of Charles Vann resigned.

James Gregory came into Court and moved for Administration on the Estate of John Gregory decd. - Granted. He to give Security in the sum of 3000 pds. William Baker and David Rice Securities.

Inventory of the Goods & etc. of the Estate of Benjamin Sumner exhibited by Thomas Garrett, Admr.

Account of the sales of part of the Estate of the orphans of Thomas Barnes decd. sold by the Extrs.

Deed of Gift of Goods & etc. Richard Bond to Thomas Smith proved by the oath of Isaac Miller.

Cyprian Cross, Jesse Vann and John Odom who were to make a division of the Estate of William Hargrove decd. made report.

David Rice and Joseph Riddick, Esqrs. who were to make a division of the Estate of John Huntor decd. made report.

Wednesday Feb. 18, 1784.

Present: Christopher Riddick, Joseph Riddick, Seth Riddick, William Baker, Justices.

Deed of land Jeremiah Jordon to Thomas Brickell proved by the oath of Jethro Miltear.

In a Disputed Entry Jonathan Roberts and Edward Brisco against John Baker. Sheriff to summon a Jury.

In a Disputed Entry David Rice and John Rice against Jacob Huntor. Sheriff to summon a Jury.

Elisha Hunter to be allowed the sum of 266 pds. 13 sh. 4 pc. for building the Court House in this County.

William Goodman records his Ear Mark. A Swallow Fork in the Right Ear and a Half Moon and a Cross off the Left Ear.

Moses Kitrell Records his Ear Mark. A Cross off the Left Year and a Nick under the Right Ear.

The Sheriff to summons Job Riddick, Amos Lassiter, Simon Stallings, Charles Rountree, Amos Trotman, William Freeman, Henry Walton, Demsey Bond, Abraham Eason, Aaron Lassiter, Benjamin Gordon, Thomas Parker, John Powell, Moses Davis, Moses Benton, George Dunn, George Hargrove, Isaac Parker, William Vann, Elisha Cross, William Odom, Kedar Riddick, Micajah Riddick, James Pruden, Thomas Smith, William Cleaves, Joseph Figg, Demsey Parker, Israel Beeman and Cyprian Cross as Jurymen.

The Sheriff to summon Demsey Trotman, Jesse Barnes, Jethro Miltear and John Odom as Jurymen at Superior Court to be held at Edenton for the District of Edenton on the 1st. day of May next.

County Trustee to pay Mr. Elisha Hunter the sum of 24 pds. part payment for building the Court House.

William Harvey and Elizabeth Harvey, his Wife, Admrs. of Docton Riddick decd. to appear at this Court at next sitting to show Cause why they should not appear and give Counter Security.

May 17, 1784.

Present: Jethro Ballard, Christopher Riddick, David Rice, Isaac Pipkin, Justices.

Deed of sale John Randolph Wilkinson to James Sumner proved by the oath of Jethro Sumner.

Deed of sale John Randolph Wilkinson to William Matthias proved by the oath of Lewis Jones and John Powell.

Deed of land Israel Beeman to James Hayes Ackd.

Deed of Gift Sarah Saunders and Benjamin Saunders to Henry Saunders proved by the oath of Joseph Speight.

James Baker Sumner orphan of Demsey Sumner decd. came into Court and made a choice of Mrs. Martha Sumner as his Guardian. She to give Bond in the sum of 2000 pds. Jethro Sumner and Wallis Baker Securities.

Last Will of James Bray Walters exhibited by William Walters Extr. therein appointed and proved by the oaths of Peter Parker and Daniel Horton two of the Witnesses.

Deed of land Guy Hill to Joseph Brinkley proved by the oath of Spencer Brinkley.

Deed of land Lott Rogers to Enos Rogers proved by the oath of Elisha Cross.

Deed of sale and receipt thereon William Walters to John Barr Ackd.

Deed of land Amos Trotman to Joseph Brinkley proved by the oath of Spencer Brinkley.

Deed of land Josiah Jordon to Peter Piland proved by the oath of Thomas Brickell.

Deed of land Peter Piland to Thomas Brickell proved by the oath of Jonathan Roberts.

Thomas Ellin appeared for begetting a Bastard Child on the Body of Edey (?) Parker. He to give Security in the sum of 100 pds. Solomon Philips and Jesse Vann Securities.

William Warren moved for Administration on the Estate of Joseph Warren, decd. - Granted. He to give Security in the sum of 100 pds. John Bethey and Hardy Wills Securities.

Inventory of the Goods & etc. of the Estate of Joseph Warren decd. exhibited by William Warren, Admr.

Ordered that Hardy Eason orphan of William Eason about the age of

14 years bound as an Apprentice to Moses Briggs to learn the business of a Taylor (NOTE- THIS ENTIRE ENTRY MARKED OUT)

Hannah Courtney moved for Administration on the Estate of John Courtney decd. - Granted. She to give Security in the sum of 1000 pds. Jacob Norfleet and Benjamin Gordon Securities.

Inventory of the Goods & etc. of the Estate of John Courtney exhibited by Hannah Courtney, Admr.

Inventory of the Goods & etc. of the Estate of John and Elizabeth Norfleet decd. was exhibited by Jacob Gordon, Admr.

Deed of Jointer between Abel Cross and Mary King proved by the oath of Moses Kittrell.

Thomas Smith appointed Overseer of the road in the room and stead of James Riddick.

James Jones moved for Administration on the Estate of Jonathan Boyce decd. - Granted. He to give Security in the sum of 50 pds. Jesse Barnes and Cyprian Cross Securities.

Inventory of the Goods & etc. of the Estate of Jonathan Boyce decd. exhibited by James Jones, Admr.

Tuesday Morning.

Present: Joseph Riddick, Christopher Riddick, Seth Riddick, Justices.

Inventory of the Estate of Joseph John Sumner who was convicted of possessing a Counterfiet Forty Shilling Bill part of the penalty enflicted on him being the forfeiture of one half of the said Sumners Estate. The Sheriff having summoned a Jury agreeable to an order of the Superior Court for the District of Edenton at May term last, ordered that this _____ be recorded.

Deed of land Moses Blanshard to Kedar Hill proved by the oath of Jacob Bagley.

Present: Jethro Ballard and Isaac Pipkin, Justices.

Deed of sale Samuel Smith to Seth Riddick proved by the oath of William Harriss.

In a Disputed Entry Jesse Barnes and Cyprian Cross against James Landing, John Harrell, James Charles and William Fryer. The Sheriff to summon a Jury.

In a Disputed Entry William Powell and Micajah Riddick against Isaac Powell. The Sheriff to summon a Jury.

Ordered that Jacob Gordon, a Searcher, sell a certain Horse (at three Months Credit) which the said Gordon took from a certain Negro Man, Jim, the property of William Sumner and that he make return of his proceedings to this Court at next sitting and that he enter with the Stray Master of this County the Colourage Mark or Brand of the said Horse.

Ordered: James Gregory Esqr. take a list of the Taxable property in the District of Capt. Joseph Riddick. Thomas Huntor Esqr. take a list of the Taxable property in the District of Capt. Jonathan Roberts. Jethro Ballard Esqr. take a list of the Taxable property in the District of Capt. Jethro Sumner. Isaac Pipkin Esqr. to take a list of the Taxable property in the District of Capt. Wm. Goodman, Seth Riddick Esqr. in the District of Capt. Christr. Riddick and that William Baker Esqr. take a list of the Taxable property in the District of Capt. Charles Euri.

Seth Eason, Simon Stallings and John Riddick to assess the Taxable property on the South side of Bennetts Creek. James Riddick, William Harriss and William Van to assess the Taxable property in this County on the North side of Bennetts Creek.

Rebecca Eure moved for Administration on the Estate of Enos Eure decd. - Granted. She to give Security in the sum of 200 pds. Thomas Harrell and Stephen Eure Securities.

Inventory of the Goods & etc. of the Estate of Enos Eure decd. exhibited by Rebecca Eure, Admr.

The Sheriff returned the verdict of a Jury in a Dispute entered relative to Lands by John Rice against Jacob Huntor. Ordered that the Clerk of the Court deliver to the said John Rice an authentick copy thereof which is as follows. We the Subscribers after being summoned, met and was qualified to determine a Disputed entry of Land made by Colos. Jacob Huntor and caveated by John Rice doth agree that the said Rice shall begin at his Beginning Tree and runing the Courses of his Pattent to a maple standing on the North side of a Branch called Homes Branch from thence down the said Branch where it was formerly looked upon to be the side of said Branch before the Mill was Built and that Colo. Jacob Huntor shall have all the vacant land and that the said John Rice shall pay all Costs given form under our hands this 20 day of March 1784. William Boyce, Isaac Harrell, William Harriss, Job Harriss, Job Riddick, Jacob Powell, Seth Eason, Joshua Small, William Cleaves, Abraham Harrell, Ephraim Griffin, John Briggs, Richard Briggs, Reuben Lassiter, William Matthews, Samuel Baker, Demsey Trotman.

The Sheriff having returned the verdict of a Jury with the Pannell in a Dispute made or entered relative to Lands by David Rice against Jacob Huntor it was then and there ordered that the Clerk of this Court deliver to the said David Rice an authentick copy thereof which is as follows (to wit) State of N. C. Gates Co. We the Subscribers after being summoned met and was qualified to determine a Disputed Entry of Land made by Colo. Jacob Hunter and was caveated by David Rice doth agree that the said Rice shall begin at a Maple standing in the Homes Branch thence down the run of said Branch to the Mouth of the Auster Tongus Branch from thence up the said Branch to the first station and that Colo. Jacob Hunter have all the vacant Land and that the said David Rice shall pay all the costs given from under our hands this 20 day of March 1784. Job Riddick, Jacob Powell, Seth Eason, Joshus Small, William Cleaves, Abraham Harrell, Ephraim Griffin, John Briggs, Richard Briggs, Reubin Lassiter, William Matthews, Samuel Baker, Demsey Trotman, William Boyce, Isaac Harrell and William Harris.

The Sheriff returned the verdict of a Jury with the Pannell thereof in a Dispute made or entered relative to Lands by Jonathan Roberts and Edward Brisco against John Baker, Ordered that the Clerk of this Court deliver to the said Jonathan Roberts and Edward Brisco an authentick copy thereof which is as follows (to wit) March 12, 1784 We the Subscribers, Juriors in a Disputed Claim of Land on the Easterly side of Bennetts Creek in the Indian Neck entered by John Baker of Hertford County and Caveated by Jonathan Roberts and Edward Brisco do say and are of the opinion that Jonathan Roberts and Edward Brisco hold and keep in possession all the land that was and is in their possession and that the Entry made by John Baker as far as intercepts with the land of the said Roberts and Brisco be and is Null and Void to all interests and purposes and that Baker pay all Costs, in Witness whereof we the Subscribers, Jurors have hereunto set our hands in the day and date above mentioned. Moses Kittrell, James Riddick, George Williams, Willis Browne, William Vann, Isaac Langston, Jonathan Smith, Jonathan Williams, James Brady, Jesse Browne, Charles Eure, Stephen Eure, Peter Harrell, Lewis Sparkman, Samuel Taylor, William Fryer, John Gatling and David Lewis.

The Sheriff to summon Kedar Hill, Jacob Bagley, Absolom Blanshard, William King, Abraham Eason, John Rice, Jacob Gordon, Jacob Eason, George Outlaw, Jacob Powell, Moses Hare, Edward Arnold, James Norfleet, Thomas Parker, James Knight, Edward Doughty, William Doughty, Jesse Benton, William Walters, James Land, William Goodman, Henry Goodman, William Gatling, Philip Lewis, Demsey Barnes, Charles Eure, Moses Carter, George Williams, Levi Lee and Jeremiah Speight as Jurymen.

William Isaac Hunter appointed Sheriff for the ensueing year. He to give Bond and Security. Joseph Riddick, Seth Riddick and William Harriss Securities.

Wednesday Morning 10 O'Clock.

Present: Thomas Hunter, Joseph Riddick, James Gregory, Justices.

A Negro Woman one half the property of the Estate of Enos Eure decd. be sold, the said one half to be sold agreeable to law.

Abel Cross and his Wife, Mary Cross, to be summoned to appear at this Court next sitting and to produce their account with the Estate of Henry King, decd.

Last Will of John Gregory decd. exhibited by James Gregory an Extr. therein appointed and proved by the oath of Josiah Granbery who says on his oath that he believed the hand riting of the said Will was the hand riting of the deceased and that the hand riting of the Witness thereto was the hand riting of John Granbery (of Js) - Granted.

Thomas Hunter Esqr. to receive a list of the Taxables from the Inhabitants of Capt. Jonathan Roberts Captaincy. Jethro Meltear Constable to warn the Inhabitants in the said Captaincy to give a list of their Taxables to him. James Gregory Esqr. to receive a list of Capt. Joseph Riddicks Captaincy. Samuel Harrell Constable to warn the Inhabitants. Jethro Ballard Esqr. to Receive a list of the Inhabitants of Capt. Jethro Sumners Captaincy and that Wm. Arnold Constable to warn the Inhabitants. Christopher Riddick Esqr. to Receive a list of Taxables from the Inhabitants of Capt. Christopher Riddicks Captaincy and that John Polson Constable to warn the Inhabitants. Seth Riddick Esqr. to Receive a list of Taxables from the Inhabitants of Capt. James Arlines Captaincy and that Jno. Polson Constable to warn the Inhabitants. Isaac Pipkin Esqr. to Receive a list of Taxables from the Inhabitants of Capt. William Goodmans Captaincy and that Charles Vann Constable to warn the Inhabitants. William Baker Esqr. to Receive a list of Taxables from the Inhabitants of Capt. Charles Eure's Captaincy and that Charles Vann Constable to warn the Inhabitants.

Book 2 - August 1784 - Nov. 1787

State of North Carolina - Gates County - At a Court of Pleas and Quarter session begun and held for the County of Gates at the Court House on the third Monday in August in the Year of our Lord One Thousand Seven Hundred and Eighty Four.

Present: James Gregory, Isaac Pipkin, Thomas Hunter, David Rice and William Baker, Justices.

Deed of land John Miller to William Crafford proved by the oath of Jesse Barnes.

Deed of Gift Nicholas King to Henry King proved by the oath of James Arline.

Last Will of William Hayes Decd. exhibited by James Hayes and Wright Hayes Estrs. therein. Proved by the oath of Thomas Brickell one of the witnesses.

Deed of Land William Hinton to Isaac Harrell proved by the oath of Absolom Blanchard.

Jethro Sumner, Moses Kittrell and William Walters Gent. who were appointed to Audit State and Settle the accounts of Jesse Benton and Eliza. Benton Extr. and Extrx. of John Benton Decd. exhibited their proceedings.

William Baker Esqr. returned a list of the taxable property in the district he was appointed.

William Baker guardian to Blake, Mary and Elizabeth Baker returned a division of the Estate of Mrs. Mary Baker decd.

William Baker guardian to Blake Baker, Mary Baker and Elizabeth Baker returned his Account Current with the said orphans.

Last Will and Testament of William Umfleet Decd. exhibited by Job Umfleet one of the Extrs. therein appointed and proved by the oath of Charles Eure one of the witnesses.

James Skinner, Mills Skinner and Uriah Skinner work on the road under Cyprian Cross instead of working on the road under Demsey Barnes.

Christopher Riddick and Seth Riddick Esqrs. returned a List of Taxes in the districts they were appointed to.

Deed of land William Hunter to Demsey Trotman proved by the oath of Ezekeal Trotman.

Deed of Sale Thomas Hunter to Demsey Trotman Ack.

Disputed Entry Jesse Barnes and Cyprian Cross against James Landing. John Harrell, James Curle and William Fryer. Jury to be summoned.

Sarah Polson to sell so much of the Estate of John Polson decd. as will pay debts.

Christopher Riddick, Seth Riddick and Robert Parker or any two of them to make a Division of the Estate of John Polson decd.

Cyprian Cross moved for leave to keep a Publick House. He to give security in the sum of 50 pds. David Cross and Abel Cross Securities.

Thomas Robertson came into Court for Begetting a Bastard Child on the Body of Katherine Simpson – he to give Security in the Sum of 100 pds. William Ritter and Stephen Piland Securities.

Jacob Gordon to pay the Warden of the Poor the Sum of 5 pds. 10 sh. and 2 pc. (which was taken from a certain Negro Man the property of William Sumner which was ordered to be sold by this Court).

William King orphan of Henry King decd. came into Court and made choice of Abel Cross for his Guardian. He to give Security in the sum of 800 pds. Cyprian Cross and David Cross Securities.

Isaac Pipkin and Jethro Ballard Esqrs. returned a list of Taxes in the districts they were appointed to.

Jesse Benton Extr. and Eliza. Benton Extrx. of John Benton decd. made return of the account of sales.

Tuesday Morning: Present David Rice, Joseph Riddick, Isaac Pipkin, James Gregory, Thomas Hunter and Seth Riddick, Justices.

Thomas Hunter Esqr. returned a list of the Taxables in the district he was appointed to.

Seth Eason appointed Overseer of the Road in the room of Jacob Gordon resigned.

Inventory of the Goods & etc. of the Estate of John Gregory decd. exhibited by James Gregory Extr.

Rebecca Eure returned an account of the Sale of half of the Negro Woman Venus belonging to the Estate of Enus Eure.

Deed of Sale Richard Bond to John Walton proved by the oath of Jeremiah Spieght.

Henry Eason orphan of William Eason decd. about the age of 14 to be bound an apprentice to Samuel Harrell to learn the business of a Cooper.

John Bunbury Walton appointed to collect the Public and County Tax in the Captaincy of Jonathan Roberts - he to give Bond in the sum of 500 pds. Thomas Hunter and David Rice Securities.

Edward Daughtee summoned to appear at this Court at next sitting to show cause why he did not attend the Grand Jury at this Court as a Juryman.

James Rice appointed to collect the Tax in Captain Jethro Sumners Captaincy. He to give Bond in the sum of 500 pds. Thomas Hunter and David Rice Securities.

John Walton Senr. appointed to collect the Tax in Capt. Joseph Riddicks and Capt. Charles Eures Captaincys. He to give Bond in the sum of 1000 pds. Jonathan Roberts and Kedar Riddick Securities.

The County Trustee to pay Elisha Hunter the sum of 143 pds. 17 sh. and 10 pc. it being the balance due him for building the Court House in this County.

John Pipkin appointed to Collect the Tax in Capt. William Goodmans Captaincy. He to give Bond in the sum of 500 pds. Isaac Pipkin and Moses Kittrale Securities.

Moses Kittrell appointed to collect the Taxes in Capt. Christopher Riddicks and Capt. James Arlines Captaincys - he to give Bond in the sum of 1000 pds. Seth Riddick and Isaac Pipkin Securities.

Wednesday Morning - Present: William Baker, Joseph Riddick, Thomas Hunter, Seth Riddick and David Rice.

Sheriff to Summon Guy Hobbs, Aaron Hobbs, William Hurdle, Simon Stallings, Demsey Bond, Jonathan Roberts, John Riddick, Kedar Ballard, Seth Esson, Amos Trotman, William Hunter, Job Riddick, Thomas Trotman, Benjamin Gordon, Amos Lassiter, Isaac Langston, George Dunn, James Phelps, William Vann, William Boyce, Lewis Walters, Isaac Miller, Anthony Matthews, Enos Rogers, William Warren, Francis Speight, Samuel Smith, Robert Parker of Demsey, Jesse Harrell and Henry King as Jurymen.

Jesse Barnes, Demsey Barnes, Jethro Miltear and George Outlaw summoned by the Sheriff to attend the Superior Court as Jurymen.

Deed of Land Jonathan Tradir to Peter Piland proved by the oath of Laurance Baker.

Thomas Garrett to be summoned by the Sheriff to attend this Court at next setting in order to Settle his Guardian Account with the orphan of Jas. Garrett decd.

John Brickell Esqr. allowed the sum of 4 pds. each Court he may attend as Attorney for the State in this County.

Lawrence Baker the Clerk of this Court allowed the sum of 16 pds. for extra services performed by him the year pased.

The sum of 3 sh. be levied on each free Male person of the age of 21 years and up and on all Slaves from the age of 12 to 50 and that the sum of 1 sh. be levied on each hundred acres land in this County for County Tax.

Third Monday in Nov. 1784

Present: Christopher Riddick, Thos. Hunter, David Rice, Isaac Pipkin and James Gregory, Justices.

Deed of land Ephraim Griffin to Thomas Trotman Ack.

Deed of land Demsey Trotman to Ephraim Griffin Ack.

Deed of land John Davis to Moses Davis Ack.

Deed of land Moses Davis to John Davis Ack.

Deed of land William Booth to Jonathan Nichols proved by the oath of John Robbins, Junr.

Deed of land Elisha Parker to James Prudin proved by the oath of Isaac Miller.

Kedar Parker records his Brand with the two first letters of his name KP.

John Walton Deed of Sale to William Hinton Ack.

Deed of Sale John Eure to Samuel Tayloe proved by the oath of Stephen Eure.

Keziah Hodges came into Court and moved for administration on the Estate of James Hodges decd. - granted. She to give Bond in the sum of 500 pds. William Berryman and Job Riddick Securities.

Inventory of the Goods & etc. of the Estate of James Hodges exhibited by Kiziah Hodges Admtrx.

Deed of Sale Mary Spivey Walton to Moses Blanshard proved by the oath of Thomas Spivey.

Deed of land Ephraim Griffin and Sarah Griffin to Moses Hill proved by the oath of Guy Hill.

Inventory of the Goods & etc. of the Estate of William Umfleet decd. exhibited by Job Umfleet Extr.

Inventory of the Goods & etc. of the Estate of William Hays decd. exhibited by Jas. Hays and Wright Hays Extrs.

Deed of land Edwin Sumner to Henry Griffin proved by the oath of William Vann.

Deed of land Prissella Lassiter to Aaron Blanshard proved by the oath of Demsey Blanshard.

Account of the Sales of the Estate of Aaron Blanshard decd. exhibited by Demsey Blanshard Extr.

Thomas Parker, Cooper, records his Brand T P.

Abraham Morgan, Cooper, records his Brand A M.

Bond: Jesse Benton to John Benton proved by the oath of Jethro Sumner.

Deed of land William Harriss to Humphry Hudgins Ack.

Abraham Sumner moved for administration on the Estate of Jacob Sumner, Junr., decd. - granted. He to give Security in the sum of 500 pds. John Powell and Thomas Hurdle Securities.

Moses Davis appointed Overseer of the Road in the room of Aaron Lassiter resigned.

Demsey Trotman appointed Overseer of the road in the room of Ezekial Trotman - Mr. James Gregorys and Mr. Demsey Trotmans hands to work on the Road under him.

Last Will and Testament of Jacob Hunter, decd. was exhibited by Isaac Hunter one of the Extrs. - proved by the oaths of William Freeman and Abner Harrell two of the witnesses.

Court Morning - Present: Christopher Riddick, Thomas Hunter and Seth Riddick, Justices.

Inventory of the Goods & etc. of the Estate of James Bray Walters decd. was exhibited by William Walters Extr.

Last Will and Testament of Joseph N_____(?) decd. exhibited by Sarah N_____(?) the Extrx. therein appointed. Proved by the oath of Thomas Brickell one of the witnesses.

William Baker, William Goodman, Seth Riddick and Moses Kittrell or any three of them to make a Division of the Estate of James Riddick, decd.

A rect.(?) John Granbery (son of Josiah) to Joseph Granbery proved by the oath of Henry Baker.

Mills Rooks a base born Child about the age of 8 years bound as an apprentice to Robert Parker to learn the business of a Cooper.

Deed of land Stephen Cross and Henry Dilday to Enos Rogers proved by the oath of Robt. Parker.

Ordered that John Powell, James Norfleet, Jacob Gordon, Thomas Parker, John Darden, James Knight, Aaron Lassiter, Jeremiah Speight, Elisha Norfleet, Thomas Brickell, James Riddick, George Williams, Kedar Hill, Henry Walton, Thomas Walton, John Riddick, David Harrell, Moses Hill, Richard Briggs, William Gatling, William Daughtie, Edward Daughtie, William Freeman, Thomas Hoffler, John Rice, Charles Rountree, William King, Jonah Lassiter, Solomon Briggs and Moses Davis be summoned to attend this Court at their next sitting as Jurymen.

Abraham Spiveys hands to work on the Road under Thomas Walton, Overseer.

William Warren Admr. of Joseph Warren decd. to sell the parishable part of the Estate of Joseph Warren.

Ordered that Bray Warren orphan of Joseph Warren about the age of 18 years bound as an apprentice to Henry Lee to learn the business of a House Carpenter and Joiner.

Third Monday in Feby. 1785

Present: Christopher Riddick, Isaac Pipkin, David Rice and Thomas Hunter, Justices.

Hardy Wills to Court for begetting a Bastard Child on the Body of Sarah Griffin - he to give Bond in the sum of 100 pds. Solomon Phelps and Robt. Parker Securities.

Ordered that Jacob Robbins Indian boy 10 years old in January Last be bound as an apprentice to Jethro Lassiter to learn the business of a Cooper.

Sanford Edwards to have leave to keep Public House at Gates Court House. He to give Bond in the sum of 100 pds. Jeremiah Speight and Jonathan Roberts Securities.

David Jones an Illigitimate Child Son of Mary Jones about twelve years old bound as an apprentice to Hardy Brown to learn the business of a taylor.

Josiah Granbery, James Gregory, Seth Riddick, David Rice and Lawrence Baker to Audit State and Settle the accounts of Thomas Garrett Extr. of James Garrett decd.

Philip Dunford to be exempt from paying a Poll Tax for the year 1784.

John Davis about the age of Seven years son of Rachel Davis bound as an apprentice to John Miller to learn the business of a Cowper(?)

Daniel Spivey to be hereafter exempt from paying a Tax in this County.

Hannah Courtney to have a license to keep a Public House at the Folly. She to give Security in the sum of 100 pds. James Norfleet and Jacob Gordon Securities.

Thomas Trotman appointed guardian to William, Miles, Joseph, Sarah, Noah and John Scott the Children of James Scott. He to give Bond in the sum of 200 pds. Charles Rountree and William Berryman Securities.

Deed of land James Parker and Wife to Samuel Thomas proved by the oath of Geo. Hargrove.

Last Will and Testament of Absolom Blanshard decd. exhibited by Mary Blanshard Extrx. therein appointed - proved by the oaths of Kedar Hill and Ameriah Blanshard two of the witnesses.

Deed of land Kedar Odom to Philip Rogers proved by the oath of William Vann.

Inventory of the Goods & etc. of the Estate of Colo. Jacob Hunter decd. exhibited by Isaac Hunter Extr.

Deed of land Caleb Savage to John Gatling proved by the oath of Philip Lewis.

Deed of land James Brady to Israel Beeman Ack.

Deed of Gift Nicholas King to Henry King proved by the oath of William Davidson.

Deed of land Thomas Smith to Jonathan Smith Ack.

Deed of land William Cleaves to Thomas Smith Acks.

Deed of land Jesse Benton to Kedar Parker proved by the oath of Edwin Sumner.

Deed of land Daniel Holland, Henry Harrison, Henry Norfleet, Anna Harrison, Elizabeth Holland and Henry Holland to John Brayshar proved by the oath of Demsey Langston.

Deed of Gift William Brinkley to Lewis Jones proved by the oaths of William Arnold and David Jones, Jur.

Deed of Gift Elizabeth Vann to Darkis Vann proved by the oath of John Parker.

Deed of land Richard Felton to Stephen Piland Ack.

Deed of land James Copeland, James Winborne and Zachariah Copeland to Joseph Speight proved by the oath of Henry Speight.

Deed of land Nicholas King to Henry King proved by the oath of William Davidson.

Deed of land Demsey Parker and Eler his Wife to Isaac Parker proved by the oath of Miles Parker.

Deed of land Charles Lawrence to Thomas Brickell Ack.

Deed of land Jesse Eason to Christopher Pierce Ack.

Deed of land Abraham Norfleet and Sarah his Wife to James Jones proved by the oaths of Seth Eason and William Ellis.

Deed of land John Felton to Noah Felton proved by the oath of John Jones.

Deed of land Samuel Harrell to Jesse Harrell proved by the oath of William Crafford.

Deed of Gift Edward Trotman to Sarah Scott proved by the oath of Thomas Trotman.

William Crafford Admr. of James Willis decd. exhibited his account Current with the said Estate.

Inventory of the Goods & etc. of the Estate of Absolom Blanshard was exhibited by Mary Blanshard Extrx.

Last Will and Testament of Kedar Riddick decd. was exhibited by Elizabeth Riddick Extrx. therein appointed and was proved by the oaths of Christopher Riddick and John Walton witnesses.

Inventory of the Goods & etc. of the Estate of Kedar Riddick decd. exhibited by Elizabeth Riddick Extrx.

Last Will and Testament of John Ross decd. was exhibited by Parthena Ross Extrx. therein appointed and proved by the oath of James Brady one of the witnesses.

Thomas Walton guardian to Theopholos Hunter exhibited his account Current where there appears to be a balance due the said orphan of 63 pds. 4 sh. 8 pc.

Tuesday morning - Present: Seth Riddick, William Baker, Isaac Pipkin and Christopher Riddick, Justices.

Sheriff returned the verdict of a Jury in a Dispute made relative to lands. James Landing, John Harrell, James Curle and William Fryer against Cyprian Cross and Jesse Barnes. Ordered that the Clerk of this Court deliver to the said Cyprian Cross and Jesse Barnes an authentick copy thereof which is as follows - - the jury accordingly after going on the premisses was qualified to settle said dispute - the verdict of said Jury is that Cross and Barnes shall have the pattents by which the entry was bounded run out the vacant land if any found to be said Crosses and Barnes the said Cross and Barnes paying all Costs. Given under our Hands this 29th. day of Jany. 1785. Francis Speight, Miles Benton, Francis Parker, Joseph Speight, William Odom, James Bristow, George Dunn, John Miller, Jesse Saunders, Thomas Norris, John Gatling and Edward Warren.

Demsey Trotman guardian to John Hunter Orphan of John Hunter, decd. exhibited his Account Current - there appears to be a balance due the said orphan of 57 pds. 11 sh. 5 pc.

Moses Kitrell, Collector of the Public County and Parish Tax in the district or Captaincy of Christopher Riddick and James Arline be exempt from accounting for the Tax which appears to be due from George Williams who is an old Decreped Man and Demsey Boyce and Zacheriah Parke who are under the age of 21 years.

Motion of Mr. Cumming Attorney at Law in behalf of Michal Lawrence for Administration on the Estate of Job Copeland, decd.- granted. He to give Bond in the sum of 100 pds. Christopher Riddick and Seth Riddick Securities.

Sheriff to summon Robert Parker, Senr., Kedar Ballard, Christopher Riddick and George Williams to attend at the Superior Court in May next as Jurors.

Elisha Hunter, James Gregory, John Gordon and Jacob Gordon appointed to make a division of the Estate of Jacob Hunter Esqr. decd.

Moses Hare appointed Constable instead of Wm. Arnold.

Kedar Hill appointed Overseer of the Road instead of Absolom Blanshard, decd.

Humphry Hudgins appointed Constable in Capt. Christopher Riddicks Captaincy.

Thomas Trotman to sell the Estate given to Sarah Scott by her Father Edward Trotman and after her decease to her Children.

A Negro Winch which was the property of Judeth Rountree to be sold and equally divided between the Children of Thomas Rountree decd.

William Baker, Josiah Granbery, Jethro Ballard, Kedar Ballard and David Rice or any three of them to Audit State and Settle the accounts of James Sumner and Henry Riddick Admrs. of Luke Sumner, decd.

Sheriff to summons Jonathan Roberts, Demsey Bond, Simon Stallings, George Outlaw, John Hare, Jacob Hobbs, William Matthias, James Norfleet, Benjamin Goodman, Reuben Hobbs, Jacob Bagley, Thomas Brickell, (John Miller, Folly), Moses Hare, Anthony Matthews, James Riddick, Joseph Figg, Isaac Miller, Jesse Benton, Moses Kittrell, Enos Rogers, John Bethey, Jesse Saunders, Philip Lewis, Francis Speight, Abel Cross, Sm'l. Eure, David Cross and Isaac Langston as Jurymen.

John Pipkin Collector of the Public County and Parish Tax be exempted from paying to the Sheriff the Taxes of John Norrington.

May 16, 1785

Present: William Baker, Isaac Pipkin, David Rice and Christopher Riddick, Justices.

John Miller and Wm. Matthias fails to appear as Jurors.

Inventory of the Goods & etc. of the Estate of John Ross decd. exhibited by Parthena Ross Extrx.

Account of Sales of part of the Estate of the Children of _____(?) Scott was exhibited by Thomas Trotman guardian.

Deed of Sale Abner Eason to Joseph Riddick Ack.

Mills Odom appointed Overseer of the Road instead of Demsey Odom resigned.

William Daughtie appointed Overseer of the Road instead of Moses Boyce resigned.

Lewis Jones moved for administration on the Estate of William Brinkley, decd. - granted. He to give surity in the sum of 500 pds. Willis Wiggons and Abraham Sumner Securities.

Josiah Phelps and Molly Phelps bound as apprentences to Reuben Sparkman to learn the business of a Planter and House Business. the Boy 9 years old Dec. 16 last the Girl 11 years old 22 March Last.

Inventory of the Goods & etc. of the Estate of Wm. Brinkly, decd. exhibited by Lewis Jones, Admr.

Last Will and Testament of John Benton, decd. exhibited by Mary Benton and Samuel Benton Extr. and Extrx. and proved by the oath of Edwin Sumner one of the witnesses.

Inventory of the Goods & etc. of the Estate of John Benton decd. was exhibited by Mary Benton and Samuel Benton Extr. and Extrx.

Moses Kitrell moved for administration in the Estate of Joseph Griffin, Junr., decd. - granted. He to give Security in the sum of 50 pds. William Goodman and Henry Goodman Securities.

Inventory of the Goods & etc. of the estate of Joseph Griffin, decd. was exhibited by Moses Kitrell, Admr.

The hands of Jacob Bagley and Kedar Hills work on the Road where Kedar Hill is Overseer of the Road.

John Vann appointed Constable in Capt. Wm. Goodmans Captaincy.

Lewis Sparkman appointed Constable in Capt. Charles Eures Captaincy.

Jesse Vann moved for administration on the Estate of Charles Vann, decd. - granted. He to give Security in the Sum of 200 pds. John Gatling and William Warren Securities.

Inventory of the Goods & etc. of the Estate of Charles Vann, decd. was exhibited by Jesse Vann, Admr.

Wm. Arnold Extr. of the Last Will and Testament of Joseph Jones, decd. to sell the parishable part of the said Estate.

Kedar Ballard appointed Overseer of the Road in the stead of Benjamin Gordon resigned.

Inventory of the Goods & etc. of the Estate of Job Copeland, decd. was exhibited by Michal Laurance, Admr.

The Last Will and Testament of Thomas Fullington, decd. was exhibited by Abraham Harrell, Extr. therein appointed and proved by the oaths of Seth Eason and Josiah Lassiter, witnesses.

The Last Will and Testament of Joseph Jones, decd. was exhibited by William Arnold one of the Extrs. therein appointed and was proved by the oath of Bathsheba Jones one of the witnesses.

Inventory of the Goods & etc. of the Estate of Joseph Jones, decd. was exhibited by Wm. Arnold, Extr.

The Last Will and Testament of Daniel Rogers, decd. was exhibited by Milley Rogers, Extrx. and John March, Extr. therein appointed and proved by the oaths of Thomas Hiatt and Jesse Hiatt two of the witnesses.

Deed of Sale Thomas Smith to William Cleaves proved by the oath of Jonathan Smith.

Deed of Sale Samuel Smith to William Boyce Ack.

Deed of Gift Christipher Pierce to Isaac Pierce proved by the oath of Jacob Gordon.

Deed of Sale Willis Wiggins and Mary Wiggins to James King Ack.

Patent to Simon Stallings.

Patent to Job Riddick.

Deed of Gift Frusannah Raby to Willis Wiggins proved by the oath of Willis Wiggins, Junr.

Simon Stallings guarding to James Walton orphan of Timothy Walton, decd. exhibited his Account Current.

James Costen and David Rice made return of their Account Current as Extrs. to the Estate of Demsey Costen, decd.

Tuesday Morning. Present: Christopher Riddick, Jesse Eason, David Rice, William Baker, Seth Riddick, Isaac Pipkin and Jethro Sumner.

Willis Browne appointed guardian to Nancy Garrett minor orphan of James Garrett, decd. He to give Security in the sum of 4000 pds. Robert Parker and Jacob Bagley Securities.

Jesse Eason Esqr. appointed Sheriff for the ensueing year for this County. He to give Security according to Law. William Baker and David Rice Securities.

Joseph Sumner came into Court for begetting a Bastard Child on the Body of Susanna Phelps, single woman of this County. He to give Security in the sum of 100 pds. John Riddick and Enos Rogers Securities.

The Last Will and Testament of Francis Saunders, decd. was exhibited by Charity Saunders and John Parker, Extrx. and Extr. therein appointed and proved by the oaths of William Odom and Uriah Odom two of the witnesses.

Mordicai Perry moved for administration on the Estate of Mary Eason, decd. - granted. He to give Security in the sum of 100 pds. Demsey Bond and Samuel Smith Securities.

Wednesday Morning. Present: Christopher Riddick, William Baker, David Rice, Justices.

John Hamilton Esqr. produced his License from the Hble. the Judges of the Superior Court, for pleading the Law in this State and at the same time took and Subscribed the oath of Government and also the oath of an Attorney.

William Baker Esqr. to take a list of the Taxable property in Capt. Charles Eures Captaincy. Isaac Pipkin Esqr. to take a list in Capt. William Goodmans Captaincy. Christopher Riddick Esqr. to take a list in Capt. Christo. Riddicks Captaincy. Seth Riddick Esqr. to take a list in Capt. Arlines Captaincy. David Rice Esqr. to take a list in Capt. Jethro Sumners Captaincy. James Gregory

73

Esqr. to take the list in Capt. Joseph Riddicks Captaincy.
Thomas Hunter Esqr. to take a List in Capt. Jonathan Roberts
Captaincy.

The Sheriff to Summons Jesse Harrell, Edward Arnold, William
Harriss, Richard Briggs, Jeremiah Speight, Moses Benton, William Walters, Thomas Parker, John Gatling, John Powell, William
Goodman, Jacob Powell, Henry Goodman, William Ellis, Abraham
Morgan, Jacob Pierce, Michal Lawrence, James Costin, Levi Lee,
Timothy Lassiter, John Odom, Reuben Lassiter, Demsey Barnes,
Thomas Trotman, Cyprian Cross, Amos Trotman, James Landing,
Aaron Hobbs, John Parker and James Freeman as Jurymen.

Jesse Harrell an Illigitemate Child Son of Martha Harrell, about
7 years old bound as an apprentice to William Booth to learn the
Plantation Business.

Easter Price about 8 years old, an Illigitemate Child, the Daughter of Keziah Price bound as an apprentice to Christopher
Riddick Esqr. to learn the business of House Work.

Rachal Price about 6 years old an Illigitimate child Daughter
of Keziah Price bound as an apprentice to William Booth to learn
the business of House Work.

August 15, 1785

Third Monday in August. Present: Isaac Pipkin, Seth Riddick and
David Rice, Justices.

Inventory of the Estate of Daniel Rogers, decd. exhibited by
Milley Rogers, Extrx.

Deed of land Israel Beeman to Isaac Pipkin Ack.

Mary Braddy moved for administration on the Estate of John Braddy,
decd. - granted. She to give Security in the sum of 400 pds.
Ebon Sears and Levi Lee Securities.

Inventory of the Goods & etc. of the Estate of John Braddy, decd.
was exhibited by Mary Braddy Extrx.

Deed of land Jesse Eason to Jacob Pierce Ack.

Deed of Sale John Rice & Usr. to David Rice proved by the oath of
Wm. Crusey (?).

Deed of land Isaac Hunter to David Rice Ack.

Inventory of the Estate of Francis Saunders, decd. was exhibited
by John Parker, Extr.

Aaron Hobbs appointed Overseer of the Road instead of Thos. Spivey,
resigned.

Inventory of the Goods & etc. of the Estate of Thomas Fullington,
decd. was exhibited by Abraham Harrell Extr.

Deed of land Samuel Smith to Wm. Vann Ack.

Deed of land Moses Spivey to Nathaniel Spivey proved by the oath of Charles Rountree.

Deed of land Nathaniel Spivey to Charles Rountree Ack.

John Gwinn bound as an apprentice to Matthias Morgan to learn the business of a Cooper the said Gwinn about 11 years of age.

Deed of land Champean Spivey to Jacob Bagley proved by the oath of Thomas Hunter.

Charity Morris moved for Administration on the Estate of Jacob Morris, decd. -granted. She to give Security in the sum of 100 ps. Henry Hill and James Freeman Securities.

Jethro Sumner, Moses Kittrell and Demsey Williams, who were appointed to make a division of the Estate of Eley Rogers, decd. made return of their proceedings.

Seth Rountree and Lavina Rountee minor orphans of Thomas Rountree, decd. came into Court and made choice of Charles Rountree as their guardian. He to give Security in the sum of 2000 pds. George Outlaw and James Freeman Securities.

Charles Rountree appointed guardian to Rachel Rountree, Priscilla Rountree and Penny Rountree. He to give Security in the sum of 2000 pds. for each of them. George Outlaw and James Freeman Securities.

Joseph Riddick, Thomas Trotman, Simon Stallings and George Outlaw or any three of them to divide the Thomas Rountree according to the Will.

Ephraim Griffin appeared for begetting a Bastard Child on the Body of Charity Lilley. He to give Security in the sum of 200 pds. Moses Hill and Jacob Bagley Securities.

David Harrell minor son of Abraham Harrell being charged with begetting a Bastard Child on the Body of Mary Taylor. He to give Security in the sum of 200 pds. Abraham Harrell and David Rice Securities.

Isaac Pipkin Esqr. returned a list of the Taxables in the Captaincy of William Goodman.

Deed of land Andrew Hambleton to Israel Beeman Ack.

James Gregory, Seth Ridditk, David Rice and Josiah Granbery who were appointed to Audit the account of Thomas Garrett Extr. of James Garrett, decd. made report.

Rect. of John Bunbury Walton by Thomas Hunter proved by the oath of Jacob Bagley.

Petition of Charles Rountree for building a water Grist Mill on Katherine Creek - granted.

Tuesday morning. Present: Isaac Pipkin, James Gregory, David Rice, Justices.

John Gatling to be exempt from paying a Tax for a Negro Boy Toney an Idiot.

Seth Riddick Esqr. returned a list of Taxables in Capt. Arlines Captaincy.

James Gregory Esqr. returned a list of Taxables in the Captaincy of Joseph Riddick.

James Gregory, Elisha Hunter and Jacob Gordon who were appointed to make a division of the Estate of Jacob Hunter Esqr., decd. made report.

David Rice Esqr. made return of the list of Taxables in the Captaincy of Jethro Sumner.

William Baker Esqr. made return of the list of Taxables in the Captaincy of Charles Eure.

Jonathan Smith appointed Constable in the stead of Humphry Hudgins.

The Sheriff to Summons Demsey Trotman, Jethro Miltear, Cyprian Cross and Miles Benton to serve as Jurymen at the next Supreme Court to be held at Edenton.

Sheriff to Summons Charles Rountree, Jacob Bagley, Moses Hill, Thomas Walton, Joseph Hurdle, John Briggs, William Matthias, Amos Parker, David Harrell, Amos Lassiter, Seth Eason, Moses Davis, Thomas _____ (?), Micajah Riddick, James Pruden, George Dunn, Robert Parker, George Williams, Jesse Browne, Samuel Smith, Thomas Trotman, Solomon King, William Odom, John Bunbery Walton, Jacob Gordon, Henry Speight, Isaac Carter, William Daughty, Jesse Benton and Demsey Williams to serve as Jurymen.

Peter Harrell exhibited his Patent for 199 acres of land.

Isaac Mill exhibited his Patent for 15 acres of land.

William Hinton exhibited his Patent for 78 acres of land.

George Dunn exhibited his Patent for 9 acres of land.

John Odom exhibited his Patent for 45 acres of land.

Docton Riddicks Patent exhibited for 325 acres of land.

Jesse Easons Patent was exhibited for 260 acres of land.

Moses Boyce exhibited his Patent for 100 acres of land.

Abraham Sumners Patent was exhibited for 640 acres of land.

William Harris appointed Overseer of the Road in the Room of John Duke, Junr. and that the hands of Jeremiah Speight work on the said road.

William Boyce and his son to work on the Road under Thomas Smith.

Disputed Entry Abraham Sumner against Abraham Hurdle - the Sheriff to summon a Jury.

James Outlaw appointed Overseer of the Old Town Road instead of William Spivey decd.

Receipt Mary Walton to Thomas Hunter her guardian proved by John Bunbery Walton.

The Extrs. of John Bentons Senr. decd. to sell so much of the perishable part of the Estate of the decd. as will pay debts.

James Landing, James Curle, John Harrell to pay all the Costs attending the disputed Entry of Cyprian and Jesse Barnes.

The parishable part of the Estate of Jacob Morris decd. to be sold to pay debts.

The Sheriff to be allowed the sum of 8 pds. for his extra services the year past.

Christopher Riddick Esqr. made return of the list of Taxables in his Captaincy.

The County Trustee to pay Lawrence Baker the Clerk of the Court the sum of 25 pds. for extra services performed by him the year past.

Blake Baker appointed guarding to Elizabeth Baker orphan of Blake Baker, decd. He to give Security in the sum of 1000 pds. William Baker and Lawrence Baker Securities.

Disputed Entry of land Reuben Riddick and Abraham Hurdle against George Eason. The Sheriff to summons a Jury.

The County Trustee to pay Timothy Lassiter the sum of 20 pds. in part for building the Jail of this County.

Deed of land James Sumner to Ezekial Trotman Ack.

Third Monday in November, 1785.

Present: Christopher Riddick, David Rice, Thomas Hunter, James Gregory, Justices.

Bill of Sale William Walters to Elizabeth Walters proved by the oath of Isaac Miller.

Bill of Sale Elisha Parker to Elizabeth Walters proved by the oath of Isaac Miller.

Deed of land Wm. Arnold to John Arnold proved by the oath of James Knight.

The Last Will of Mary Felton, decd. exhibited by John Thomas Extr. therein appointed and proved by the oaths of Isaac Miller and James Pruden two of the witnesses.

William Williams an Illigetimate Child Son of Elizabeth Carter about the age of 16 years Oct. Last, bound as an apprentice to William Lenier (?) to learn the Business of House Carpenter.

Charles Rountree appointed Overseer of the Road instead of Kedar Hill and the hands of the said Rountree keep the same.

Kedar Hill and all his hands that work on the Road under him work on the Road that Aaron Hobbs is Overseer of.

Deed of Sale John Walton to Jethro Miltear proved by the oath of Robt. Parker, Junr.

Deed of land Jethro Ballard to Joshua Small proved by the oath of Daniel Gwinn.

Isaac Benton appointed Overseer of the Road instead of Moses Benton resigned.

Joseph Riddick, Thomas Trotman, Simon Stallings and George Outlaw who were appointed to make division of the Estate of Thomas Rountree decd. made report.

Deed of land William Freeman to Lemuel Taylor Ack.

James Davis appointed guardian to James Hodges son and orphan to James Hodges, decd. He to give Security in the sum of 500 pds. Job Riddick and Thomas Walton Securities.

David Rice Esqr., Job Riddick, Thomas Walton and William Berryman make a division of the Estate of James Hodges, decd.

James Davis guarding to James Hodges orphan of James Hodges, decd. to sell the perishable part of the Estate of the said Orphan.

Charles Rountree guardian to Seth Rountree, Levina Rountree, Rachel Rountree, Priscilla Rountree and Penny Rountree orphans of Thos. Rountree, decd. to sell the perishable part of the Estate of the said Orphans.

Deed of Sale Moor Carter to Charles Eure Ack.

Deed of Sale Daniel Hayes to Jacob Hayes Ack.

Tuesday Morning. Present: Christopher Riddick, David Rice, James Sumner, Justices.

Deed of Sale Thomas Green to James Piland proved by the oath of John Felton.

Motion of Mr. Jas. Brickell Att. at Law on behalf of William Crafford who moved for administration on the Estate of John Wallis, decd. - granted. He to give Bond in the sum of 200 pds. George Dunn Security.

Deed of land Jessey Dilday to Jacob Walters proved by the oath of John March.

George Dunn, Joseph Speight and Francis Speight or any two of them to make a division of the Estate of John Wallis, decd. now in the hands of Wm. Crafford.

Deed of land Wm. Sumner to Job Riddick proved by the oath of Jonathan Lassiter.

Deed of land William Crafford to James Crafford Ack.

William Baker guardian to Eliza. Baker orphan of Blake Baker, decd. exhibited his account Current with the said orphan.

Deed of Sale John Walton to Jacob Powell Ack.

James Sumner, Jethro Ballard and James Norfleet to Audit State and Settle the account Current of John Norfleet Extr. of John and Elizabeth Norfleet decd. and Jacob Gordon Admr. on the Estate of Elizabeth Norfleet, decd.

Deed of land Benjamin Barnes to John Odom Ack.

On Motion of Christopher Riddick Esqr. ordered that a Se Fa Issue to Mary Riddick to show cause why a new guardian should not be appointed to the orphans of Mills Riddick, decd.

Aaron Smith an Illigetimate Child Son of Rose Smith about the age of 15 years bound as an apprentice to Saml. Smith to learn the Business of a Cooper.

Sales of the Estate of Joseph Jones, decd. exhibited by Wm. Arnold Extr.

Deed of Sale William Crafford to David Cross proved by the oath of Cyprian Cross.

Wednesday Morning. Present: Christopher Riddick, James Gregory, Isaac Pipkin, David Rice, Justices.

The Sheriff returned the verdict of a Jury in a dispute made relative to lands entered by Abraham Hurdle and Reuben Riddick against Abraham Sumner. The Clerk of the Court to deliver to Abraham Sumner a copy which is as follows: That as each party is agreed that Abraham Sumner holds all the land that Hurdle and Riddick entered and that Sumner pays all cost. Charles Rountree, Thos. Walton, Jacob Bagley, William Hunter, Timothy Lassiter, James Costen, Richard Briggs, Benjamin Gordon, Abraham Eason, John Rice and Jacob Gordon.

William Crafford appointed Overseer of the Road in the room of Samuel Thomas resigned.

Abraham Reid an Illigetimate Child Son of Jammimy Reid about 18 years of age bound as an apprentice to John Duke, Junr. to learn the Business of a Cooper.

Christopher Riddick Esqr. Public Register of this County entered into Bond for the collection of the Tax on Grants.

Lawrence Baker Clerk of this Court entered into Bond for the Collection of Certain Taxes laid by Genl. Assembly in Oct. 1784.

Jesse Spivey appointed guardian to Frederick Blanshard, Sarah Blanshard, William Blanshard and Polly Blanshard orphans of Absolom

Blanshard decd. He to give Bond in the sum of 1000 pds. Charles Rountree and Thomas Walton Securities.

Thomas Hunter Esqr., Charles Rountree, Thomas Trotman and Joseph Riddick or any three to make a division of the Estate of Absolom Blanshard decd. agreeable to the will.

The perishable part of the Estate of the orphans of Absolom Blanshard decd. to be sold by their guardian.

James Gregory, Charles Rountree, Isaac Hunter and Thomas Trotman or any three of them Audit State and Settle the accounts of Thomas Hunter Extr. of Aaron Blanshard decd.

The Sheriff to summons the following persons as Jurymen: John Riddick, Solomon Briggs, Alexr. Eason, Jacob Powell, James Jones, Joshua Small, Abraham Eason, Benjamin Gordon, Aaron Lassiter, James Costen, Timothy Lassiter, Henry Hobbs, Saml. Green, Wm. Berryman, William Hunter, Amos Trotman, William Harriss, William Walters, Edward Daughty, Jeremiah Speight, Anthony Matthews, Isaac Miller, Lewis Walters, Peter Harrell, George Williams, John Gatling, Demsey Barnes, Henry Lee, Henry Goodman and Jesse Harrell.

The Sheriff of this County to summons a Jury to lay off a Road from or near Bass's Branch on the Direct Road the most convenient courses to Josiah Granberys.

Feby. 20, 1786

Third Monday in Feb. Present: Seth Riddick, Isaac Pipkin, Christopher Riddick, David Rice, Justices.

Deed of land Thomas Hambleton to William Vann Ack.

Deed of Sale Samuel Green to Isaac Green Ack.

John Baker to have licence to keep Public House. He to give Bond and Security agreeable to Law. Josiah Granbery and James Maney Securities.

No person be allowed to sell Spiriteous Liquors on the Court House Ground.

George Outlaw Deed of Gift to James Outlaw Ack.

Thomas Walton guardian to Theopholos Hunter returned his account Current with said orphan.

John Bunbery Walton appointed Overseer of the Road in the stead of Americas Blanshard resigned.

Account of Sales of part of the Estate of John Benton decd. exhibited by Saml. Benton one of the Extrs.

Inventory of the Goods & etc. of the Estate of Jacob Morris decd. was exhibited by Charity Morris Admrx.

Bill of Sale William Rawls to John Goodman proved by the oath of John Pipkin.

The Last Will and Testament of John Brinkley decd. was exhibited by Jacob Brinkley one of the Extrs. therein appointed and proved by the oath of Joseph Thompson one of the witnesses.

Inventory of the Goods & etc. of the Estate of John Brinkley decd. exhibited by Jacob Brinkley Extr.

Deed of land Jesse Barnes to Demsey Barnes proved by the oath of John Pipkin.

James Knight, Edward Arnold, Wm. Parker and Thomas Parker or any three of them to make a division of the Estate of Joseph James, decd. agreeable to the Will.

Deed of land Josiah Parker to James Parker proved by the oath of Lawrence Baker.

William Wallis Deed of Sale to David Cross proved by the oath of Demsey Barnes.

George Dunn and Joseph Speight who were appointed to make a division of the Estate of John Wallis decd. made report.

Deed of land John Arnold to James Pruden proved by the oath of Abraham Morgan.

Deed of land Peter Piland to Edward Piland Ack.

Deed of Sale Isaac Hunter to Anthony Matthews Ack.

The Last Will and Testament of Sarah Dunn was exhibited by Katherine Benton, Extrx. therein appointed and proved by the oath of James Knox one of the Evidences thereto.

Inventory of the Goods & etc. of the Estate of Sarah Dunn, decd. was exhibited by Miles Benton Extr. in right of his Wife.

Henry Dilday, Junr. came into Court for begetting a Bastard Child on the Body of Christian Wills. He to give Security. Thomas Piland and John Wills Securities.

Deed of land William King to William Wallis proved by the oath of Richard Arnold.

Account of Sales of the Estate of Absolom Blanshard decd. was exhibited by Isaac Hunter, Sheriff.

William Booth appointed Overseer of the Road instead of Amos Lassiter.

Mary Braddy, Extrx. of John Braddy decd. to sell part of the Estate of the decd. to pay debts.

On Motion of John Brickell Esqr. Att. at Law in behalf of Samuel Harrell, ordered that Cyprian Cross, Charles Eure, Jesse Vann and Stephen Eure or any three of them make a division of the Estate of Thomas Harrell, decd.

David Rice, Thomas Walton and William Berriman who were appointed to make a division of the Estate of James Hodges decd. make report.

John Ellis orphan of John Ellis decd. bound as an apprentice to Cyprian Cross (the orphan about 14 years old) to learn the Business of Husbandry.

James Freeman, Jonathan Roberts, Demsey Bond and Thomas Hunter or any three of them to make a division of the Estate of Jacob Morris, decd.

John Gwinn orphan of Isreal (?) Gwinn about 16 years old bound as an apprentice to Peter Parker to learn the Business of a Cooper.

Bill of Sale William Wallis to Demsey Barnes proved by the oath of Jesse Vann.

Tuesday Morning. Present: Seth Riddick, William Baker, Christo. Riddick, James Gregory, Jethro Ballard, Justices.

James Davis guardian of James Hodges orphan of James Hodges decd. made return of his account Sales of the said orphans Estate.

Deed of Sale John Baker to Elisha Norfleet Ack.

John Baker, Christopher Riddick and Lawrence Baker or any two of them to let the Bridge to build at Lawrence Bakers Mill to the Lowest Bidder.

Jethro Ballard, James Norfleet and James Sumner who were appointed to Audit State and Settle the accounts of John Norfleet, Extr. of John & Elizabeth Norfleet decd. and the account of Jacob Green Admr. of Elizabeth Norfleet decd. made report.

Hannah Courtney moved for a license to keep a Public House at the Folly. William Bethey and Anthony Matthews Securities.

Deed of Sale Benjamin Saunders to Jesse Saunders proved by the oath of Henry Speight.

Deed of Sale James Skinner to John Odom Ack.

Deed of Sale John Norfleet to Jacob Gordon Ack.

Deed of Sale Hezekiah Norfleet to Jacob Gordon proved by the oath of John Norfleet.

Wednesday Morning. Present: David Rice, Thomas Hunter, Isaac Pipkin, William Baker, Jethro Ballard, Justices.

Joseph Dilday moved for administration on the Estate of Elisha Odom decd. -granted. He to give Security in the sum of 100 pds. Christopher Riddick Esqr. and Enos Rogers Securities.

Inventory of the Goods & etc. of the Estate of Elisha Odom decd. was exhibited by Joseph Dilday Admr.

Joseph Dilday Admr. of Elisha Odom to sell the personal Estate of the decd. to pay debts.

John Bunbery Walton to Receive the Public and County Tax in Capt. Jonathan Robert's Muster Bounds for the year 1785. Joseph Riddick to receive the Tax in the district of Capt. Joseph Riddick. John Riddick to receive the Tax in Capt. Jethro Sumners Captaincy. Isaac Miller to receive the Tax in Capt. James Arlines Captaincy. William Harris to receive the Tax in Capt. Christopher Riddick's Captaincy and Miles Benton receive the Tax in Capt. William Goodman's Captaincy and Capt. Charles Eure's Captaincy.

The following persons to receive a list of white and black persons in the County and Captaincys as follows: Simon Stallings the list in Capt. Jonathan Roberts Captaincy. Reuben Riddick in Capt. Joseph Riddicks Captaincy. Benjamin Gordon in Capt. Jethro Sumners Captaincy, Humphry Hudgins in Capt. Christopher Riddicks Captaincy. Moses Kittrell in Capt. Jas. Arlines Captaincy. William Davidson in Capt. Capt. Charles Eures Captaincy and John Pipkin in Capt. William Goodmans Captaincy.

Deed of land Demsey Rooks to Joseph Rooks proved by the oath of Charles Eure.

Thurs. Morning. Present: Thomas Hunter, Seth Riddick, Isaac Pipkin, David Rice, Justices.

On motion of James Walton by Simon Stallings his guardian for leave to build a water grist mill which was built by Thomas Walton and given by him to his son Richard and by the said Richard to James Walton Minor and that Charles Rountree as appears to the Court having some pretentions to build a mill on the same stream. Ordered that the said Charles be summoned to appear next term and show reasons to this Court why an order may not be granted to the said James Walton to rebuild the said Mill.

The Sheriff to summons William Walters, Seth Eason, John Powell and James Norfleet to appear at Edenton as Jurymen.

The Sheriff to summons Kedar Hill, James Outlaw, Jacob Bagley, Demsey Trotman, Thomas Walton, Thomas Hurdle, Aaron Hobbs, Moses Davis, Isaac Harrell, Richard Bond, William Booth, William Arnold, Thomas Parker, James Knight, Thomas Trotman, Robert Parker, Wright Hayes, William Cleaves, William Daughtie, Moses Kittrell, William Goodman, Elisha Cross, Enos Rogers, Philip Lewis, Jesse Vann, Francis Speight, Samuel Smith, Benjamin Barnes, Joseph Figg and Willis Browne as Jurymen.

Moses Hare to be allowed the sum of 3 pds. 12 sh. for summoning the Inhabitants to give the list of their property and for attending six days on this Court as a Constable.

Ordered that the sum of 3 sh. be Levied on each free Male Person of the age of 21 years and upwards and on all Slaves from the age of 12 years of age to 50 and that 1 sh. be Levied on each Hundred Acres of land in this County for the County Tax.

May 15, 1786.

Third Monday. Present: Christopher Riddick, William Baker, Jethro Ballard, Justices.

The Last Will and Testament of James Riddick decd. was exhibited by Christopher Riddick Esqr. one of the Extrs. therein appointed and was proved by the oaths of Seth Riddick and James Hayes witnesses.

Inventory of the Goods & etc. of the Estate of James Riddick decd. was exhibited by Christopher Riddick Extr.

William Baker, Seth Riddick and Robert Parker or any two of them to make division of the Estate of James Riddick decd. agreeable to the Will.

Deed of Sale Edward Allen, Betty Allen, Mary Reid and Caty Reid to Henry Forrest proved by the oaths of Demsey and Jonathan Smith.

Deed of Sale Saml. Smith to Henry Forrest proved by the oath of Jonathan Smith.

The Last Will and Testament of Guy Hoss exhibited by Moses Hill and Moses Hobbs Extrs. there appointed and was proved by the oath of Aaron Hobbs one of the witnesses.

James Small appointed Overseer of the Road instead of Kedar Ballard resigned.

Deed of Sale George Dunn to Francis Speight proved by the oath of Joseph Speight.

Deed of Sale John Miller to Francis Speight proved by the oath of Philip Lewis.

Deed of Sale Elisha Copeland to Henry Speight proved by the oath of Francis Speight.

On motion of John Brinkley Esqr. Att. at Law on behalf of Pases (?) Turner it was ordered that Jethro Ballard, Jethro Sumner and Kedar Ballard Audit State and Settle the accounts of Pases (?) Turner Extr.

Deed of land Thomas Brickell to William Lewis proved by the oath of Isaac Hunter. Ceneson (?) Brickell relinquished her right of Dower.

Inventory of the Goods & etc. of the Estate of Guy Hobbs decd. was exhibited by Moses Hobbs one of the Extrs.

Sarah Saunders to pay a Tax on 152 acres of land instead of 400 acres.

Shadrick Ellis to be exempt from paying a Tax for the present year.

Deed of Sale Elisha Parker to Peter Parker proved by the oath of Jonah Benton.

Edward Arnold appointed Overseer of the Road instead of James Jones resigned.

Deed of Sale Samuel Thomas to James Thomas proved by the oath of William Harris.

Account of Sales of a Negro Winch belonging to the Estate of Thos. Rountree was exhibited by Charles Rountree on oath.

Account of Sales of the Estate of Elisha Odom was exhibited by Joseph Dilday Admr.

Account of Sales of the Estate of John Braddy decd. exhibited by Charles Dilday Admr.

Benjamin Gordon who was appointed to take a list of the Inhabitants in Capt. Jethro Sumners Captaincy made report.

Humphry Hudgins who was appointed to take a list of the Inhabitants in Capt. Christopher Riddicks Captaincy made report.

Elizabeth Riddick to be appointed guardian to Thomas Riddick, Edward Riddick, Sarah Riddick and James Riddick. She to give Security in the sum of 200 pds. Christopher Riddick and Seth Riddick, Esqr. Securities.

Deed of Sale William Arnold to John Arnold Ack.

Moses Kitrell who was appointed to take a list of Inhabitants in Capt. James Arlines Captaincy made report.

Simon Stallings who was appointed to take a list of the Inhabitants in Capt. Jonathan Robert's Captaincy made report.

Joseph Riddick, Thomas Trotman, Thomas Hunter and Charles Rountree or any three of them make a division of the Estate of Guy Hobbs decd.

Jethro Ballard, Jethro Sumner and Kedar Ballard who were appointed to Audit State and Settle the accounts of Pases (?) Turner Extr. of Daniel Pugh decd. made report.

Augustine Minshew orphan of John Minshew decd. about 14 years of age bound as an apprentice to John Robbins to learn the Business of a Blacksmith.

Deed of Sale Charles Vaughan to George Hargrove proved by the oath of John Harrell.

Reuben Davidson who was appointed to take a list of the inhabitants in Capt. Charles Eures Captaincy made return.

Thomas Hunter, Joseph Riddick and Thomas Trotman who were appointed to make division of the Estate of Absolom Blanshard decd. made report.

Robert Smith an Illigetimate Child Son of Selah Smith about 10 years of age bound as an apprentice to Isaac Miller to learn the Business of Husbandry.

Jethro Ballard, Kedar Ballard, David Rice and Jethro Sumner to make a division of the Estate of Daniel Pugh decd.

Tuesday Morning. Present: William Baker, Jethro Ballard, Seth Riddick, David Rice, Isaac Pipkin, Justices.

Deed of Sale Moses Blanshard to John Hoffler proved by the oath of Moses Hill.

Deed of Sale James Lassiter to John Wills Ack.

Deed of Sale Demsey Bond to Geo. Outlaw proved by the oath of James Freeman.

Deed of land George Eason to Timothy Lassiter proved by the oath of Job Riddick.

Bill of Sale George Eason to William Baker proved by the oath of Jeremiah Speight.

John Pipkin who was appointed to take a list of the Inhabitants in Capt. Wm. Goodmans Captaincy made return.

John Bunbery Walton Collector of the Tax in the District of Capt. Jonathan Roberts to be allowed in the Settlement of his accounts for the Tax assessed on William Bristow and William Kelly.

Deed of Sale Deonshews Minshew to Demsey Bond proved by the oath of Richd. Bond.

Demsey Trotman guardian of John Hunter orphan of John Hunter decd. made return of his guardian Accounts.

Deed of land Jethro Sumner former Sheriff of this County to Cyprian Cross Ack.

Petition of Jesse Spivey and Mary Spivey his Wife late widow of Absolom Blanshard decd. - it is ordered that the Sheriff summons a Jury to lay out the thirds of the land agreeable to Law.

In a suit Thomas Gregorys Extrs. vs. Jethro Benton, Senr. it was agreed on by the parties that the Deposition of John Glover a witness for the Plantiff be taken.

Mills Lewis appointed Overseer of the Road instead of Philip Lewis resigned.

Isaac Pipkin Esqr. appointed Sheriff for the present year. He to give Bond agreeable to Law. Wm. Baker and Seth Riddick Securities.

Isaac Hunter Sheriff of this County allowed the sum of 8 pds. for extra services.

Isaac Mill appointed Constable instead of Jonathan Smith resigned.

William Harriss allowed the sum of 4 pds. for carrying Wm. _____ (name smeared) to the Jail in Halifax after his breaking jail from there.

Weds. Morning. Present: Christopher Riddick, William Baker, Seth Riddick, Jethro Ballard, Justices.

The County Trustee to pay Lawrence Baker the sum of 35 pds. for building a Bridge across the Creek below Laurance Bakers Mill.

Deed of Sale Wm. Booth to Demsey Jones proved by the oath of Joseph John Sumner and William Gordon.

Christopher Riddick appointed guardian to Mills Riddick, Nathaniel

Riddick, Elizabeth Riddick and David Riddick orphans of Mills Riddick decd. He to give Security in the sum of 3000 pds. Seth Riddick and William Baker Esqr. Securities.

Deed of land Jethro Benton, Junr. to Thos. Coke and Francis Asbury proved by the oath of Thomas Parker.

Demsey Bond to be exempt from paying a Tax on a certain Negro named Jacob which tax has already been paid in Chowan where the said Negro was listed.

Moses Kittrell Admr. of the Estate of Joseph Griffin, Junr. decd. made return of his account current.

Samuel Harrell allowed 16 sh. for summonsing inhabitants of Capt. Joseph Riddicks Captaincy to give their lists.

Timothy Lassiter to be allowed the sum of 30 pds. it being part of the balance due to him for building the jail of this County.

Thurs. Present: Christopher Riddick, William Baker, Seth Riddick, David Rice, Justices.

John Pipkin (who was appointed Deputy Sheriff of this County) took the oath prescribed by Law.

The Sheriff to summons the following persons to serve as Petty and Grand Jurymen: Jacob Gordon, Peter Harrell, Miles Benton, Demsey Odom, Isaac Walters, Edwd. Daughty, Zadock Hinton, Robert Taylor, Kedar Hill, Jesse Spivey, Thomas Barnes, Demsey Blanshard, Benjamin Gordon, Joseph Speight, John Gatling, Cyprian Cross, Charles Eure, Henry Goodman, David Cross, Jesse Saunders, William Harriss, James Freeman, Simon Stallings, Thomas Trotman, Kedar Ballard, John Riddick, Thomas Walton, Joshua Small, John Odom and Timothy Lassiter.

Miles Benton Collector of Taxes in the Captaincy of Capt. William Goodman and Capt. Charles Eure be allowed in the Statement of his accounts for the Tax assessed on Joseph Plats, Junr., Henry Delday and Jesse Ellis.

Following Persons to take a list of Taxables in the different Captaincys in this County (to wit) Thomas Hunter Esqr. in Capt. Jonathan Roberts Captaincy, James Gregory in Capt. Joseph Riddicks Captaincy, Jethro Ballard in Capt. Jethro Sumners Captaincy, Jethro Sumner in Capt. Arlines Captaincy, Seth Riddick in Capt. Eures Captaincy, Christopher Riddick Esqr. in Capt. Christopher Riddicks Captaincy and William Baker in Capt. Wm. Goodmans Captaincy.

Samuel Harrell to be allowed the sum of 32 sh. for his attendance as a Constable on the Court this Term.

John Riddick Collector of the Tax in the Captaincy of Capt. Jethro Sumner to be allowed the settlement of his accounts for the Tax assessed on Joseph Thompson.

Christo. Riddick to be allowed the sum of 20 sh. for a Book he purchased to enter the records of this County.

Isaac Hunter late Sheriff of this County to be summoned to appear at this Court next sitting and to bring his accounts for the collection of County Tax.

Third Monday in August 1786

Present: William Baker, Christopher Riddick, David Rice, Thomas Hunter and Seth Riddick, Justices.

William Berryman appointed Overseer of the Road instead of Thomas Trotman resigned.

Deed of Sale Moses Hare to Moses Benton proved by the oath of Jethro Sumner, Esqr.

Deed of Sale Josiah Parker to Stephen Shepherd proved by the oath of Israel Beeman.

Deed of Gift Margaret Colly to Limuel Colley proved by the oath of James Outlaw.

Last Will and Testament of Solomon Hiatt decd. presented by Rebecca Hiatt and Henry Goodman Extr. and Extrx. therein appointed and proved by the oath of John Bethey.

Last Will and Testament of Joel Goodman decd. exhibited by James Goodman and John Goodman Extrs. therein appointed and proved by the oaths of Jethro Bethey and William Goodman two of the witnesses.

Inventory of the Goods & etc. of the Estate of Joel Goodman decd. exhibited by James Goodman and John Goodman Extrs.

Mary Haslett Deed of Sale to Henry Mironey proved by the oath of John Powell.

Account of Sales of the Estate of Thomas Harrell decd. exhibited by Samuel Harrell Extr.

Jonathan Lassiter orphan of Ozea (?) Lassiter about the age of 16 years bound as an apprentice to Abraham Hurdle to learn the Business of a Blacksmith.

Josiah Benton appointed Overseer of the Road instead of James Pruden resigned.

Levin Philips to be exempt from paying a Public County and Parish Tax in this County he being rendered unable to pay the said Tax from a wound he received in the Continental Army.

Deed of Sale William Hinton to Isaac Harrell Ack.

John White moved for Admr. on the Estate of William Spivey decd. - granted. He to give Surity in the sum of 100 pds. James Outlaw and Thomas Walton Securities.

William Arnold appointed Overseer of the Road instead of James Knight resigned.

Inventory of the Goods & etc. of the Estate of William Spivey decd.

exhibited by John White Admr.

The perishable part of the Estate of the orphans of Kedar Riddick decd. which was given them by James Riddick decd. to be sold agreeable to Law.

John White Admr. of Wm. Spivey decd. to sell so much of the Estate of the decd. as will pay debts.

Deed of Sale Jacob Bagley to Demsey Trotman proved by the oath of Thomas Trotman.

Deed of Sale Demsey Trotman to James Walton Ack.

Deed of land Keziah Blanshard to Joseph Alphin proved by the oath of Moses Lassiter.

Deed of Sale Lewis Jones to David Brinkley proved by the oath of John Brinkley.

Jethro Sumner Esqr. returned a list of Taxables in the Captaincy of James Arline.

Tues. Morning. Present: Christopher Riddick, Jethro Sumner, James Gregory, David Rice, Justices.

Charles Rountree guardian to the orphans of Thos. Rountree decd. made return of the Sale of the personal Estate of the said orphans.

Inventory of the Goods & etc. of the Estate of Solomon Hiatt decd. exhibited by Henry Goodman one of the Extrs.

James Gregory Esqr. returned the list of Taxables taken by him in the Captaincy of Capt. Joseph Riddick.

Patrick Hegity appointed Surveyor for the County of Gates. He to give Bond agreeable to Law. Joseph Riddick and George Eason Securities.

The Hands of Josiah Granbery to work on the road where John Riddick is Overseer.

Abraham Harrell appointed Overseer of the New Road leading from the Desert Road to Josiah Granberys and that the following persons and their hands work on the said road under him. John Rice, Isaac Hunter, Isaac Harrell, Noah Harrell, Josiah Lassiter, Jacob Gordon, Samuel Harrell, John Gordon, Isaac Pearce and Aaron Lassiter.

Deed of Sale Seth Stallings to Simon Stallings proved by the oath of James Walton.

Last Will and Testament of Elisha Hunter decd. exhibited by Thomas Hunter and Joseph Riddick, Extrs. therein appointed. Proved by the oath of John Gordon one of the witnesses.

Inventory of the Goods & etc. of the Estate of Elisha Hunter decd. exhibited by Thos. Hunter and Joseph Riddick Extrs.

Thomas Hunter, Thomas Trotman and Charles Rountree who were appointed to make division of the Estate of Guy Hobbs decd. made report.

Thomas Hunter and Joseph Riddick Esqr., Thomas Trotman and Simon Stallings or any three of them to make division of the Estate of William Spivey decd.

William Baker Esqr. returned his list of Taxables in the district of Capt. William Goodmans Captaincy.

Christopher Riddick Esqr. returned the list of Taxables in the Captaincy of Christopher Riddick.

Thomas Hunter Esqr. returned the list of Taxables taken by him in the Captaincy of Capt. Jonathan Roberts.

Seth Riddick Esqr. returned the list of Taxables taken by him in the Captaincy of Capt. Charles Eure.

James Gregory Esqr., Isaac Hunter and Thomas Trotman who were appointed to Audit State and Settle the accounts of Thomas Hunter Extr. of the Last Will of Aaron Blanshard decd. made report.

Henry Goodman Extr. of Solomon Hiatt decd. to sell so much of the Estate of the said decd. as will pay debts.

Mourning Phelps daughter of Aaron Phelps decd. about the age of 11 years bound as an apprentice to Thomas Travis to learn the Business of a Weaver.

Moses Hobbs Extr. of Guy Hobbs decd. to sell the perishable part of the Estate of the said decd.

Weds. morning. Present: Christopher Riddick, James Gregory, William Baker, Seth Riddick and Jethro Sumner, Justices.

Bill of Sale Thomas Hays and Wife to Thomas Hunter, James Freeman and Thomas Hoffler proved by the oaths of Demsey Bond and John B. Walton.

Christopher Riddick, John Baker Esqrs. and Lawrence Baker to let the repairing of the Bridge below Lawrence Bakers Mill to the lowest bidder.

John Brickell Esqr., State Att. for this County to be allowed the sum of 16 pds. for his services in the year 1785.

The Sheriff to summons Thomas Hunter, Timothy Lassiter, William Harriss and David Small to attend as Jurymen for the Superior Court of Law and Equity to be held at Edenton.

Sheriff to summons Moses Hill, Henry Harrell, Simon Stallings, Aaron Hobbs, Mordicai Perry, Demsey Trotman, William Freeman, James Outlaw, Kedar Hill, Richard Bond, Thomas Parker, James Knight, Edward Arnold, William Arnold, John Darden, John Powell, William Doughty, Jesse Benton, Peter Parker, Micajah Riddick, James Pruden, Wm. Walters, William Goodman, Moses Kittrell, Anthony Matthews, Miles Benton, Henry Lee, Francis Speight, More Carter and George Williams as Inferior Court Jurymen.

On motion of Thos. Vail Esqr. Att. of Law in behalf of James Walton ordered that James Walton build or repair a Water Grist Mill across Catherine Creek at the place where Thomas Walton formerly had a Mill.

John Warren Extr. and Priscilla Rogers Extrx. of Stephen Rogers decd. to sell the perishable part of the Estate of the decd.

County Trustee to pay Lawrence Baker Clerk of this Court the sum of 20 pds. for the extra services performed by him this year past.

Third Monday in November 1786

Present: Thomas Hunter, Seth Riddick, David Rice, Justices.

Deed of land Zackarias Copeland and William Porter to William Goodman proved by the oath of Henry Goodman.

Deed of land Isaac Croom, Mary Croom, Richard Croom and Ann Croom to Francis Parker proved by the oath of Abraham Saunders.

Deed of land George Gatling to Jesse Saunders proved by the oath of John Pipkin.

Present: Christopher Riddick, Justice.

Joseph Davis son of Mary Davis an Illegitimate Child, bound as an apprentice to Edward Barreman (?) to learn the Business of a Shoemaker.

Sarah Davis daughter of Mary Davis an illegitimate child about the age of 7 years bound as an apprentice to Edward Berryman to learn House Business.

Liddy Spivey Widow of Thomas Spivey moved for administration on her decd. Husbands Estate - granted. She to give Security in the sum of 1000 pds. Kedar Hill and Jesse Spivey Securities.

Inventory of the Goods & etc. of the Estate of Thomas Spivey decd. was exhibited by Liddey Spivey Admr.

Thomas Hunter and Joseph Riddick Esqrs. and Thomas Trotman who were appointed to make division of the Estate of William Spivey decd. made report.

Account of Sales of part of the Estate of William Spivey was exhibited by John White Admr.

William Griffin orphan of Joseph Griffin bound as an apprentice to William Boyce until he arrives to 21 years of age to learn the Business of Husbandry.

The Hands of Francis Speight to work on the road under Jesse Saunders

Marriage Contract between James Sumner and Mourning Blanshard proved by the oath of Starkey Shark one of the witnesses.

Thomas Trotman, Charles Rountree, Kedar Hill and Thomas Hunter to make division of the Estate of Thomas Spivey decd.

Liddey Spivey appointed guardian to Jacob Spivey and Sarah Spivey orphans of Thomas Spivey decd. She to give Security in the sum of 1000 pds. Thomas Walton and Jacob Bagley Securities.

Israel Miller to be allowed the sum of 30 sh. for conveying two prisoners to Hertford County Jail.

Liddey Spivey guardian to Jacob Spivey and Sarah Spivey to sell the perishable part of the Estate of the said orphans.

John White moved for guardianship of Seth Spivey and Smith Spivey. He to give security in the sum of 500 pds. Mordica Perry and Thomas Walton Securities.

Andrew Matthews came into Court for begetting a Bastard Child on the Body of Ruth Wiggins. He to give Security in the sum of 100 pds. for the keeping of the said Child from becoming chargable to the County. William Boyce and Isaac Walters Securities.

Deed of Gift John Raby to Kedah Raby proved by the oath of Henry Mironey.

Deed of land John Raby to Kedar Raby proved by the oath of Henry Mironey.

John White guardian to Seth Spivey and Sarah Spivey to sell the perishable part of the Estate of the orphans.

Tues. morning. Present: Christopher Riddick, Seth Riddick, David Rice, Thomas Hunter, Justices.

Deed of land Jacob Pierce to Aston Nickson Ack.

Present: James Gregory and Jethro Ballard, Justices.

Account of Sales of the Estate of the orphans of Guy Hobbs decd. exhibited by Moses Hobbs.

The Hands of John Gordon to work on the Road he formerly worked on under Demsey Trotman.

John Swann Esqr. produced his license and qualified himself as a practicing Att. in this Court.

Deed of land John Harrell to Cyprian Cross proved by the oath of John Odom.

Cyprian Cross, Stephen Eure and Charles Eure who were appointed to make division of the Estate of Thomas Harrell decd. made report.

Weds. morning. Present: Thomas Hunter, James Gregory, Seth Riddick, Christopher Riddick, David Rice, Jethro Ballard and William Baker, Justices.

The County Treasurer to pay Wm. Lewis the sum of 13 pds. 10 sh. for repairing the Bridge below Lawrence Bakers Mill.

John Warren and Priscilla Warren his Wife Admrs. of Stephen Rogers, decd. summoned to attend this Court at next sitting to show cause if any they have why they have not made a settlement with the Estate of the decd.

Sheriff to summon the following persons to attend this Court next sitting as Jurymen. Jonathan Roberts, William Matthews, Joshua Small, Jacob Gordon, Richard Briggs, John Briggs, Aaron Lassiter, James Costen, Thomas Hurdle, William King, Amos Trotman, William Hunter, Job Riddick, John Arnold, Edward Doughty, Henry Speight, Isaac Walters, Peter Harrell, Elisha Parker, Willes Parker, Charles Eure, John Bethey, Reuben Lassiter, William Hinton, William Harriss, Henry Forrest, Samuel Smith, Jeremiah Speight, Michael Lawrence and Henry Goodman.

Edward Arnold to collect the Taxes both public and County in the Captaincy of Jethro Sumner. Samuel Harrell in Capt. Isaac Hunters Captaincy. Kedar Hill in Capt. Jonathan Roberts Captaincy, Moses Kittrell in Capt. James Arlines Captaincy. Isaac Miller in Capt. William Harriss's Captaincy. Lewis Sparkman in Capt. Charles Eures Captaincy. John Pipkin in Capt. William Goodmans Captaincy.

Deed of land Jesse Spivey to Henry Harrell proved by the oath of Abraham Hurdle.

Thurs. morning. Present: Christopher Riddick, William Baker, Thomas Hunter, Seth Riddick, Justices.

William Baker, Christopher Riddick and Jethro Sumner Esqr. to Audit and State the account of William Harvey and Elizabeth Harvey his Wife Admrs. of Docton Riddick decd.

Blake Baker Esqr. impowered to purchase the following Books for the use of this Court: Blackstons Commentaries, Washingtons Abridgment of the Statutes, Davies's last Edition of the Revial of the Acts of Assembly, Jacobs Law Dictionary, Burns Justice of the Peace and Swinburn of Wills or Godslphines Orphans Legacy, and that the County Trustee pay him for the same.

Christopher Riddick, William Baker and Lawrence Baker to Audit and State the accounts of Jethro Sumner one of the late Sheriffs of this County and that they Audit State and Settle the accounts of Isaac Hunter Sheriff and that they call on the said Sheriff to attend with their accounts.

William Baker appointed County Trustee.

Third Monday in Feb. 1787

Present: William Baker, Seth Riddick, David Rice, Jethro Sumner, Justices.

Deed of land John Goodman to Solomon King proved by the oath of William Odom.

Abraham Saunders appointed Overseer of the Road instead of William Odom resigned.

Mary Hill deed of Gift to Henry Hill Ack.

Deed of land William Vann and Samuel Brown to Charles Eure proved by the oath of William Davidson.

Deed of land William Vann to William Davidson proved by the oath of Charles Eure.

Last Will and Testament of John Miller decd. was exhibited by Rachal Miller and proved by the oath of Patrick Hegerty one of the witnesses.

Deed of land Peter Piland and Charley Piland to Willis Moor proved by the oath of William Polson.

Thomas Walton guardian to Theopholas Hunter made return of his account Current with said orphans.

Last Will of James Piland decd. exhibited by James Piland one of the Extrs. therein appointed and proved by the oath of Eleanor Davis one of the witnesses.

Deed of Sale David Cross to Abel Cross Ack.

Deed of Sale John Felton to Asa Harrell proved by the oath of Lawrence Baker.

Shadarack Ellis to be exempt form paying a poll Tax in this County for the year 1786.

Kedar Hinton moved for administration on the Estate of Richard Freeman decd. -granted. He to give Security in the sum of 600 pds. (no Securities given).

Deed of Sale Edward Arnold to Thomas Parker Ack.

Deed of Sale William Arnold to Abraham Morgan proved by the oath of Edward Arnold.

William Booth, Christo. Riddick Esqr. and James Freeman Securities. (this for Kedar Hinton on the Estate of Richard Freeman decd.)

Kedar Hinton Admr. of Richard Freeman decd. to sell part of the Estate of the decd. to pay debts.

Deed of land Job Riddick to James Costen Ack.

Last Will of Henry Smith decd. exhibited by Samuel Smith and Thomas Smith Extrs. therein appointed and proved by the oaths of Henry Forrest and Charles Smith two of the witnesses.

Inventory of the Goods & etc. of the Estate of Henry Smith decd. exhibited by Saml. and Thomas Smith Extrs.

Deed of land Kedar Hill to Moses Blanshard proved by the oath of Thos. Trotman.

Account Sales of the Estate of the orphans of William Spivey decd. exhibited by Thomas Hunter Esqr.

Account Current James Davis guardian of James Hodges orphan of James Hodge decd. exhibited by the said James Davis.

Rachal Miller moved for administration on the Estate of John Miller decd.--granted. She to give Security in the sum of 500 pds. Samuel Harrell and Moses Davis Securities.

Inventory of the Goods & etc. of the Estate of John Miller decd. exhibited by Rachel Miller, Admr.

Rachel Miller to sell part of the perishable Estate of the decd. John Miller.

Thomas Trotman, Charles Rountree, Kedar Hill and Thomas Hunter who were appointed to make a division of the Estate of Thomas Spivey decd. made report.

Christopher Riddick, Moses Kittrell and William Vann to make division of the Estate of Elisha Odom.

Sam'l. Robbins and Illigetimate Child Son of Lucy Robbins about the age of 15 years bound to Jethro Miller (?) to learn the Business of a Cooper.

Deed of Sale James Sumner to Joseph John Sumner proved by the oath of James Jones.

David Jones, Junr. gave Security in the sum of 500 pds. for his good behavior and keeping the peace for one year from this date. James Jones and Willis Wiggings Securities.

Tues. morning. Present: Christopher Riddick, James Gregory, Jethro Ballard, William Goodman, William Baker, John Baker, Justices.

Simon Stallings guardian of James Walton orphan of Richard Walton decd. made return of his accounts.

Deed of land Joseph Riddick to Charles Matthews Smith Ack.

Isaac Miller to be allowed 48 sh. for summoning the Inhabitants in the Captaincy of Cept. William Harris and Capt. Arlines.

John Weatherby appointed Inspector of Tar Pitch & Terpertine. He to give Bond and Security agreeable to Law. Henry King and Henry Goodman Securities.

Deed of land Joseph Scott to Josiah Granbery proved by the oath of John Rice.

Account of Sale of the Estate of the orphans of Thos. Spivey decd. exhibited by Thos. Hunter.

Disputed Entry David Rice against Samuel Harrell. The Sheriff to summon a Jury.

Inventory of the Goods & etc. of the Estate of Ricd. Freeman decd. exhibited by Kedar Hinton Admr.

Willis Browne guardian to Nancy Garrett orphan of James Garrett decd. made return of his Account Current.

Joseph Riddick and David Rice Esqrs. to make division of a Certain

95

Tract or parcel of land adjoining the land of Josiah Granbery, John Rice and Isaac Hunter which was left by James Jones decd. in his last will to be equally divided between his two daughters.

William Baker and Lawrence Baker to audit state and settle the accounts of Blake Baker Guardian to Elizabeth Baker orphan of Blake Baker decd.

Wednesday morning. Present: William Baker, Seth Riddick, James Gregory, David Rice and John Baker, Justices.

Deed of land Timothy Lassiter and Jethro Lassiter to Robert McCullok proved by the oath of Isaac Hunter.

Deed of Sale John Briggs to Josiah Granbery proved by the oath of James Baker.

Thursday morning. Present: Jethro Sumner, David Rice, John Baker, James Gregory, Christopher Riddick, Seth Riddick and William Baker.

Ordered that the sum of 2 sh. be levied on each free Male Person of the age of 21 years and upwards and on all Slaves from 12 years to 50 and that 6 pc. be levied on each hundred acres of land in this County as County Tax.

The Sheriff to summons the following persons to attend this court at the next sitting on the third Monday in May next. William Booth, Demsey Bond, Simon Stallings, Jacob Bagley, Demsey Trotman, Thomas Walton, John Rice, John Riddick, Richard Briggs, Alexander Eason, James Knight, Thomas Parker, William Walton, Aaron Lassiter, Anthony Matthews, Peter Parker, Samuel Barker, Demsey Williams, James Bristow, Francis Speight, Francis Parker, David Lewis, Cyprian Cross, John Gatling, Jesse Browne, Robert Parker, Demsey Odom, William Odom, Jesse Benton and David Harrell.

The Sheriff to summons the following persons to attend at the next Superior Court of Law and Equity to be held at Edenton on the third day of May next. Moses Hare, Thomas Trotman, Benjamin Gordon and Philip Lewis.

The County Trustee to pay Moses Hare 5 pds. 12 sh. for attending the Court and warning the inhabitants to give a list of Taxables in the Captaincy of Jethro Sumner.

Jethro Ballard appointed guardian to Elizabeth Riddick orphan of James Riddick decd. He to give bond in the sum of 1000 pds. Jethro Sumner and Thomas Hunter esqrs. Securities.

Third Monday in May 1787

Present: Thomas Hunter, Christopher Riddick, John Baker, William Baker, Justices.

Deed of land John Goodman to William Goodman proved by the oath of Henry Goodman.

Deed of land Silas Copeland, John Copeland, James Copeland and Jesse Copeland to Francis Parker proved by the oath of Abraham Saunders.

Charles Rountree guardian to Priscilla Rountree, Penney Rountree, Livina (?) Rountree and Rachel Rountree made a return of his accounts.

William Blair Esqr. produced his license for practicing the Law in the County Courts in this State and took the oath agreeable to law.

Last Will and Testament of Stephen Thomas decd. exhibited by Jacob Thomas Extr. therein appointed and proved by the oath of William Felton one of the witnesses.

Inventory of the goods & etc. of the Estate of Stephen Thomas decd. exhibited by Jacob Thomas Extr.

Isaac Miller to be allowed the sum of 30 sh. for conveying James Sullivan to the Jail of Edenton.

Solomon Alphin to be exempt from the payment of his Public County and Parish Tax.

John Baker Esqr. appointed as Overseer of the road instead of Willis Brown resigned.

Milley Harrell to be exempt from the payment of a Tax on a Negro woman named Pegg she being infirm.

Lemuel Kein to be exempt from the payment of his Poll Tax for the year 1786 he being underage.

James Parker in the district of Moor Kittrell to be exempt from the payment of a Double Tax he being returned rong.

Deed of Sale Thomas Felton, John Felton and Elizabeth Felton to John Piland proved by the oath of Stephen Harrell.

Henry Saunders and Joseph Saunders to be exempt from the payment of a Poll Tax for themselves they being underage when listed.

Jesse Benton appointed Overseer of the road instead of William Daughtie resigned.

Sophia Frost appeared for having a Bastard child. She to give security in the sum of 50 pds. for keeping said child from becoming chargeable to the Parish. Thomas Hiatt Security.

John Parker allowed the sum of 45 sh. for assisting in conveying a prisoner to Halifax Jail.

Willis Parker to pay only a single Tax on two hundred and fifty acres of land instead of a Double Tax on five hundred acres it being a mistake in the return.

Thomas Trotman guardian to Miles, Joseph, Sally, Noah and John Scott orphans of James Scott made a return of his guardianship.

Deed of land Lawyer Lawrence, George Lawrence, Thomas Campbell, Nancy Campbell and Benjn. Powell to Thomas Marshall proved by the oath of William Brooks.

Jethro Meltear allowed the sum of 48 sh. for warning the Inhabitants in the Captaincy of Capt. Jonathan Roberts in the year 1785 and 1786.

Jesse Saunders appeared on behalf of Meriam Saunders for her having a Bastard. She to give Security in the sum of 150 pds. for keeping said child from becoming chargeable to this Parish. William Odom and Jesse Saunders Securities.

Thomas Hurdle guardian of Christian Rountree made return of his Accounts.

Deed of land Isaac Pipkin to John Parker Acknowledged.

Lewis Sparkman to be exempt from accounting with the County Treasurer for 3 pds. 3 sh. 8 pc. for Insolvants.

The sum of 3 pds. 4 sh. allowed to Edward Arnold Tax-Insolvant.

Hezekiah Jones appointed Overseer of the road instead of Edward Arnold resigned.

Tuesday morning. Present: William Baker, Jethro Ballard, David Rice, John Baker, Justices.

Account of the Sales of part of the Estate of John Millder decd. exhibited.

Thomas Hobbs moved for administration on the Estate of Amos Hobbs decd.-granted. He to give Security in the sum of 300 pds. Henry Hobbs and Jacob Hobbs Securities.

Inventory of the Goods & etc. of the Estate of Amos Hobbs decd. exhibited by Thomas Hobbs Admr.

Thomas Hunter and Joseph Riddick Esqrs. and Thomas Trotman to make a division of the Estate of Amos Hobbs decd.

Thomas Hobbs to sell the perishable part of the Estate of Amos Hobbs decd.

James Gregory to be exempt from the payment of his Tax on Chain Wheels. Also Seth Eason, Thomas Hunter, William Baker, John Baker and Lawrence Baker to be exempt from the payment of those Public Taxes returned on their Chain Wheels, being not lawful.

William Matthias, Moses Davis, David Harrell and John B. Walton to be fined 5 pds. each unless they appear at the next court to be held for this County and show cause & etc.

Kedar Hill, Tax Gatherer to be exempt from accounting for the tax on Ephrain Griffin he being insolvant. (written along edge of page- Sam Harrell)

Disputed Entry made by Samuel Harrell and cavented by David Rice in behalf of the orphans of James Jones decd. The Sheriff haveing summoned a Jury and met on the premises, say the orphans of James Jones decd. be entitled to the said land in Dispute between the parties. It was also agreed that Samuel Harrell pay all costs. 7 April 1787.

Jacob Powell, Benjamin Gordon, John Briggs, Aaron Lassiter, Richard Briggs, Josiah (X) Lassiter, William Harris, Humphry Hudgins, Moses Davis, Saml. Smith, Henry Forrest and William Ellis.

A Writ of Dower having been issued to set apart and allot to Ann Vann Relict and Widow of Charles Vann decd. the Sheriff returned the proceedings which are as follows: This may certifie that we the Subscribers Free Holders after being duly summoned and qualified for that purpose have laid off alloted and set apart to Ann Vann Widow and Relict of Charles Vann decd. one third of the lands the said Charles Vann decd. seized and possessed. Viz. Beginning at a Red Oak in the Pattent line from thence along a line of marked trees to a Walnut Tree in the plantation then along a line of marked trees through the Swamp to Isaac Langstons line thence down Langstons line to Langstons Corner from thence up the said Patent line to the first Station - - - includes the house the said Charles Vann decd. usually dwelt agreeable to a petition exhibited to the Inferior Court of Pleas and Quarter Sessions 28 April 1787. Joseph Speight, Edward Warren, Henry Speight, Benjamin Barnes, Cyprian Cross, John Odom, Isaac Langston, Demsey Langston, William Gatling, Henry Goodman, William Ellis, Thomas Barnes.

A Writ of Dower having issued to set apart and allot to Mary Riddick Widow and Relict of Mills Riddick decd. The Sheff. having returned the proceedings as follows: This may Certify that we the Subscribers free holders - - have laid off and alloted and set apart to Mary Riddick Widow and Relict of Mills Riddict decd. one third part of the lands the said Mills Riddick decd. seized and possessed of. Viz. Beginning at the main Desert and running through the Orchard to a post from thence to a persimmon tree thence along a line of marked trees to the Horse Pool Swamp to a pine from thence across the Swamp thence along a line of marked trees to Abram Harrells line to a pine a corner from thence the old line to the first Station - - includes all the houses buildings & etc. 20 April 1787. James Costen, Abraham Eason, Isaac Pierce, Abram Harrell, John Davis, Thomas Walton, William Hunter, Samuel Green, Jacob Pearce, Isaac Harrell, Christopher Pierce, Joshua Small.

Bill of sale Lewis Jones and Sarah Jones for a Negro Woman named Lucia to Jacob Powell proved by the oath of Bery (?) Gordon.

William Baker, Christopher Riddick, William Goodman and Seth Riddick, Esqrs. or any three of them to make a division of the Estate of Stephen Rogers decd.

Isaac Pipkin appointed guardian to Elizabeth, Stephen and Sarah Rogers orphans of Stephen Rogers decd. He to give Security in the sum of 1000 pds. John Gating and Lawrence Baker Securities.

John Gatling appointed guardian to Priscilla, William and John Rogers orphans of Stephen Rogers decd. He to give Security in the sum of 1000 pds. Isaac Pipkin and Lawrence Baker Securities.

Charity Morris Admrx. to Jacob Morris decd. returned the account of the sales of part of the Estate of the decd.

The Extrs. of Solomon Hiatt decd. to sell as much of the Estate of the decd. as will be sufficient to maintain a Bastard Child begot on the Body of Martha Rogers by the said Hiatt for three years from the date hereof.

James Freeman, Jonathan Roberts, Thomas Hunter and Demsey Bond or any three of them to make a division of the Estate of Jacob Morris.

Inventory of the Goods & etc. of the Estate of James Piland decd. exhibited by James Piland Extr.

Deed of land William Booth to Joel Foster Acknowledged.

David Rice Esqr. Unanimously elected Sheriff for the present year.

Bill of sale Henry Mironey to Kedar Raby Ack.

Jesse Harrell to be exempt from the payment of a Tax on one hundred acres land which was returned more than he has.

John Warren returned an account of Sales of part of the Estate of Stephen Rogers decd.

Jesse Spivey guardian to Frederick Blanshard, William Blanshard, Sarah Blanshard and Mary Blanshard returned his Account Current.

Wednesday morning. Present: Christopher Riddick, John Baker and William Goodman, Justices.

Deed of sale Joseph Browne to Abraham Riddick proved by the oath of James Hayes.

Samuel Harrell, Jethro Meltear, Moses Hare and Lewis Sparkman who were appointed constables came into Court and entered into Bond for the faithful discharge of their duty.

Lawrence Baker with William Baker and Christo. Riddick, Esqrs. to Audit State and Settle the account of Wm. Harvey Admr. of Docton Riddick decd.

Thomas Hunter Esqr. to take a list of Taxables and Taxable property in the District of Capt. Jonathan Roberts. James Gregory Esqr. in Capt. Isaac Hunters Captaincy. Jethro Ballard in Capt. Jethro Sumners Captaincy. William Goodman in Captaincy of William Goodman, John Baker Esqr. in Capt. Jesse Bentons Captaincy. Christopher Riddick Esqr. in Capt. William Harrisses District.

The Sheriff to summons Henry Goodman, Miles Benton, William Gatling, Samuel Smith, Micajah Riddick, James Phelps, Enos Rogers, Robert Parker of Demsey, Charles Eure, Israel Beeman, Peter Harrell, John Powell, Kedar Ballard, Samuel Green, William Freeman, John Bethey, Henry Lee, Benjamin Barnes, Isaac Miller, James Pruden, Isaac Parker, Philip Rogers, Elisha Cross, Stephen Eure, Samuel Eure, Jesse Harrell, Jacob Gordon, Abraham Harrell, James Norfleet and James Freeman as Jurymen.

Moses Kitrell Tax Gatherer to be exempt from accounting with the County Treasurer for the Tax on Saml. Parker and Edward Polson. Parker having moved away. Polson Insolvant.

Isaac Pipkin Esqr. late Sheriff of this County to be allowed the sum of 20 pds. for extra services.

Samuel Harrell to be allowed the sum of 3 pds. 4 sh. for his services attending this Court as Constable and summoning Inhabitants of Capt. Isaac Hunters Captaincy.

Third Monday in August 1787

Present: Christopher Riddick, Seth Riddick, Wm. Goodman, William Baker, John Baker, Justices.

Deed of land John Norfleet to Elisha Darden proved by the oath of Charles Hedgpeth.

Deed of land Robt. H. Fisher to John Anderson proved by the oaths of Elisha Darden and Jethro Darden.

Isaac Pipkin and William Goodman Esqrs., Henry Goodman and Cyprian Cross to make a division of the Estate of William Copeland decd.

William Baker Esqr. returned the list of Taxables in the Captaincy of Capt. Jesse Benton.

Deed of land Andrew Hamilton to William Davidson proved by the oath of William Vann.

Deed of land Demsey Trotman to Charles Rountree ack.

William Copeland, Junr. orphan of William Copeland decd. came into Court and made choice of Bryan Hare as his guardian. Bryan Hare to give Security in the sum of 800 pds. John Shepherd and Henry Goodman Securities.

Deed of land James Hayes to Seth Riddick Ack.

Deed of land Israel Beeman to James Hayes Ack.

Deed of land James Sumner to Jacob Powell proved by the oath of Kedar Ballard.

Last Will and Testament of Guy Hill decd. exhibited by Richard Bond one of the Extrs. therein appointed and proved by the oath of Kedar Hill one of the witnesses.

Inventory of the Goods & etc. of the Estate of Guy Hill decd. was exhibited by Richard Bond Extr.

Mary Carter an Illegitimate Child Daughter of Ann Carter about 4 years of age bound as an apprentice to Richard Rawlings to learn Spining and Weaving.

Deed of land Joseph John Sumner to Jethro Sumner Ack.

Bill of Sale for a Negro Joseph John Sumner to Jethro Sumner Ack.

Bill of Sale John Rice to Shadrack Felton proved by the oath of Josiah Granbery.

Last Will and Testament of James Sumner decd. exhibited by Jethro Ballard, David Rice and Timothy Hunter Extrs. therein appointed and proved by the oaths of Kedar Ballard, James Norfleet and William Matthias three of the witnesses.

James Norfleet, Jethro Sumner and Kedar Ballard to make a division of the Estate of James Sumner decd.

Deed of land Jonathan Roberts to Jethro Miltear proved by the oaths of William Gordon and David Harrell.

On Motion of Mr. William Cumming Esqr. Atto. at Law it is ordered that Mr. Jethro Ballard, David Rice and Timothy Hunter Extrs. of James Sumner decd. be appointed Administrators of all and singular the Goods & etc. of the Estate of Luke Sumner which has been unadministred by James Sumner and Henry Riddick former Administrators of Luke Sumner decd. They to give Security in the sum of 20,000 pds. Jethro Sumner and Josiah Granverry Esqrs. Securities.

Tuesday morning. Present: Christopher Riddick, Seth Riddick, John Baker, James Gregory, Justices.

James Curle appointed Admr. of all the Goods & etc. of the Estate of Richard Curle decd. He to give Security in the sum of 150 pds. Jesse Vann and Lewis Sparkman Securities.

Inventory of the Goods & etc. of the Estate of Richard Curle decd. was exhibited by James Curle Admr.

James Curle Admr. of Richard Curle decd. to sell the perishable part of the Estate of the decd.

Richard Bond Extr. of Guy Hill decd. to sell the perishable part of the Estate of the decd. as will pay debts.

Jesse Vann Admr. of Charles Vann decd. returned his Acc. Current.

The Sheriff to summons the following persons as Jurymen: Willis Browne, George Williams, William Brooks, Jesse Harrell, William Hinton, Simon Stallings, Richard Mitchell (?), James Outlaw, Seth Rountree, Charles Rountree, Ezekiel Trotman, John Hoffler, Henry Harrell, Moses Kittrell, Timothy Lassiter, Isaac Hunter, James Knight, William Daughtie, Samuel Baker, William Harriss, Peter Parker, Joseph Figg, James Costin, Isaac Harrell, Edwin Sumner, Jesse Saunders and Joshua Small.

The Sheriff to summons the following persons as Jurymen at the next session of the Court of Law and Equity to be held at Edenton; on the 3rd. day of November next. John Gatling, Philip Lewis, Kedar Hinton and Moses Hare.

William Goodman Esqr. returned his list of Taxables in the Captaincy of Capt. Wm. Goodman.

John Baker Esqr. returned his list of Taxables in the Captaincy of Capt. Charles Eure.

A Noncupative Will of Priscilla Russell decd. was exhibited by James Braddy and proved by the oath of Elizabeth Delday and Rachel Laurence.

Ordered that John Arnold move the Road as to straighten said road.

Bill of sale for a Negro Girl Job Riddick to John Gardiner Ack.

Deed of land Richard Bond to William Hinton proved by the oath of Reuben Riddick.

William Matthias appointed overseer of the road instead of James Sumner Esqr. decd.

Deed of Contract between Elisha Norfleet and Elizabeth Benton proved by the oath of Jesse Benton.

Account of Sales of part of the Estate of Richard Freeman decd. was exhibited by Kedar Hinton Admr.

List of Taxables taken by Thomas Hunter Esqr. in the Captaincy of Capt. Jonathan Roberts was returned.

Account of sale of the Estate of the orphans of Stephen Rogers decd. was exhibited by Isaac Pipkin Esqr.

Mr. Reuben Riddick Entrytaker for this County resigned his appointment to that office.

Bill of sale for a Negro Boy Harry, Charles Rooks and Thomas Rooks proved by the oath of Blake Baker.

Wednesday morning. Present: William Baker, Seth Riddick, John Baker.

Christopher Riddick made return of List of Taxables in the Captaincy of Capt. William Harris.

Christopher Riddick, Moses Kittrell and William Vann who were appointed to make a division of the Estate of Elisha Odom decd. made report.

James Gregory Esqr. to take a list of Taxables and Taxable property in the Captaincy of Capt. Isaac Hunter he having not taken it before.

David Rice Sheriff of this County rendered the Account of Sale of the orphans part of the Estate of Amos Hobbs decd.

An Additional Inventory of the Estate of Amos Hobbs decd. was exhibited by Thomas Hobbs Admr.

Joseph Riddick, Thomas Hunter Esqrs. and Mr. Thomas Trotman who were appointed to make a division of the Estate of Amos Hobbs decd. made report.

John Brickell Esqr. State Attorney of this County to be allowed the sum of 16 pds. for his services in the year 1786.

The County Trustee to pay Lawrence Baker the sum of 20 pds. for extra services for the year passed.

William Baker, Christopher Riddick and Lawrence Baker to make a division of the Estate of Docton Riddick decd.

Ordered that a Jury of Men and two Surveyers chosen by Priscilla Walton Plaintiff and Thomas Walton Defendant in a Suit now pending for Title of a certain lands in this Court the following persons were chosen by the said parties: Joseph Hurdle, Charles Rountree, Saml. Harrell Freeholders and Patrick Higerty Surveyor chosed by Danl. Stallings in behalf of Plaintiff and Jacob Briggs, Moses Hill and Saml. Harrell Freeholders and John Moran Surveyor chosen and that they go on the primisses and proceed agreeable to Law.

Third Monday in November 1787

Present: Christopher Riddick, Issac Pipkin and Seth Riddick.

Deed of land Benjamin Harrell and James Parker to John Whitehead proved by the oath of William Barnes.

James Gregory Esqr. returned his list of Taxables in the District of Capt. Isaac Hunter.

Jesse Odom orphan of Elisha Odom about nine years old is bound as an apprentice to Joseph Delday to learn the business of a Cooper.

Jacob Odom orphan of Elisha Odom about seven years old is bound as an apprentice to Joseph Dilday to learn the business of a Shoemaker.

Account of Sales of the Estate of Guy Hill decd. was exhibited by David Rice Esqr.

Jethro Benton, Jur. appointed Overseer of the road instead of Isaac Benton resigned.

Bond Job Riddick and Noah Harrell to Samuel Harrell proved by the oath of David Rice Esqr.

Isaac Hunter appointed Overseer of the road instead of Abram Harrell resigned.

The list of Taxables of Richard Mitchell to be added to the list of Taxables taken by Thomas Hunter Esqr. for the present year.

Deed of Sale Benj. Harrell, Aaron Harrell and Elizabeth Harrell to Peter Piland proved by the oath of William Polson.

Bill of Sale for a Negro Lad named Joseph John, Randolph Wilkinson to Seth Eason proved by the oath of Jacob Gordon.

Deed of Gift of lands Goods and Chattels Moses Hare to Elisha Dare proved by the oath of Kedar Ballard.

William Baker, Christopher Riddick, Seth Riddick and William Goodman or any three of them to make a division of the Estate of Stephen Rogers decd. among his widow and children.

Inventory of the Goods & etc. of the Estate of James Sumner decd. exhibited by Jethro Ballard, David Rice and Timothy Hunter Extrs.

Mary Rountree, John Rountree and James Norfleet moved for Administration on the Estate of Charles Rountree decd. -They to give Bond in the sum of 4,000 pds. Seth Eason, Jethro Ballard and Thomas Hurdle Securities.

Inventory of the Goods & etc. of the Estate of Charles Rountree exhibited by Mary Rountree, James Norfleet and John Rountree, Admrs.

Deed of land Charles Rountree to Jacob Eason proved by the oath of Levy Eason.

Jethro Ballard Esqr. returned the list of Taxables in the Captaincy of Jethro Sumner Esqr.

Seth Rountree appointed guardian to Rachel Rountree, Priscilla Rountree, Penina Rountree and Livina Rountree orphans of Thomas Rountree decd. He to give Security in the sum of 200 pds. Thomas Trotman and Jacob Bagley Securities.

Humphry Hudgins appointed Overseer of the road instead of William Harris resigned.

Pasco (?) Turner (?) moved for Administration on the Estate of Filesca Jones. He to give bond in the sum of 3000 pds. William Harris and Jethro Sumner Securities.

Tuesday Morning. Present: Thomas Hunter, James Gregory, Jethro Ballard, Isaac Pipkin, Seth Riddick, Justices.

Deed of land Richard Baker to John Rochell proved by the oath of Elisha Darden.

Deed of sale James Parker to James Thomas proved by the oath of John Odom.

Account of Sales of the Estate of Solo. Hiatt decd. exhibited by Henry Goodman Esqr.

Deed of land Moses Hare to Jethro Sumner proved by the oath of Joseph John Sumner.

Bill of Sale Moses Hare to Jethro Sumner for a Negro Girl named Venus proved by the oath of Joseph John Sumner.

Deed of land Jethro Meltear to Jonathan Roberts proved by the oath of William Gordon.

Deed of land Jesse Barnes to David Cross proved by the oath of Cyprian Cross.

Deed of land William Ellis to Jacob Gordon proved by the oath of James Baker.

Richard Mitchell moved that he have leave to keep a Public House and that he enter into Bond with Security for his faithful performance of the duty of a Public House Keeper. Simon Stallings Security.

Jacob Bagley appointed Overseer of the road instead of Charles Rountree decd. and that the hands of the said Jacob Bagley and the Estate of Charles Rountree work on the same.

Deed of land William Ellis to Jacob Gordon proved by the oath of James Baker.

Cyprian Cross exhibited his Account Current with Thomas Smith orphan of James Smith decd.

Kedar Ballard, Seth Eason, Thomas Hunter and Thomas Trotman or any three of them to make division of the Estate of Charles Rountree decd.

William Harvey Admr. of Docton Riddick decd. to be summoned to appear at this Court to show cause why he has not produced his Accounts with the said Estate.

Wednesday morning. Present: Thomas Hunter, James Gregory and Jethro Ballard, Justices.

Deed of land Joseph Rooks to Willis Hiatt (?) proved by the oath of Lawrence Baker.

Samuel Smith appointed Coroner by the Court of this County.

Sheriff to summon the following persons to serve as Petit and Grand Jurors. Thomas Hurdle, Abraham Eason, Demsey Trotman, William Hunter, Timothy Lassiter, Aaron Hobbs, James Walton, Thomas Parker, John Darden, Isaac Harrell, Moses Benton, Richard Briggs, John Riddick, Richard Mitchell, William Mathias, Kedar Ballard, William Walters, Edward Daughtie, James Phelps, William Cleaves, Thomas Smith, Michal Lawrence, James Brady, Senr., Demsey Williams, Cyprian Cross, John Odom, Stephen Eure, Peter Harrell, Demsey Barnes and Isaac Parker.

Henry Harrell and his hands to work on the road where Demsey Trotman is Overseer.

Isaac Hunter to collect the Public and County Tax in the Captaincy where he is Capt. Jonathan Roberts in the Captaincy where he is Capt. John Riddick in the Captaincy of Capt. Jethro Sumner. Micajah Riddick in the Captaincy of Capt. Jesse Benton. Isaac Miller in the Captaincy of Capt. William Harris. Lewis Sparkman in the Captaincy of Capt. Charles Eure. John Pipkin in the Captaincy of Capt. William Goodman.

Michal Lawrence appointed Overseer of the road instead of Robert Parker.

INDEX

Allen 83
Alphin 3,23,52,88,96
Alston 3
Anderson 100
Arline 21,29,30,39,44,47,48,
  49,50,51,56,62,64,69,72,
  75,82,84,86,88,92,94
Arnell/Arnel/Arnall 2,4,5,10,
  18,19,22,29,30
Arnold 12,13,16,17,22,24,32,
  33,35,37,38,39,41,44,45,
  47,48,53,55,56,61,62,68,
  70,71,73,76,78,80,82,83,
  84,87,89,92,93,97,101
Asbury 86
Baccus 5
Bagley 10,15,17,18,20,22,27,
  29,32,33,42,43,44,45,46,
  51,53,54,59,61,70,71,72,
  74,75,78,82,88,91,95,104
Baker 1,2,3,4,5,7,8,9,10,12,
  13,14,15,20,24,25,26,27,
  29,30,31,32,33,37,38,39,
  40,41,42,43,44,45,46,47,
  48,50,53,54,55,56,57,58,
  60,61,64,66,67,69,70,72,
  75,76,78,79,81,82,83,84,
  85,86,87,89,90,91,92,93,
  94,95,96,97,98,99,100,
  101,102,103,104,105
Ball 16,
Ballard 1,4,10,11,12,15,16,
  18,22,24,25,34,35,49,50,
  51,53,56,58,59,60,62,63,
  64,69,70,71,77,78,81,82,
  83,84,85,86,91,94,95,97,
  99,100,101,103,104,105
Barker 95
Barnes 2,3,7,8,9,10,11,12,13,
  22,24,27,30,31,33,35,36,
  37,38,39,40,41,42,46,47,
  49,55,57,59,61,62,63,64,
  69,73,76,78,79,80,81,82,
  86,98,99,103,104,105
Barnett 49
Barr 58
Barrett 56,
Bassard 56
Beacon 48
Beeman 3,35,42,49,50,57,58,
  68,73,74,87,99,100
Bell 54
Bennet 24
Benson 55
Benton 1,3,5,6,7,8,9,10,11,12,
  13,16,19,20,22,23,30,32,
  33,35,37,39,40,41,44,57,61,
  62,63,66,68,69,70,71,73,75,
  76,77,79,80,82,83,85,86,87,
  89,95,96,99,100,102,103,105
Berryman/Berriman/Berreman/Bereman
  24,33,40,43,65,67,77,79,80,
  87,90
Best 5
Bethey/Bathey 8,10,11,12,17,20,
  33,44,50,51,58,70,81,87,92,
  99
Blair 96
Blanshard 3,6,7,8,15,17,18,19,
  27,31,38,40,45,50,52,59,
  61,62,65,67,69,70,78,79,
  80,84,85,86,88,89,90,93,
  99
Blyth/Blythe 14,19,
Bond 2,3,5,6,9,10,11,15,16,18,
  32,36,42,44,50,51,53,57,63,
  64,70,72,81,82,85,86,89,95,
  100,101,102
Booth 19,24,26,27,31,37,46,47,48,
  50,65,73,80,82,85,93,95,99
Bowin 27
Boyce 3,9,16,18,19,20,24,30,31,
  43,44,52,53,59,60,64,69,70,
  72,75,90,91
Braddy/Brady 2,4,12,30,31,32,35,
  39,42,43,46,47,49,61,68,69,
  73,80,84,101,105
Banbery 31
Brayshar 25,68
Brickell 3,12,20,21,24,26,27,28,
  36,37,38,40,41,49,50,51,52,
  57,58,62,64,66,68,70,77,80,
  83,89,102
Briggs 7,8,12,15,18,19,27,28,35,
  39,42,46,48,53,55,59,60,66,
  73,75,78,79,92,95,98,103,
  105
Brinkley 12,21,22,31,42,43,49,58,
  68,70,71,80,83,88
Briscow/Brisco 24,35,57,61
Bristow 26,38,52,55,69,85,95
Brooks 25,26,27,29,46,55,96,101
Brown/Browne 3,23,25,29,31,33,34,
  42,45,46,51,56,61,67,72,75,
  82,92,94,95,96,99,101
Burgess/Burgas/Burges 13,19,20,35
Buses 37
Byrd/Bird 4,8
Cally 11
Campbell 96
Carter 2,10,14,16,18,23,24,29,33,
  34,36,38,42,45,50,51,52,61,

75,76,77,89,100

Case 13
Casey 37
Caspey 13
Caswell 1
Clark 40
Cleaves 10,11,32,34,44,48,57,
    60,68,71,82,105
Coke 86
Colley/Colly 87
Collins 31,47,49,56
Copeland 5,15,43,56,68,69,71,
    83,90,95,100
Costants 50
Costen/Costin 2,4,10,11,12,
    13,15,18,19,20,23,25,35,
    36,37,43,50,53,72,73,78,
    79,92,93,98,101
Cotten 15
Courtney 22,59,67,81
Cowper 10,19,20,28,30,50
Crafford 14,28,34,37,47,50,
    53,62,68,77,78
Croom 90
Cross 3,8,13,19,37,38,42,43,
    48,49,54,55,56,57,58,59,
    61,62,63,66,69,70,73,75,
    78,80,81,82,85,86,91,93,
    95,98,99,100,104,105
Crusey 73
Cullins 31
Cumming 101
Curle 11,31,37,63,69,76,101
Daniel 20,28
Dardin/Darden 6,7,8,27,30,35,
    37,55,66,89,100,104,105
Dare 103
Davidson 68,82,84,93,100
Davis 7,8,11,17,18,28,29,35,
    36,37,40,52,53,57,65,66,
    67,75,77,81,82,90,93,94,
    97,98
Dickinson 15
Dilday/Delday 47,66,77,80,81,
    84,86,101,103
Doughty/Doughtie/Daughtie/
Daughtee 2,3,4,5,7,8,16,22,24,
    30,33,35,39,41,43,48,49,
    51,61,64,66,70,75,79,82,
    86,89,92,96,101,105
Draper 8
Duke 8,41,42,48,75,78
Dunford 67
Dunn/Dun 2,3,4,5,12,13,14,19,
    24,30,33,43,46,48,50,57,
    64,69,75,77,80,83

Eason 1,2,3,4,8,10,11,12,13,16,
    18,19,20,21,23,24,26,27,28,
    19,20,21,23,24,26,27,28,39,
    40,41,42,43,44,46,49,50,54,
    55,56,57,58,60,61,63,64,68,
    70,71,72,73,75,76,78,79,82,
    85,88,95,97,98,103,104,105
Edwards 67
Ellin 58
Ellis/Elliss 8,9,12,14,15,18,34,
    37,38,41,42,68,73,81,83,86,
    93,98,104
Eure/Euri 2,5,7,8,10,16,17,18,20,
    23,25,27,29,30,31,32,33,34,
    35,37,38,39,44,45,46,47,49,
    51,52,53,54,56,60,61,62,63,
    64,65,70,71,72,75,77,80,82,
    84,86,89,91,92,93,99,101,
    105
Felton 11,56,68,76,77,93,100
Figg 10,19,20,24,29,33,35,37,57,
    70,82,101
Fisher 100
Forrest 83,92,93,98
Foster 99
Frank 31
Frankling 41
Freeman/Freman 2,4,5,10,11,14,17,
    20,22,24,28,31,37,39,40,43,
    44,50,52,53,54,55,57,66,73,
    74,77,81,85,86,89,93,94,99,
    102
Frost 96
Fryer/Fryor 14,47,49,53,59,61,
    63,69
Fullington 43,71,73
Gardiner 101
Garott/Garrott/Garrett 4,7,8,12,
    13,17,18,19,22,24,25,26,27,
    28,37,41,42,54,57,64,67,72,
    74,94
Gatling 10,12,13,19,20,23,28,29,
    39,44,47,48,50,52,55,61,66,
    68,69,71,73,75,79,86,90,95,
    98,99,101
Giles 20
Glover 85
Goodman 10,12,13,14,16,17,18,19,
    20,24,27,29,30,31,32,33,35,
    37,38,39,41,42,44,45,47,48,
    49,50,51,52,55,57,60,61,62,
    64,66,70,71,72,73,74,79,82,
    85,86,87,88,89,90,92,94,95,
    98,99,100,101,103,104,105
Gordon 2,7,12,19,22,27,32,33,35,
    39,41,43,44,46,51,52,55,57,
    59,61,63,64,66,67,69,71,72,
    75,78,79,81,82,84,85,86,88,

91,92,95,98,101,103,104
Granbery/Granverry 1,4,12,19,20,
    21,30,31,61,66,67,70,74,79,
    88,94,95,100,101
Green 4,10,11,16,17,18,23,25,31,
    34,40,43,44,46,55,56,77,79,
    81,98,99
Gregory 12,15,19,23,27,31,34,35,
    37,40,43,44,45,49,52,56,57,
    60,61,62,63,65,66,67,69,72,
    74,75,76,78,79,81,85,86,88,
    89,91,94,95,97,99,101,102,
    103,104,105
Griffin 20,27,30,39,42,49,53,60,
    65,67,71,74,86,90,97
Gwinn 21,43,44,52,74,77,81
Hambleton 11,23,37,74,79
Hamilton 11,72,100
Hare 7,8,10,12,13,14,15,19,20,
    27,32,39,43,44,52,53,61,70,
    82,87,95,99,100,101,103,104
Hargrove/Hargroves 9,53,54,55,
    57,67,84
Harrell 1,3,5,6,7,8,9,10,11,12,
    13,14,16,18,19,23,25,27,28,
    29,30,31,33,34,35,38,39,40,
    42,44,46,47,48,50,52,54,55,
    59,60,61,62,63,64,66,68,69,
    71,73,74,75,76,79,80,82,84,
    86,87,88,89,91,92,93,94,95,
    96,97,98,99,100,101,103,105
Harris/Harriss 2,4,5,6,7,9,10,11,
    12,16,18,20,22,23,24,25,30,
    34,35,37,39,41,44,48,49,50,
    53,54,59,60,61,66,73,75,79,
    82,83,85,86,89,92,94,98,99,
    101,102,104,105
Harrison 68
Harvey 58,92,99,105
Haslett 87
Hays/Hayes/Hase 2,35,42,43,48,
    50,58,62,65,77,82,83,89,99,
    100
Hedgpeth 100
Hegity/Hegerty/Higerty 88,93,103
Hiate/Hiatt 42,52,71,87,88,89,
    98,104,105
Hill 2,5,7,8,9,10,11,14,15,17,
    20,21,23,27,33,34,37,40,44,
    46,47,48,49,50,51,53,58,59,
    61,65,66,67,70,71,74,75,77,
    82,83,84,86,89,90,92,93,94,
    97,100,101,103
Hinton 6,9,14,15,17,27,28,29,31,
    35,37,38,42,49,50,53,56,62,
    65,75,86,87,92,93,94,101,
    102

Hobbs 5,7,10,11,33,42,44,55,
    64,70,73,77,79,82,83,84,
    89,91,97,102,105
Hodges/Hodge 4,65,77,81,93
Hoffler 22,40,45,46,66,84,89,
    101
Holland 46,68
Horton 58
Hoss 83
Howell 48,49
Hudgins 66,70,75,82,84,98,104
Hughes 38
Hunter 1,2,3,4,5,6,7,9,11,12,
    13,14,15,16,17,18,19,21,
    23,24,26,27,28,29,30,31,
    32,33,34,35,36,37,38,39,
    40,41,43,44,46,47,48,49,
    50,51,52,53,54,55,57,60,
    61,62,63,64,65,66,67,68,
    69,73,74,75,76,78,79,80,
    81,82,83,84,85,86,87,88,
    89,90,91,92,93,94,95,97,
    98,99,100,101,102,103,
    104,105
Hurdle 2,4,6,10,12,13,14,19,
    20,24,33,40,44,46,53,64,
    66,75,76,78,82,87,92,97,
    103,105
Iredell 13,19
James 80
Johnston 52,53,54
Jones 3,12,14,20,21,31,33,35,
    41,42,43,44,46,55,56,58,
    59,67,68,70,71,78,79,83,
    85,86,94,95,97,98,104
Jordon 37,40,41,57,58
Kein 96
Kelly 44,85
Ketherell/Kitherell 6,7,19,20
King 3,7,8,10,12,13,14,16,18,
    20,23,24,29,33,43,45,46,
    59,61,62,63,64,66,68,72,
    75,80,92,94
Kitrell/Kittrell/Kittrale 27,
    35,36,38,41,44,51,56,57,
    59,61,62,64,66,69,70,71,
    74,82,84,86,89,92,94,96,
    99,101,102
Knight 2,4,5,6,7,30,31,32,44,
    49,61,66,76,80,82,87,89,
    95,101
Knox 80
Land 12,61
Landing 16,23,30,31,35,37,46,
    54,59,63,69,73,76
Lang 10,33,50

Langston 3,11,49,51,61,64,68,
    70,98
Lassiter 2,3,4,6,11,15,18,19,
    21,24,27,29,30,32,35,36,
    37,39,40,42,45,46,48,50,
    52,53,55,57,60,64,65,66,
    67,71,73,75,76,78,79,80,
    84,85,86,87,88,89,92,95,
    98,101,105
Lawrence/Laurance 52,68,69,71,
    73,92,96,101,105
Lee 14,17,33,53,61,67,73,79,
    89,99
Lenier 77
Lewis 2,3,4,5,7,9,12,19,20,33,
    35,36,42,44,46,55,61,68,
    70,82,83,85,91,95,101
Lilley 74
McCullok 95
McKee 15
Magner 52
Maney 79
Mansfield 37,40
March 71,77
Marshall 96
Martin 20,24, 26,27,44
Matthews 4,14,15,16,18,20,23,
    29,32,33,39,45,48,53,60,
    64,70,79,80,81,89,91,92,
    95
Matthias 31,58,70,75,97,100,
    102,105
Mayner 52
Meltear/Miltear 4,6,14,16,19,
    26,30,35,39,41,47,48,57,
    61,64,75,77,97,99,101,
    104
Menya 36
Miles 67
Mill 75,85
Miller/Millder 4,11,12,13,15,
    17,18,24,28,29,32,33,39,
    48,52,57,62,64,65,67,69,
    70,76,79,82,83,84,91,92,
    93,94,96,97,99,105
Minard 55
Mingard 44
Minshew 6,53,84,85
Minyard 44
Mironey 87,91,99
Mitchell 101,103,104,105
Moore/Moor 5,93
Moran 103
Morgan 7,8,9,12,19,32,42,46,
    55,66,73,74,80,93
Morris 74,76,79,81,98,99
Mortan 13
Murphry/Murfree 47,52

Nichols 4,8,14,55,65
Nixon/Nickson 20,91
Norfleet 2,3,4,5,6,10,11,14,18,
    19,20,22,24,25,27,28,35,44,
    50,52,59,61,66,67,68,70,78,
    81,82,99,100,101,102,103
Norrington 70
Norris 18,37,49,69
Odom/Ohdon 3,6,7,8,9,12,14,16,17,
    18,20,21,22,25,27,29,32,33,
    36,39,41,42,44,46,50,53,54,
    55,56,57,67,69,70,72,73,75,
    78,81,84,86,91,92,94,95,97,
    98,102,103,104,105
Only 20,27
Outlaw 2,4,5,10,11,14,15,18,20,
    22,29,32,33,35,42,43,48,54,
    61,64,70,74,76,77,79,82,87,
    89,101
Parke 69
Parker 3,7,8,10,13,14,16,17,18,
    19,21,22,25,26,27,28,29,30,
    31,32,33,35,36,37,41,44,46,
    49,50,51,53,54,55,57,58,61,
    63,64,65,66,67,68,69,72,73,
    75,76,77,80,81,82,83,86,87,
    89,90,92,93,95,96,97,99,101,
    103,104,105
Pearce 39,88,98
Perry 1,2,4,5,15,18,23,24,26,27,
    46,50,72,89,91
Perryman 11
Phelps 24,64,67,70,72,89,99,105
Philips 58,87
Pierce 11,29,32,48,53,68,72,73,
    91,98
Piland 28,30,31,40,47,53,58,63,
    64,68,77,80,93,96,99,103
Pipkin 1,2,3,8,9,10,12,13,14,16,
    17,18,19,20,21,23,24,27,29,
    30,33,34,36,38,39,40,41,43,
    44,45,46,47,48,49,50,51,52,
    53,55,56,58,59,60,62,63,64,
    65,66,69,70,72,73,74,78,79,
    80,81,82,84,85,86,90,92,97,
    98,99,100,102,103,104,105
Plats 86
Polson 7,8,20,24,30,35,36,39,48,
    55,62,63,93,99,103
Porter 90
Powell 2,4,7,8,10,11,15,16,18,20,
    21,22,24,30,32,34,35,36,37,
    40,42,46,50,53,55,57,58,59,
    60,61,66,73,78,79,82,89,96,
    98,99,100
Price 73
Pruden 6,7,10,11,33,39,40,57,65,
    75,76,80,87,89,99

Pugh 84
Raby 20,31,72,91,99
Rawlings 100
Rawls 79
Reid 78,83
Rice 2,8,10,12,15,18,21,23,24,
    25,28,29,30,31,32,33,34,
    35,36,38,39,40,41,43,44,
    45,46,47,48,49,50,51,52,
    53,54,56,57,58,60,61,62,
    63,64,65,66,67,70,72,73,
    74,75,76,77,78,79,80,81,
    82,84,86,87,88,90,91,92,
    94,95,97,99,100,101,102,
    103
Richardson 5
Riddick/Ridditk 1,2,3,4,5,6,7,
    8,9,10,11,12,13,14,15,16,
    17,18,19,20,21,22,23,24,
    25,26,27,28,29,30,31,32,
    33,34,35,36,38,39,40,41,
    42,43,44,45,46,47,48,49,
    50,51,52,53,54,55,56,57,
    58,59,60,61,62,63,64,65,
    66,67,69,70,72,73,74,75,
    76,77,78,79,81,82,83,84,
    85,86,87,88,89,90,91,92,
    93,94,95,97,98,99,100,
    101,102,103,104,105
Ritter 63
Roberts/Robberts 10,11,18,26,
    29,30,32,33,36,39,41,44,
    45,47,48,49,51,53,54,55,
    57,58,60,61,64,67,70,73,
    81,82,84,85,86,89,92,97,
    99,101,102,104,105
Robertson 63
Robins/Robbins 8,26,27,40,43,
    46,48,54,65,67,84,94
Rochell 104
Rogers 10,12,16,18,19,27,31,
    32,39,46,52,56,58,64,66,
    67,70,71,72,73,74,81,82,
    90,91,98,99,102,103
Ronals 28
Rooks 26,36,66,82,102,105
Ross 69,70
Rountree 1,2,6,7,8,10,12,14,
    17,20,22,23,24,25,28,29,
    30,32,35,39,44,48,53,57,
    66,67,70,74,75,77,78,79,
    82,83,84,88,90,94,96,97,
    100,101,103,104,105
Russell 41,101
Saunders 2,3,4,6,7,8,10,12,29,
    33,48,52,55,58,69,70,72,
    73,81,83,86,90,92,95,96,
    97,101

Savage 53,68
Scott 67,70,94,96
Sears 73
Shark 90
Shepherd 5,23,43,87,100
Simpson 63
Skinner 55,56,62,81
Slavin 21,43
Small 6,12,18,19,22,27,28,30,31,
    39,43,46,51,60,77,79,83,86,
    89,92,98,101
Smith 7,9,12,13,14,16,19,20,22,
    23,24,25,26,32,34,35,36,38,
    39,42,45,48,49,51,53,54,55,
    57,59,61,64,68,71,72,73,75,
    78,82,83,84,85,92,93,94,98,
    99,104,105
Sparkman 10,16,18,19,28,34,40,50,
    53,61,70,71,92,97,99,101,105
Speight 2,3,4,6,8,10,11,12,13,14,
    16,17,18,19,22,24,25,26,30,
    31,32,33,34,35,37,40,42,43,
    44,45,48,50,52,53,54,58,61,
    63,64,66,67,68,69,70,73,75,
    77,79,80,81,82,83,85,86,89,
    90,92,95,98
Spivey 5,17,20,21,30,32,42,43,44,
    45,48,50,65,66,67,73,74,76,
    78,85,86,87,89,90,91,92,93,
    94,99
Stallings 6,7,10,11,14,15,19,22,
    24,28,29,32,34,35,39,42,44,
    47,50,51,56,57,60,64,70,72,
    74,77,82,84,86,88,89,94,95,
    101,103,104
Sullivan 96
Sumner 1,3,5,7,8,9,10,11,12,13,
    14,15,16,21,22,25,26,27,28,
    29,30,31,33,34,35,36,38,39,
    40,41,42,44,45,46,47,48,49,
    50,51,53,54,55,56,57,58,59,
    60,62,63,64,66,68,70,71,72,
    74,75,76,77,78,81,82,83,84,
    85,86,87,88,89,90,92,94,95,
    99,100,101,102,103,104,105
Swann 91
Tayloe 65
Taylor 5,9,27,28,34,35,37,45,46,
    61,74,77,86
Thomas/Tommas 11,14,20,34,43,50,
    67,76,78,83,96,104
Thompston/Thompson 52,80,86
Trader/Tradir 25,64
Travis 46,47,89
Trotman 2,4,5,12,14,15,17,18,19,
    20,22,24,27,29,32,33,35,36,
    37,42,44,46,47,50,55,57,58,
    60,63,64,65,66,67,68,69,70,

73,74,75,76,77,79,82,84,
85,86,87,88,89,90,91,92,
93,94,95,96,97,100,101,
102,104,105
Tugwell 4,5,27
Turner 83,84,104
Twine 35
Tynes 46
Umfleet 7,24,30,31,47,50,62,
65
Vann/Van 2,3,4,5,7,8,10,11,
12,13,14,16,19,20,27,30,
31,34,35,36,39,40,42,44,
49,54,55,56,57,58,60,61,
62,64,65,67,68,71,73,79,
80,81,82,92,94,98,100,
101,102
Varnell 37
Vaughan 84
Voil/Vail 11,90
Wallis 34,37,46,53,55,77,80,
81
Walters 2,4,8,16,18,19,20,27,
29,30,31,32,33,39,41,46,
48,50,51,53,58,61,62,64,
66,73,76,77,79,82,89,91,
92,105
Walton 2,5,6,10,12,15,16,17,
18,22,23,24,27,28,29,31,
33,34,35,36,37,42,43,45,
46,47,48,49,50,51,53,55,
56,57,63,64,65,66,69,72,
74,75,76,77,78,79,80,82,
85,86,87,88,89,90,91,93,
94,95,97,98,102,105
Ward 5
Warner 42
Warren 6,11,12,19,29,30,31,
33,39,40,51,55,58,64,67,
69,71,90,91,98,99
Watson 3,17,18,23,27
Weatherby 94
White 87,88,90,91
Whitehead 103
Wiggins/Wiggons 18,32,43,70,
72,91,94
Wilkinson 20,26,31,58,103
Williams/William 3,4,6,7,12,
19,24,25,27,28,29,32,33,
34,35,36,38,39,42,43,45,
46,48,54,55,56,61,66,69,
74,75,76,79,89,95,101,
105
Willis 68
Wills 13,47,58,67,80,84
Wilson 4,8,37,46

Winborne 34,68
Witherill 8
Woods 48
Woodward 5
Worrell 11
Wright 15
Wynns 15
Zelf 5

Gates County North Carolina

Court Minutes

- 1779-1793 -

(2 Volumes in 1)

By:
Marilyn Poe Laird, Vivian Poe Jackson
& Judith Krause Reid

Southern Historical Press, Inc.
Greenville, South Carolina

GATES COUNTY, NORTH CAROLINA

MINUTES OF COUNTY COURT

Feb. 1788 - Aug. 1793

Feby. 18, 1788. Third Monday in February.

Present: Christopher Riddick, John Baker, William Goodman, Justices.

Shadrack Ellis to be exempt from the payment of a Poll Tax for the year 1787.

Isaac Walton records his Ear Mark. Swallow fork in the right Ear and a Half Moon under the left Ear.

Deed of land Josiah Granbery to Robert Riddick proved by the oath of Isaac Miller.

Deed of land Henry Copeland to Demsey Langston acknowledged.

Deed of Gift of Goods & etc. Rebecca Eure to Ann Eure proved by the oath of Thomas Harrell.

Deed of land William Davidson to Elisha Harrell proved by the Oath of Stephen Eure.

Deed of land William Morris to Henry Goodman proved by the oath of William Goodman.

Receipt. Josiah Granbery to Josiah Rogerson for a Negro Wench proved by the oath of William Felton.

Deed of land James Wright to John Wright proved by the oath of Henry Wright.

Deed of land John Wright to Lewis Meredith proved by the oath of Henry Wright.

Deed of land John Arnold to James Pruden affirmed by William Draper.

James Walton appointed Overseer of the Road instead of Aaron Hobbs resigned.

Asa Harrell appointed Overseer of the Road instead of Moor Carter resigned.

Last Will and Testament of Jesse Eason decd. exhibited by Alexander Eason and James Jones Extrs. thereto appointed and proved by the oath of David Small one of the witnesses.

Inventory of the Goods & etc. of the Estate of Jesse Eason decd. exhibited by Alexander Eason and James Jones Extrs.

Deed of land John Benbury Walton to Moses Davis acknowledged.

Deed of Trust Richard Mitchell bearing date the 18th. day of Feb. 1788 to William McDonald proved by the oath of Seth Rountree.

On Motion of William Cumming Esqr. Att. at Law ordered that John Baker Esqr. one of the members of this Court take the private examination of Easther Mitchell whether she executed the said deed freely and willingly of her own accord without fear or threat of her husband.

Christmas Parry to have a License to keep a Public House at the Folly in this County. He to give Security agreeable to Law. Josiah Granbery Security.

Ordered that John Powell have License to Keep a Public House at his Dwelling House in the Crepeak Swamp. He to give Security agreeable to Law. Seth Eason and David Small Securities.

Deed of land George White, Joshua White and John White to Thomas White proved by the oath of Jacob Spivey.

Deed of Sale John Brayshar to William Crafford proved by the oath of James Landing.

Deed of land William Crafford to Patrick Garvey acknowledged.

James Davis Guardian to James Hodges orphan of James Hodges decd. made return of his Account Current.

Peter Harrell, William Davidson, Charles Eure and Elisha Ellis or any three of them to make a division of the Estate of Enos Eure decd.

John White Guardian to Seth Spivey returned his Account Current.

John White Guardian to Smith Spivey returned his Account Current.

John Baker Esqr. who was appointed to take the private examination of Easther Mitchell wife of Richard Mitchell made return thereon as follows: Feb. 18, 1788. I do hereby Certify that in virtue of the within order of Court to me directed as one of the members and acting Justices thereof, that I did take the private examination of Esther Mitchell the wife of the within Mitchell whether she did Execute the within Deed willingly freely and of her own accord without being aduced thereto by fear of threats of ill usage by her said husband who therein did acknowledge, being private and apart from her said husband and all other persons did acknowledge and say that she did acknowledge the said Deed willingly and of her own accord without being aduced thereto by threats of ill usage from her said husband and that she had full and perfect knowledge of the operation and consents of the said Deed.

John Baker Esqr. who was appointed to take the private examination of Esther Mitchell wife of Richard Mitchell made return thereon as follows: (READS EXACTLY AS THE ABOVE EXAMINATION).

Mildred Harrell to be exempt from the payment of a Tax on a Negro Wench called Pegg for the year 1787.

Deed of Sale John Arline, Junr. to Moses Kittrell proved by the oath of Edward Drake.

Last Will and Testament of Thomas Walton decd. exhibited by Henry Walton, Benjamin Gordon and Samuel Harrell three of the Extrs. therein appointed and proved by the oath of James Gregory one of the witnesses.

Inventory of the Goods & etc. of the Estate of Thomas Walton decd. exhibited by the Extrs.

Henry Goodman, Isaac Pipkin and William Goodman who were appointed to make a division of William Copelands Estate made a report.

Alexander Eason and James Jones Extrs. of Jesse Eason decd. to sell the perishable part of the Estate of the decd.

Henry Walton, Benjamin Gordon and Samuel Harrell Extrs. of Thomas Walton decd. to sell the perishable part of the Estate of the decd.

William Gatling, Junr. appointed Constable instead of John Vann resigned. He to give Bond agreeable to Law. William Gatling Security.

Christopher Riddick, William Goodman and Seth Riddick who were appointed to make a division of the Estate of Stephen Rogers decd. made report.

Deed of land William Freeman to John Hobbs acknowledged.

Last Will and Testament of Demsey Bond decd. exhibited by Richard Bond and John Bunbery Walton two of the Extrs. therein appointed and proved by the oath of James Walton one of the witnesses.

Inventory of the Goods & etc. of the Estate of Demsey Bond decd. exhibited by Richard Bond and Jno. Benbury Walton Extrs.

Richard Bond and Jno. Bunbury Walton Extrs. of Demsey Bond decd. to sell so much of the perishable part of the Estate of the decd. as will pay debts.

Joseph Riddick and John Pipkin two Gentm. who were put into the Commission of the Peace came into Court and qualified themselves for that office and took seats accordingly.

Mary Rountree appointed Guardian to Mary Rountree orphan of Charles Rountree decd. She to give Security in the sum of 1000 pds. Joseph Riddick and Thos. Trotman Securities.

Tuesday morning. Present: Christopher Riddick, Seth Riddick and Joseph Riddick, Justices.

Thomas Hunter, Thomas Trotman and Seth Eason who were appointed to make a division of the Estate of Churles Rountree decd. made report.

Deed of land Henry Dilday to William Gatling proved by the oath of William Goodman.

Moses Benton appointed Guardian to William Jones orphan of Joseph Jones decd. He to give Bond in the sum of 200 pds. Richard Briggs and Moses Hare Securities.

Last Will of Mary Hare decd. exhibited by Joseph Spight and proved by him as one of the witnesses.

Agreeable to a Writ of Dower directed to the Sheriff of this County for the purpose of laying off the Dower of Mary Hill Widow and Relict of Guy Hill decd. made return as follows: Beginning on the North side of Catherine Creek Swamp at a pine and thence across the Cornfield to a Locus Tree thence near a North Course of Blazed trees to Joseph Brinkleys line to a White Oak thence down the said Brinkleys line an easterly course to a blazed White Oak on a branch, thence Southwardly course by a line of blazed Trees to Catherine Creek Swamp to a Maple and Ellm to the Run of the Swamp thence down the run of the Swamp to the first Station. All the land included in the said bounds to the Widow. (signed) Abraham Hurdle, James Costen, George Outlaw, James Outlaw, William Hunter, Demsey Trotman, Ezekial Trotman, John Rountree, Simon Stallings, James Freeman, John Hoffler, Seth Rountree. Jan. 18, 1788 - David Rice, Sheriff.

Deed of land Joseph Scott, Junr. and Mary his Wife and Judith Jones to David Rice acknowledged. Mary Scott relinquished her right of Dower.

Deed of land Joseph Scott, Mary Scott his Wife and Judith Jones to Moses Hare acknowledged. Mary Scott Wife of the said Joseph Scott relinquished her right of Dower.

Miles Rountree orphan of Charles Rountree decd. came into Court and made choice of James Norfleet as his Guardian. He to give Security in the sum of 1000 pds. David Rice and Seth Eason Securities.

Simon Stallings records his Ear Mark a Swallow form in the Right Ear and a Half Moon under the left Ear.

The Guardians of Josiah and Polly Rountree orphans of Charles Rountree decd. to sell the perishable part of the Estate of the said orphans.

Theopholus Hunter orphan of John Hunter decd. came into Court and made choice of William Hunter as his Guardian. He to give Security in the sum of 500 pds. Demsey Trotman and Seth Eason Securities.

Wednesday morning. Present: Christopher Riddick, Joseph Riddick, Jethro Sumner, John Baker, Justices.

Agreeable to the Petition of Sundry Inhabitants of this County for the laying off a Public Road issuing out of the Old Sumnerton Road at or near the place where the Old Mill Road issued out of the Old Sumnerton Road aforesaid and to be layed off at or near the Old Mill Road to the Virginia line near the fork of the Road that leads to Sumnerton Creek Bridge it is therefore ordered that the Sheriff summon a Jury to lay off the said Road and make report of their proceedings to this Court at next sitting.

Account of Sales of part of the Estate of Richard Freeman decd. exhibited by David Rice Esqr. Sheriff.

Willis Browne Guardian to Nancy Garrett orphan of James Garrett decd. returned his Account Current.

The Sheriff to summon William Harriss, Humphry Hudgins, Philip Lewis and Moses Hare to appear at Edenton on the 3rd. day of May next as Jurymen at the Superior Court.

Henry Goodman appointed Entry Taker of this County. He to give Security agreeable to Law. William Goodman Security.

Seth Eason appointed Guardian to Josiah Rountree orphan of Charles Rountree decd. He to give Security in the sum of 1000 pds. John Powell and David Rice Securities.

David Rice Esqr. appointed Sheriff of this County and that the appointment take place at May term next.

One sh. 6 pc. to be Levied on each Poll in this County and 6 pc. on each 100 acres of land for County Tax.

Moses Hare Constable of this County to be allowed the sum of 4 pds. for his services for summoning the inhabitants in the Captaincy of Jethro Sumner to return the list of Taxables for the year 1787 and for attending the Court seven days.

William Walters appointed Constable in the Captaincy of Jesse Benton.

The Sheriff to summon the following persons as Petit and Grand Jurymen: Abraham Eason, Jonathan Williams, Henry Speight, Seth Eason, Jacob Gordon, Moses Devis, Alexander Eason, William Ellis, Amos Trotman, John Rountree, Zadoc Hinton, William Booth, Willis Browne, Amos Lassiter, Job Riddick, Kedar Hinton, Samuel Smith, Henry Forrest, William Daughtee, Elisha Parker, Jesse Benton, Micajah Riddick, James Pruden, Thomas Barnes, Henry Goodman, Demsey Odom, Miles Benton, William Arnold, Charles Eure and Francis Speight.

<u>Thursday morning.</u> Present: John Baker, Seth Riddick, Joseph <u>Riddick, Justices.</u>

James Outlaw appointed Inspector on Katherine Creek and at Hunters Mill and also on Bennetts Creek as far up as Hintons landing. He to give Security agreeable to Law. Seth Rountree and John B. Walton Securities.

Timothy Lassiter records his Ear Mark a Swallow fork in the Right Ear and a Slope under the Left Ear.

David Rice Esqr. Sheriff of this County enters his protest against the Jail of this County it being unfit for public services.

<u>May 19, 1788. Third Monday in May.</u>

Present: Thomas Hunter, Seth Riddick, John Baker and William Goodman, Justices.

Deed of land Job Riddick to Isaac Costen acknowledged.

The County Trustee to pay Jethro Meltear Constable the sum of 4 pds. for his services.

Deed of land Job Riddick to Samuel Harrell acknowledged.

Deed of land William Crafford to Francis Speight acknowledged.

Deed of land Samuel Green to Uriah Eure proved by the oath of Daniel Eure.

Bill of Sale for a Negro Winch Hannah and her Child Lucy - William Granbery to Moses Hare, Senr. proved by the oath of Josiah Granbery.

Deed of land Judith Jones to Josiah Granbery proved by the oath of Isaac Hunter.

Abraham Eason appointed Overseer of the Road instead of Seth Eason resigned.

The County Trustee to pay Moses Hare the sum of 5 pds. 16 sh. 4 pc. for his services attending the Sept. Court.

Willis Sparkman only to pay a single Tax instead of a double Tax for which he was returned.

William Scott to be exempt from the payment of a Tax on a Negro Woman Jude who being infirm.

Samuel Thomas, Senr. to be exempt from the payment of a Tax on 50 acres of land which is returned as a double Tax and also that he pay only a single Tax on his Poll.

Deed of land John Rice to Josiah Granbery proved by the oath of Benjamin Gordon.

Noah Harrell appointed Overseer of the Road instead of Isaac Hunter resigned.

Deed of Gift Martha Sumner to James Baker Sumner for a Negro proved by the oath of Joseph John Sumner.

William Speight and Illigetimate Child, Son of Elizabeth Speight about 5 years old bound as an apprentice to Thomas Barnes to learn the business of a Cooper.

Deed of land Amos Lassiter to Israel Menyard proved by the oath of Demsey Blanshard.

Bill of Sale Josiah Benton to James Knight proved by the oath of John Saunders.

William Booth to be exempt from the payment of a Tax on 250 acres of land the said Tax being paid by Joel Foster.

Inventory of the Estate of Jacob Spivey decd. which was left in his last Will to his Widow was exhibited by Abraham Spivey Extr.

Thomas Hunter, Thomas Trotman, Simon Stallings, Joseph Riddick or any three of them to make a division of the Estate of Jacob Spivey decd.

Deed of land Henry Copeland to Isaac Langston acknowledged.

William Davidson, Elisha Ellis and Peter Harrell who were appointed to make a division of the Estate of Enos Eure decd. made report.

Deed of land Samuel Green to David Lewis proved by the oath of Uriah Eure.

Deed of land Jethro Meltear to Ephraim Morris proved by the oath of Demsey Jones.

Lidia Spivey Guardian to Jacob Spivey orphan of Thomas Spivey decd. made return of her Account Current. At the same time the said Liddy Spivey Guardian to Sarah Spivey orphan of Thomas Spivey decd. made return of her Account Current.

Disputed Entry made by Jeremiah Speight against Anthony Matthews. The Sheriff to summons a Jury.

Deed of land Abner Blanshard to Samuel Browne proved by the oath of Ameriah Blanshard.

Seth Eason moved for administration on the Estate of Elisha Summer decd. - granted. He to give Security in the sum of 2000 pds. Josiah Granbery and Samuel Smith Securities.

Thomas Hunter, Thomas Trotman, Jonathan Roberts and Simon Stallings or any three of them to make division of the Estate of Guy Hill decd.

Richard Bond Extr. of Guy Hill decd. to sell the perishable part of the Estate.

Account of the Sales of the Estate of Thomas Walton decd. was exhibited by David Rice Esqr. Sheriff.

Account of Sale of part of the Estate of Mary Rountree orphan of Charles Rountree decd. was exhibited by David Rice Esqr. Sheriff.

On a Petition of Lidia Spivey Widow of Thomas Spivey for Dower. Ordered the Sheriff summons a Jury and go on the premises and proceed agreeable to Law.

Deed of Gift Moses Blanshard to Zelphia Blanshard proved by the oath of Alexander Eason.

Account of Sales of the Estate of Jesse Eason decd. was exhibited by Alexander Eason Extr.

Samuel Eure appointed Guardian to Nancy Eure orphan of Enos Eure decd. He to give Security in the sum of 200 pds. Elisha Ellis and Stephen Piland Securities.

Samuel Eure Guardian to Nancy Eure orphan of Enos Eure decd. to sell the Estate of the said orphan.

Tuesday May 20, 1788.

Present: William Baker, John Baker, Jethro Ballard, Christopher Riddick, Joseph Riddick, Justices.

Thomas Finney moved by John Brickell Esqr. Att. at Law for leave to keep a Public House at Gates Court House. He to give security agreeable to Law. John Baker Security.

The Sheriff of this County to forewarn all persons whatsoever from selling any Spiritous Liquors or provisions but by license on the Court House Ground.

David Rice moved for administration on the Estate of John Jones decd. - granted. He to give Security in the sum of 100 pds. Seth Eason and Samuel Smith Securities.

Inventory of the Goods & etc. of the Estate of John Jones decd. was exhibited by David Rice Admr.

Bill of Sale for a Negro Boy called Hall - Demsey Rooks to John Vann acknowledged.

John Pipken the Collector in the Dictrict of Capt. William Goodman allowed in the settlement of his Account with the County Treasurer the Tax on Josiah Skite and Benjamin Dewpres(?) they being Insolvent.

Micajah Riddick the Collector of Tax in the Captaincy of Jesse Benton allowed in the Settlement of his Accounts with the County Treasurer the Tax on Arthur Williams he having moved out of this State.

John Riddick the Collector of the Tax in the Captaincy of Jethro Sumner allowed in the settlement of his Accounts with the County Treasurer the Tax on Elvy Brinkley, David Jones, Junr., William Phelps and George Bowing they being Insolvants.

James Gregory, Joseph Hurdle, Thomas Trotman and Kedar Ballard or any three of them to make a division of the Estate of Elisha Hunter decd.

Inventory of the Estate of Luke Sumner decd. was exhibited by Jethro Ballard, David Rice and Timothy Hunter.

The County Trustee to pay Lewis Sparkman 2 pds. 16 sh. for his services attending on this Court seven days as Constable.

Wednesday May 21, 1788.

Present: James Gregory, John Baker, Joseph Riddick, Justices.

David Rice Esqr. appointed as Sheriff of this County produced his Commission from the Governor and took the oath. He entered into Bond with John Baker and James Gregory as Securities.

Isaac Miller the Collector of the Tax in the Captaincy of William Harriss allowed in the settlement of his Account with the County Treasurer the Tax on Abraham Wilder and on John Swann(?) Parker. Wilder having removed himself out of this County and Parker an Insolvant.

Christopher Riddick Esqr. returned his account Current with the orphans of Miles Riddick decd.

The County Trustee to pay Isaac Miller the sum of 16 sh. for his services as Constable two days.

Ebran Sears appointed Overseer of the New Road that leads from the Old Somerton Road to the Virginia Line lately layed off and that the Hands of William Goodman, Henry Goodman, John Bethey, William Gatling, Anness Goodman, Henry Lee, Jacob Walters, William March, Thomas Hiatt, Henry Delday, Samuel Collings and Watson Howell work on the same.

Seth Eason and William Hurdle against Richard Mitchell see No. 10 trial Dockett verdict having been given for $100.00 and cost. Mr. Cummings moved for an appeal in behalf of the Defendant and tendered James Gregory and Thos. Hunter esqrs. for the prosecution of his appeal who were excepted off by the Court and appeal granted accordingly - Reasons for appeal filed.

James Walton, John Rountree and Richard Mitchell appointed commissioners to lay off Katherine Creek as high up said Creek as to them shall seem just for the passage of Fish up the same and to keep clear from hedges stops or dams otherwise that the Law directs and make report.

John B. Walton, Thomas Hunter and Jacob Bagley appointed commissioners to examine and lay off Warwick Creek as high up said Creek they may think necessary for the passage of Fish up the same and that the said bank be kept clear from any obstructions and that they make report.

Robert Taylor, William Hinton and Jonathan Roberts appointed commissioners to examine and lay off Bennetts Creek as high up as to them shall seem just for the passing of Fish up the same and see that the said Creek be kept clear from Hedges, Stops or Dams otherwise than the Law allows and that they make report.

The Tavern Keepers of this County to take the following Rates for Entertainment: for Breakfast 2/6 dinner 5/ with Grog or Toddy Supper 2/6 lodging for a person alone / for ditto with two in a Bed /9 each for every quart Toddy 2/6 for Grog by the quart 1/6 for Horse feed with 1 gill Oats corn or Hommony 1/6 for each skaf of Fodder /6.

The following Justices to take the list of Taxables in the different Captaincies in this County: Joseph Riddick Esqr. in Capt.

Isaac Hunters Captaincy. Thomas Hunter in Capt. Roberts Captaincy. Jethro Sumner in the Captaincy where he is Capt. John Baker in Capt. Eures Captaincy. Christo. Riddick in Wm. Harriss's Captaincy. Seth Riddick in Capt. Jesse Bentons Captaincy. John Pipkin in Capt. William Goodmans Captaincy.

The Sheriff to summon Henry Lee, Elisha Cross, Enos Rogers, John Bethey, William Gatling, George Williams Gluc(?), Samuel Eure, William Brooks, John Vann, Willis Parker, Thomas Smith, William Harriss, Israel Beeman, Cyprian Cross, James Landing, Benjamin Barnes, Michal Lawrence, Lewis Walters, James Freeman, Thomas Hoffler, Thomas Trotman, Josiah Granbery, David Cross, James Outlaw, Kedah Hill, Isaac Hunter, Aaron Lassiter, William Hurdle, Henry Harrell and John B. Walton as Jurymen.

The County Trustee to pay Samuel Harrell the sum of 5 pds. 4 sh. for his attendance on this Court 13 days as Constable.

David Rice Esqr. Sheriff of this County to be allowed the sum of 20 pds. for extra services for the year 1787.

Third Monday in August, 1788.

Present: Christopher Riddick, William Baker, John Baker, John Pipkin, William Goodman, Justices.

John Parker Esqr. who was appointed to take a list of Taxables in the Captaincy of Charles Eure returned his proceedings.

The Last Will and Testament of William Vann decd. was exhibited by Rachel Van, Jesse Vann and William Vann who were appointed Extrs. therein and proved by the oath of James Bristow one of the witnesses.

Inventory of the Goods &etc. of the Estate of William Vann decd. was exhibited by Rachel Vann, Jesse Vann and William Vann Extrs.

Moses Speight, Junr. appointed Overseer of the Road instead of John Riddick resigned.

Deed of land Joel Foster to Humphry Hudgins Senr. acknowledged.

Deed of land William Davidson to Aaron Harrell proved by the oath of Saml. Eure.

Inventory of the Goods & etc. of the Estate of Elisha Sumner decd. was exhibited by Seth Eason Admr.

Tuesday morning. Present: Christopher Riddick, William Baker, John Baker, William Goodman, John Pipkin, Justices.

Jethro Sumner Esqr. who was appointed to take a list of Taxables made report.

Thomas Hunter, Thomas Trotman and Jonathan Roberts three of the Gent'l. who were appointed to make a division of the Estate of Guy Hill decd. made report.

James Gregory, Thomas Trotman and Joseph Hurdle three of the Gent'l.

who were appointed to make a division of the Estate of Elisha Hunter decd. made report.

Bill of Sale Joseph Vollentine to Solomon King proved by the oath of Miles Benton.

John Pipkin Esqr. who was appointed to take a list of Taxables in the Captaincy of Capt. William Goodman made return.

Deed of Gift Willis Wiggins, Senr. to Willis Wiggins, Junr. was acknowledged.

Account of Sales of the Estate of John Hill and Elizabeth Hill was exhibited by James Bond and proved by the oath of David Rice Sheff.

Richard Bond appointed Guardian to John and Elizabeth Hill orphans of Guy Hill decd. He to give Security in the sum of 500 pds. Simon Stallings and Demsey Trotman Securities.

Samuel Eure Guardian of Nancy Eure orphan of Enos Eure made return of the Account of Sales of the perishable part of the Estate.

Grand Jury Discharged.

<u>Wednesday morning.</u> Present: Christopher Riddick, William Baker, Joseph Riddick, John Baker, Justices.

Petition of Milley Hobbs that her Dower may be layed off in the lands of Amos Hobbs decd. her late Husband Thomas Hobbs the Admr. being present in Court and acknowledging due notice of the Petition. The Sheriff to summons a Jury to Lay off the said Pettitioners Dower.

A Writ of Dower Directed to the Sheriff for the purpose of laying off the Dower of Liddey Spivey Widow and Relict of Thomas Spivey decd. set off certain lands which the decd. died seized and possessed with. Beginning at a Red Oak on the New Road in Demsey Trotmans line, thence runing an Easterly Course to a Shinkapin Tree on the side of a Branch thence up the said Branch by a line of marked trees to a Sweet Gum on the East Side of Edenton Road thence along the said Road Southwardly to a pine on the West side thence West course through an old field to a pine in the woods, thence a straight Westerly course to the back line, thence Southwardly and Eastwardly along the old line to the first station. John B. Walton, Richard Bond, Jr., Thomas Trotman, James Walton, John Hoffler, Ezekial Trotman, Demsey Trotman, William Hunter, John Hunter, James Costen, Noah Harrell, John Rountree and David Rice, Sheriff.

The Sheriff to summons the following persons as Jurymen: John Riddick, Joshua Small, Amos Parker, Noah Harrell, Isaac Costen, Jeremiah Speight, William Cleaves, Edward Daughtie, Edward Arnold, Isaac Harrell, William King, Abraham Hurdle, William Hunter, Demsey Trotman, Abraham Harrell, Thomas Parker, James Knight, Wm. Boyce, James Norfleet, Charles Eure, Peter Parker, _____ Minshew, Robert Parker, Senr., Robert Parker of Demsey, Francis Speight, Demsey Williams, Demsey Odom, Demsey Barnes, John Odom and William Odom.

Humphry Hudgins, Thomas Trotman, James Walton and Seth Rountree to be summoned to attend the Superior Court to be held at Edenton the 3rd. Nov. next.

Seth Riddick Esqr. who was appointed to take a list of Taxables in the District of Capt. Jesse Bentons Captaincy made return.

James Walton, John Rountree and Richard Mitchell who were appointed Commissioners to Lay off Katherine Creek made report.

Robert Taylor, William Hunter and Jonathan Roberts who were appointed Commissioners to Lay off Bennetts Creek made report.

Christopher Riddick Esqr. who was appointed to take a list of Taxables in the Captaincy of Capt. William Harriss made report.

Joseph Riddick Esqr. who was appointed to take a list of Taxables in the Captaincy of Capt. William Harris made report.

John Brickell Esqr. allowed the sum of 12 pds. for his service as Att. for the year 1787.

Richard Mitchell to be exempt from the payment of his Public, County and Parish and Edenton Jail Tax on his Negroes and land listed in this County it being before listed to Jethro Ballard one of the Extrs. of James Sumner decd. to whom the said property lately belonged.

James Walton, John Rountree, Seth Rountree, Jesse Spivey, Americas Blanshard, William Freeman and Thomas Hoffler appointed Searchers in the Captaincy of Capt. Jonathan Roberts.

Abraham Hurdle, John B. Walton, Abraham Sumner, Abram Eason, Joseph Riddick and Saml. Green appointed Searchers in the Captaincy of Capt. Isaac Hunter.

Jesse Saunders, Abram Saunders, Abel Cross, Benjamin Barnes, Jesse Vann and Luten Lewis appointed Searchers in the Captaincy of Capt. Wm. Goodman.

Humphry Hudgins, William Harriss, John Duke, Willis Browne, Willis Parker and James Browne appointed Searchers in the Captaincy of Capt. William Harris.

Isaac Carter, John Parker, Mills Eure appointed Searchers in the Captaincy of Capt. Charles Eure.

William Ellis, Benjamin Gordon, James Norfleet, Edwin Sumner, John Riddick and Kedar Ballard appointed Searchers in the Captaincy of Capt. Jethro Sumner.

Philip Rogers, Jesse Benton, Elisha Cross, Jonathan Rogers, Enos Rogers and Hillard(?) Willey(?) appointed Searchers in the Captaincy of Capt. Jesse Benton.

Nov. 17, 1788 - Third Monday in November.

Present: Christopher Riddick, Seth Riddick, John Baker, Justices.

Moses Hill appointed Overseer of the Road instead of William Berryman resigned.

David Lewis appointed Overseer of the Road instead of Levi Lee.

Deed of Sale Thomas Brickell to William Lewis proved by the oath of Thomas Marshall.

Last Will and Testament of Jacob Powell decd. was exhibited by Daniel Powell and James Powell Extrs. therein appointed and proved by the oath of Jethro Ballard and Benjamin Gordon witnesses.

Inventory of the Goods & etc. of the Estate of Jacob Powell decd. was exhibited by the Extrs.

Deed of Sale Nathaniel Spivey to James Outlaw acknowledged.

Moses Kittrell, Jonathan Williams, Demsey Williams and James Bristow or any three of them to make a division of the Estate of Arthur Williams decd.

Milley Harrell to be exempt from the payment of a Tax on a Negro Woman named Pegg for the year 1788.

Deed of Sale Jesse Barnes to Cyprian Cross proved by the oaths of Demsey Barnes and Jesse Vann.

James Gregory, Isaac Hunter, Jacob Gordon and John Rice or any three of them to Audit State and Settle the Accounts of Samuel Harrell and Benj. Gordon Extrs. of Thomas Walton decd.

Deed of land Samuel Thomas to Nancy Vann proved by the oath of Reuben Harrell.

Deed of Lease William Odom to Hardy Howard proved by the oath of Abraham Saunders.

Deed of Gift Elizabeth Chaney to Francas Brooks proved by the oath of William Brooks.

Kedar Odom moved by Blake Baker Att. at Law for Administration on the Estate of Sarah Odom decd. - granted. He to give Security in the sum of 200 pds. Lewis Sparkman and Willis Hines Securities.

Inventory of the Goods & etc. of the Estate of Sarah Odom was exhibited by Kedar Odom Admr.

<u>Tuesday morning.</u> Present: Christopher Riddick, William Baker, Seth Riddick, James Gregory, Justices.

Bill of Sale Job Riddick and Benj. Perry to Simon Stallings proved by the oath of Daniel Stallings.

Mourning Rooks Relict of Thomas Rooks decd. moved for administration on the Estate of her decd. Husband. - granted. She to give Security in the sum of 200 pds. William Hawes and William Warren Securities.

Inventory of the Goods & etc. of the Estate of Thomas Rooks decd. was exhibited by the Admr.

Deed of Sale Thomas Brickell to William Booth acknowledged.

Christopher Riddick, John Baker and Law Baker to let the repairing of the Public Jail in this County to the lowest bidder.

Wednesday morning. Present: Christopher Riddick, William Baker, John Baker, Justices.

The Sheriff to summons the following persons as Grand and Petit Jurymen: Timothy Lassiter, Isaac Hunter, Simon Stallings, Thomas Trotman, John B. Walton, James Freeman, Robert Taylor, Jacob Gordon, William Ellis, Reuben Riddick, Abraham Hurdle, Job Riddick, John Darden, James Knight, John Arnold, John Weatherly, Francis Parker, Solomon King, David Watson, George Hargrove, William Crafford, Demsey Harrell, Josiah Harrell, Uriah Eure, Asa Harrell, Isaac Parker, Enos Rogers, William Daughtie, Moses Kittrell and Jonathan Williams.

1 sh. and 6 pc. to be Levied on each Poll in this County and each 100 acres of land 6 pc. Tax.

David Rice Esqr. Sheriff of this County appointed to collect the Public and County Tax for the year 1788. He to give Security in the sum of 4,000 pds. William Baker and Christopher Riddick Esqrs. Securities.

William Baker Esqr. who was appointed County Trustee exhibited his Account with this County where there appears to be a balance due from the said Trustee to the County the sum of 2 pds. 9 sh. 8 pc. and half penny.

Disputed Entry - Anthony Matthews against William Harriss. The Sherriff summoned a Jury and went on the premises - - - agree that Capt. William Harriss's Pattents to have their cources run out and if there should be any vacant land for Anthony Matthews to have it. John Riddick, John Arnold, Micajah Riddick, Noah Felton, Lewis Walters, Abraham Morgan, James Pruden, Humphry Hudgins, William Cleaves, Henry Forrest, Robert Riddick, Timothy Lassiter. 20 Sept. 1788. David Rice, Sheriff.

Abraham Harrell Extr. of the Last Will and Testament of Thomas Fullington decd. exhibited the Inventory of the Estate of the decd. after the death of his widow.

Abraham Harrell Extr. of the Estate of Thomas Fullington decd. to sell the perishable part of the Estate for the benefit of the Legatees agreeable to the Will.

A Writ of Dower directed to the Sheriff for Laying off the Dower of Milley Hobbs Relict of Amos Hobbs decd. - Jury Summoned - Qualified - set apart one third of the land and Improvement that Amos Hobbs decd. possessed to Milley Hobbs his Widow as follows: Beginning at a Oak on the North Side of the land thence a Southwardly course to a Chinkapin Tree from thence to a Stake a corner, thence to a Stake in the yard thence Southwardly to a small Black Oak in the woods thence a short corner to the back line all the part of the land to the East to his Widow except two thirds of the apple orchard beginning at a persimmon tree on the north side of the orchard thence through the orchard Southwardly to a persimmon tree all that part of the said orchard to the East with the fence about it as it now stands to orphans. Ezekiel Trotman, William Hunter, Kedar Hill, John Rountree, James Walton, Seth Rountree, J. B. Walton, Richard Bond, Abner Blanshard, Ameriah Blanshard, Thomas Trotman. - David Rice, Sheriff.

On the resignation of John Brickell Esqr. Att. for the State, Thomas Iredell Esqr. was appointed as Attorney for this County in behalf of the State.

William Booth to turn the Public Road that leads by his plantation to go on or near the line between him and Thomas Marshall.

Kedar Odom Admr. of Sarah Odom decd. to sell the perishable part of the Estate of the Decd.

Seth Riddick, John Baker and John Pipkin Esqrs. and Charles Eure or any three of them to make a division of the Estate of Jacob Odom decd. agreeable to the Will of the decd.

Willis Browne appointed Inspector of Navil Stores and other articles in this County. He to give Security agreeable to Law. Charles Eure and Moses Hare Securities.

Feb. 16, 1789 - Third Monday in Feb.

Present: Christopher Riddick, Seth Riddick, Jethro Sumner, Justices.

Deed of Sale Moses Kittrell to Samuel Baker acknowledged.

Deed of land Edward Arnold to Thomas Parker proved by the oath of John Darden.

Deed of land John R. Wilkinson to Elisha Copeland proved by the oath of Josiah Granbery.

Seth Eason Guardian to Jonah Rountree exhibited his Account.

Deed of land Mary Riddick to Seth Eason proved by the oath of Alexander Eason.

Deed of Gift Joshua Small to James Small proved by the oath of Seth Eason.

Joseph Freeman orphan of Solomon Freeman decd. of Bertie County came into Court and made choice of Joseph Speight as his Guardian He to give Security in the sum of 1000 pds. William Gatling and Henry Speight Securities.

Joseph Speight appointed Guardian to John Freeman, David Freeman and Anne Freeman. He to give Security in the sum of 1000 pds.

William Gatling and Henry Speight Securities.

Deed of land James Skinner to John Odom proved by the oath of Cyprian Cross.

Benjamin Edwards moved for Administration on the Estate of Ann Gibson. - granted. He to give Security in the sum of 2000 pds. William Harris and Jethro Sumner Securities.

Inventory of the Goods & etc. in the possession of Ann Gibson was exhibited by Benjamin Edwards.

Deed of Sale Samuel Green to David Lewis proved by the oath of Andrew Gootie.

Sale of land Peter Piland and Edward Piland to Hardy Browne proved by the oath of Wright Hayes.

Deed of land Francis Parker to Benjamin Saunders proved by the oath of Uriah Odom.

Deed of land Thomas Travis to Jeremiah Jordon proved by the oath of Henry Hill.

John Gatling Guardian to William Rogers, John Rogers and Priscilla Rogers orphans of Stephen Rogers decd. exhibited his Accounts Current.

Isaac Pipkin Guardian to Stephen Rogers, Elizabeth Rogers and Sarah Rogers orphans of Stephen Rogers decd. exhibited his Accounts Current.

Aaron Hobbs appointed Overseer of the Road instead of Jacob Bagley decd.

Jacob Spivey Guardian to Jacob Spivey and Sarah Spivey orphans of Thomas Spivey exhibited his Account Current.

Deed of Sale Abel Cross to David Cross acknowledged.

Deed of Sale Michale Howell and Edward Howell to Abel Cross proved by the oath of David Cross.

Deed of Sale Samuel Green to Samuel Taylor acknowledged.

John White Guardian to Seth Spivey and Smith Spivey orphans of William Spivey decd. exhibited his Accounts.

Last Will and Testament of Jacob Bagley exhibited by Amos Trotman, Thomas Hunter and Kedar Hill the Extrs. therein appointed and proved by the oath of Thomas Trotman one of the witnesses.

Inventory of the Goods & etc. of the Estate of Jacob Bagley decd. was exhibited by Amos Trotman, Thomas Hunter and Kedar Hill Extrs.

George Outlaw Guardian to Richd. Freeman orphan of Demsey Freeman exhibited his Accounts Current.

James Davis Guardian to James Hodges orphan of James Hodges decd. exhibited his accounts.

Judith Wilkinson moved by John Brickell Esqr. Attorney at Law for Administration on the Estate of John Wilkinson decd. Granted. She to give Security in the sum of 200 pds. Kedar Ballard and James Baker Sumner Securities.

Account of Sales of property sold belonging to the orphans of William Spivey was exhibited by David Rice Sheriff.

Account of Sale of property belonging to the orphans of Thomas Spivey decd. exhibited by David Rice Sheriff.

Deed of land John Anderson to Jesse Saunders proved by the oath of John Pipkin.

Deed of land Jonah Parker to James Parker proved by the oath of James Rice.

Henry Copeland moved that Wm. Rogers orphan of Stephen Rogers be bound to him to learn the business of a Cooper.

William Hunter Guardian to Theopholis Hunter orphan of John Hunter decd. exhibited his accounts.

On Motion of Abraham Harrell ordered that James Gregory, Isaac Hunter and Benjamin Gordon audit State and Settle the accounts of the said Abraham Harrell with Estate of Thomas Fullington decd.

Deed of land Abraham Sumner to Abraham Eason proved by the oath of Patrick Hagerty.

Bill of Sale Abraham Sumner to Abraham Eason proved by the oath of Patrick Hergety.

Tuesday morning. Present: Joseph Riddick, William Goodman, John Pipkin, Justices.

Moses Hobbs appointed Guardian to William Hobbs orphan of Guy Hobbs decd. He to give Security in the sum of 250 pds. Moses Hill and William Hunter Securities.

Moses Hobbs appointed Guardian to Jesse Hobbs orphan of Guy Hobbs decd. He to give Security in the sum of 250 pds. Moses Hill and William Hunter Securities.

Moses Hobbs moved for Administration on the Estate of Penny Hobbs decd. - orphan of Guy Hobbs - granted. He to give Security in the sum of 100 pds. Moses Hill and William Hunter Securities.

Thomas Trotman, Amos Trotman, Joseph Riddick and Simon Stallings or any three of them to Audit State and Settle the accounts of Moses Hobbs Extr. of Guy Hobbs decd.

Thomas Trotman, Amos Trotman, Simon Stallings and Joseph Riddick or any three of them to make Division of the Estate of Penny Hobbs orphan of Guy Hobbs decd.

Deed of Gift Lewis Outlaw to James Outlaw proved by the oath of Thomas Hunter.

Deed of Sale Arthur Williams to Samuel Williams proved by the oath of Moses Kittrell.

Daniel Gwinn a witness in a Suit Henry Mironey vs. Seth Eason in behalf of the Plaintiff the said Daniel Gwinn failed to appear - fined.

Deed of Sale Job Riddick to Timothy Lassiter acknowledged.

Deed of Sale Samuel Baker to Timothy Lassiter proved by the oath of Geo. Hamilton.

Willis Brown Guardian to Nancy Garrett orphan of James Garrett decd. exhibited his accounts.

Edward Gatling appointed Constable instead of William Gatling resigned. He to give Security agreeable to Law. John Gatling Security

Joseph Riddick allowed to alter a Eastern Course in a Pattent belonging to Moses Carter wherein a Course in said Pattent was by Joseph Riddick entered by mistake instead of the Course runing No. 68 East it ought to be No. 68 West.

John Pipkin, John Baker and Charles Eure who were appointed to make a division of the Estate of Jacob Odom decd. made report.

David Rice Admr. of John Jones decd. exhibited the account of Sales of the Estate of the decd.

Kedar Odom Admr. of the Estate of Sarah Odom decd. returned his account of Sales of the Estate of the decd.

Mary Rountree Guardian to Mary Rountree orphan of Charles Rountree decd. exhibited her account current.

Abraham Phelps about 15 years of age bound as an apprentice to John Rice to learn the business of a House Carpenter.

Wednesday morning. Present: Christopher Riddick, Seth Riddick, William Baker, John Baker, William Goodman, Jethro Sumner, Justices.

Isaac Costen appointed Overseer of the road instead of Thomas Walton decd.

Jonah Speight an Illigitimate child of Elizabeth Speight about 13 years bound as an apprentice to Willis Moor to learn the business of a Shoemaker.

Thomas Finney appointed Overseer of the Road instead of John Baker Esqr. resigned.

Laurance Baker allowed the sum of 35 sh. for Plank and puting the same on Bennetts Creek Bridge.

Henry Speight appointed Overseer of the road instead of William Warren resigned.

Moses Hare allowed the sum of 5 pds. 12 sh. for his Services as Constable attending this Court and warning the Inhabitants for Capt. Jethro Summers Captaincy to give list of taxable property.

The Sheriff to summons Jonathan Roberts, Seth Eason, Edward Daughtie and John Odom as Jurymen at the Superior Court of Land and Equity to be held at Edenton 3rd. day of May next.

The Sheriff to summons Joseph Speight, Thomas Barnes, John Riddick, Joshua Small, Amos Parker, Benjamin Barnes, Abel Cross, Jeremiah Speight, William Cleaves, Edward Arnold, Demsey Trotman, Thomas Trotman, Peter Parker, Richd. Bond, Robert Parker Senr., Francis Speight, Samuel Smith, William Boyce, David Harrell, William Booth, George Williams, Charles Eure, Peter Harrell, John Vann, Philip Rogers, Demsey Barnes, Jas. Landing, Willis Parker, James Bristow and Henry Goodman as Jurymen.

Jesse Spivey Guardian to Frederick Blanshard, William Blanshard, Sarah Blanshard and Mary Blanshard orphans of Absolom Blanshard exhibited his Accounts Current.

Cordel Norfleet orphan of James Norfleet bound as an apprentice to Henry Lee to learn the business of a Carpenter.

May 18, 1789, Third Monday in May.

Present: Christopher Riddick, Seth Riddick, James Gregory, Justices.

Deed of Gift Mary Riddick to Mills, Nathl. and David Riddick acknowledged.

Deed of land Mordicai Perry to Shaderack Felton proved by the oath of William Felton.

Deed of Sale and Rect. thereon Charles Russell to Samuel Brown affirmed to by Stephen Shepherd one of the witnesses.

Kedar Hinton appointed Overseer of the Road where William Booth was formerly Overseer.

Whereas Benjamin Edwards Guardian to William Edwards Webb made application to his Excellency the Governor, the Secretary of State hath issued a Grant to William Ellis, John Riddick, the Heirs of Docton Riddick and Thomas Smith for 200 acres in this County, No. 33 joining William Hinton, Samuel Taylor, John Riddick, John Webb and Docton Riddicks land. The Sheriff of this County to summons a Jury to go on the premisses and proceed agreeable to Law and to make return.

John Warren and William Warren Extrs. to the last Will of Edward Warren exhibited the said Will and was proved by the oath of William Warren and John Warren two of the witnesses.

Deed of land Edwd. Arnold to Thomas Parker proved by the oath of

Mills Ellis.

Deed of Sale Edwd. Arnold to Mills Ellis proved by the oath of Thos. Parker.

Whereas Benjamin Edwards Guardian to William Edwards Webb made application to His Excellency the Governor for a Suspension of a certain Grant to William Ellis, John Riddick, the Heirs of Docton Riddick and Thomas Smith Entry No. 34 in this Co. for 300 acres. The Secretary of State hath issued a Caviat for the Suspension of the same. The Sheriff to summons a Jury and go on the premisses and proceed agreeable to Law and to make report.

Deed of Sale Moor Carter to William Williams proved by the oath of George Williams.

Inventory of the goods & etc. of the Estate of John Wilkinson decd. exhibited by Judith Wilkinson Admr.

Thomas Trotman, Simon Stallings and Joseph Riddick three of the Gent. who were appointed to make a division of the Estate of Penny Hobbs made report.

Bill of Sale John Bethey to James Bethey acknowledged.

Deed of land Daniel Ellis to Elisha Ellis proved by the oath of Josiah Stallings.

James Gregory, Thomas Hunter, Isaac Hunter and Simon Stallings or any three of them to Audit State and Settle the accounts of the administration of Charles Rountree decd.

Bill of Sale Thomas Vann to Enos Rogers proved by the oath of John Vann.

Judith Wilkinson Admr. of John Wilkinson decd. to sell so much of the perishable part of the Estate of the decd. as will pay his just debts.

Last Will of William Parker decd. exhibited by William Parker and Amos Parker Extrs. and proved by the oath of Kedar Parker and Willis Parker who relinquished their rights as Legatees at the same time.

Inventory of the Goods & etc. of the Estate of William Parker decd. exhibited by William Parker and Amos Parker Extrs.

Deed of Gift Isaac Pipkin to John Pipkin acknowledged.

Deed of Sale Thomas Vann to Mills Lewis proved by the oath of Edward Gatling.

Hugh and Purnall King orphans of Nehemiah King (Hugh King 16 years of Age the 13 March last and Purnal 15 years old the 18 day of Oct. next) bound as apprentices to James Piland to learn the business of a Cooper.

Tuesday morning. Present: Thomas Hunter, James Gregory, Joseph Riddick, William Goodman, John Pipkin, Justices.

Deed of Land Samuel Brown to Henry Goodman proved by the oath of William Gatling.

Bill of Sale Nathl. Griffin to Edward Daughtie proved by the oath of Jethro Sumner.

Henry Lee moved for Administration on the Estate of Sarah Drury- granted. He to give Security in the sum of 100 pds. William Gatling Security.

John Slavin to be exempt from the payment of a poll tax for the year 1788 and that Jethro Slavin be exempt from the payment of a poll tax for the above year he having had the misfortune to break his leg.

Shaderack Ellis to be exempt for the payment of a poll tax for the year 1788 he being very lame and infirm.

Henry Lee Admr. on the Estate of Sarah Drury to sell the perishable part of the Estate.

The Extrs. of William Parker to sell so much of the perishable part of the Estate of the decd. as will pay his just debts.

Deed of land Willis Wiggins to Josiah Granbery acknowledged.

Lewis Outlaw to be exempt from paying a poll tax he being very old and that John Harris also be exempt for paying his tax he being blind.

Noah Harrell to be exempt from the payment of tax on a Negro the property of Richard Bond the said Bond having listed the said Negro.

Thomas Trotman, Richard Mitchell, Moses Hill and Amos Trotman or any three of them to Audit State and Settle the Accounts of the Extrs. of Guy Hill decd.

The Sheriff to summon Kedar Hill, Richard Mitchell, George Outlaw, Isaac Hunter, Henry Speight, William Gatling, Jesse Vann, James Lang, John Bethey, Benjamin Barnes, Abel Cross, John Gatling, Timothy Lassiter, Richard Bond, Amos Trotman, James Freeman, George Eason, Senr., Seth Sumner, John Powell, _____ Ballard, Jonathan Roberts, William Harriss, Jesse Spivey, Henry Walton, Moses Hill, Robert McCullgh (?), Willis Brown, Edwin Sumner, Jesse Benton and Abraham Saunders as Jurymen.

Joseph Riddick, Simon Stallings and Francis Trotman three of the Gent. who were appointed to make a division of the Estate of Jacob Spivey decd. made report.

Wednesday morning. Present: Christopher Riddick, Seth Riddick, William Goodman, Justices.

William Hunter appointed Overseer of the road instead of Demsey Trotman resigned.

Deed of land George Piland to Saml. Baker acknowledged.

Thomas Finney to have a license to keep a Public House at Gates Court House. Josiah Granbery Security.

Seth Riddick Esqr. to act as Sheriff of this County. He to give Security agreeable to Law. Christopher Riddick and Jos. Riddick Esqrs. Securities.

William Walters Constable to be allowed 6 pds. for his attendance on this Court 15 days.

Jethro Meltear Constable to be allowed 2 pds. 8 sh. for his attendance on this Court 6 days.

Seth Eason appointed Deputy Sheriff of this County by Seth Riddick Esqr. Sheriff.

The following Gent. were appointed to take the list of taxables for the present year to wit: James Gregory Esqr. in Capt. Isaac Hunters Captaincy. Thomas Hunter Esqr. in Capt. Jon. Roberts Captaincy. Jethro Ballard Esqr. in Capt. Jethro Sumners Captaincy. William Goodman Esqr. in the Captaincy where he is Capt. William Baker Esqr. in Capt. Charles Eures Captaincy. Christopher Riddick in Capt. William Harrisses Captaincy. Jethro Sumner Esqr. in the Captaincy of Capt. Jesse Benton.

David Rice Esqr. late Sheriff of this County to be allowed 20 pds. for extra Services performed by him.

An additional Inventory of the Goods & etc. of the Estate of Jacob Sumner decd. exhibited by Abraham Sumner Admr.

Accounts of Sales of the Estate of Jacob Sumner, Jr., decd. exhibited by Abraham Sumner Admr.

17 Aug. 1789. Third Monday in August.

Present: Christopher Riddick, John Baker, David Rice, Justices.

Deed of land William Walters to James Matthews acknowledged.

Last Will of Maxamilian Minshew decd. exhibited by Bond Minshew and Zachariah Minshew Extrs. therein appointed and proved by the oaths of Christopher Riddick and Seth Riddick witnesses.

An Inventory of the Goods & etc. of the Estate of Maxamilian Minshew decd. exhibited by Bond Minshew and Zachariah Minshew Extrs.

James Gregory, Benjamin Gordon and Isaac Hunter who were appointed to Audit State and Settle the Accounts of Abraham Harrell Extr. of Thomas and Judith Fullington decd. made report.

Thomas Trotman, Amos Trotman and Moses Hill who were appointed to Audit State and Settle the accounts of Richard Bond Extr. of Guy Hill decd. made report.

Account of Sales of the Estate of Thomas and Judith Fullington decd. exhibited by Abraham Harrell Extr.

James Gregory, Jacob Gordon and Isaac Hunter three of the Gent. who were appointed to Audit State and Settle the Accounts of Benjm. Gordon and Saml. Harrell Extrs. of Thomas Walton decd. made report.

Deed of land Thomas Sparkman to Lewis Sparkman proved by the oath of Samuel Taylor.

Deed of land Miles Wallis to James Outlaw proved by the oath of James Freeman.

Deed of land James B. Sumner to John Gatling acknowledged.

Deed of land George Hargroves and Amela Hargroves to Jesse Vann proved by the oath of John Odom.

Bill of Sale Edward Dudley to William Gatling for a Negro Girl proved by the oath of John Pipkin.

Deed of Sale Alexander Eason and Mary Eason his Wife to Seth Eason proved by the oath of Elisha Norfleet and Jacob Gordon.

Jacob Gordon appointed Overseer of the Road instead of Noah Harrell.

Whereas Elizabeth Norfleet was returned for the year 1788 as not having given in her list and was chargable for a Double Tax ordered that she only pay a single Tax.

The Hands of Christopher Riddick Esqr. to work on the road where Michal Lawrence is Overseer.

Last Will of Joseph Parker decd. exhibited by John Robbins, Junr. Extr. therein appointed and proved by the oath of John Robbins, Senr. one of the witnesses.

John Hare to pay only a Tax in one District in this County he having by mistake been returned in two.

Inventory of the Estate of Sarah Drury decd. was exhibited by Henry Lee Admr.

Account of Sales of the Estate of Sarah Drury decd. was exhibited by Henry Lee Admr.

Deed of land David Lewis to Samuel Green acknowledged.

Bray Saunders appointed Overseer of the Road instead of Jesse Saunders resigned.

Thomas Hurdle Overseer of the Road is to keep the Public Road from the Indian Branch to the fork of the Road and the Hands of Jos. Riddick Esqr. and Abraham Hurdle work on the Road under the said Thomas Hurdle.

David Watson moved by John Brickell Esqr. Atto. at Law for Administration on the Estate of William Boyce decd. - granted. He to give Security in the sum of 300 pds. Jesse Saunders and Abraham Saunders Securities.

Deed of land John Hunter to Ezekiel Trotman proved by the oath of Abraham Hurdle.

Inventory of the Goods & etc. of the Estate of William Boyce decd. was exhibited by David Watson Admr.

Winny Lang to be allowed the sum of 5 pds. a year for the maintinace of a Bastard Child begot on her Body by William Boyce decd. until the said Child should arrive to the age of 6 years.

David Watson Admr. of the Estate of William Boyce decd. to sell so much of the Estate of the said decd. as will pay debts.

Joseph Riddick and Jethro Ballard Esqrs. and Joseph Hurdle and Benjamin Gordon or any three of them to Audit State and Settle the Accounts of the Extrs. of Colo. Jesse Eason decd.

Inventory of the Estate of Edward Warren decd. was exhibited by John Warren and William Warren Extrs.

Hardy Griffin orphan of Joseph Griffin about 16 years of age bound as an apprentice to Jonathan Rogers to learn the business of a Blacksmith.

Mary Griffin orphan of Joseph Griffin about the age of 13 years bound as an apprentice to William Boyce to learn House Business.

Richard Bond appointed Guardian to Elisha Bond orphan of Demsey Bond decd. He to give Security in the sum of 1000 pds. John B. Walton and David Harrell Securities.

Deed of land Abraham Eason to James Gregory proved by the oath of Thos. Hunter.

August 18, 1789. Tuesday morning.

Present: James Gregory, John Baker, Joseph Riddick, William Baker, Jethro Sumner, Christopher Riddick, Jethro Ballard, Justices.

James Gregory, Joseph Riddick, Jethro Sumner and Josiah Granbery or any three of them to Audit State and Settle the Account of Abraham Sumner Admr. of Jacob Sumner decd. and make report.

Deed of Gift of land Joshua Small to John Small proved by the oath of Jethro Ballard.

Deed of Gift Joshua Small to John Small for Goods & Chattels proved by the oath of Jethro Ballard.

Samuel Harrell Extr. of Thomas Walton decd. exhibited his Accounts with Miles Walton orphan of the decd.

Stephen Copeland orphan of William Copeland decd. came into Court and made choice of Whitson Jones as his Guardian. Whitson Jones to give Security in the sum of 600 pds. William Goodman and Demsey Odom Securities.

Kedar Hinton to be exempt from paying a Tax on a certain Negro which was listed by him and Robert Taylor. The said Taylor having paid.

Samuel Harrell appointed Guardian to Miles Walton, Thomas Walton, John Walton, Milicent Walton, Amelia Walton and William Walton minor orphans of Thomas Walton decd. He to give Security in the sum of 1000 pds. William Harriss and Seth Eason Securities.

Miles Walton orphan of Thomas Walton decd. about 16 years of age bound as an apprentice to Samuel Harrell to learn the business of a Cooper.

John Walton orphan of Thomas Walton decd. about the age of 11 years bound as an apprentice to Robert McCullok to learn the business of a Taylor.

Jethro Haslett to be exempt from the payment of a Double Tax and that he pay only a Single Tax on himself and Two Negros.

Sarah Piland to be exempt from the payment of a Tax on 100 acres.

John Baker, William Baker, William Goodman and Cyprian Cross or any three of them to divide the Estate of Elisha Odom decd. and make report.

Bill of Sale Lewis Jones to Kedar Raby proved by the oath of James Knight.

Deed of Gift Rachel Bond to Elisha H. Bond, Selah Bond, Demsey Bond and Thomas Bond proved by the oath of Richard Bond.

On Motion of Kedar Ballard ordered that Judtih Wilkinson Admr. of J. R. Wilkinson decd. be summoned to appear before this Court at next sitting to give Counter Security so that the said Ballard may be released.

Account of Sales of the Estate of Elisha Hunter decd. was exhibited by Thomas Hunter Extr.

Account of Sales of the perishable Estate of the orphans of Sarah Freeman decd. which was left them by Elisha Hunter decd. was exhibited by Thomas Hunter.

James Gregory, Samuel Harrell, Jacob Gordon and Henry Walton or any three of them to Audit State and Settle the Accounts of Thomas Hunter and Joseph Riddick Extrs. of Elisha Hunter decd.

The Sheriff returned the verdict of a Jury in a dispute relative to lands by Benjamin Edwards Guardian to William Edwards Webb, orphan of John Webb decd. against William Ellis, John Riddick, the Heirs of Docton Riddick and Thomas Smith. Entry No. 33 for 200 acres of land joining William Hinton, Samuel Taylor, John Riddick, John Webb and Docton Riddicks land and also Entry No. 34 for 300 acres joining Daniel Gwinn, Moses Hare, Ann Gibson, William Hinton, Richard Bond, John Webb, William Speight, John Riddick and William Ellis. The Clerk of the Court to deliver to Benjm. Edwards Guardian to William Edwards Webb an authentic copy thereof which is as follows - - - We the Jury are of the opinion and do say that the

Deed of land John Hunter to Ezekiel Trotman proved by the oath of Abraham Hurdle.

Inventory of the Goods & etc. of the Estate of William Boyce decd. was exhibited by David Watson Admr.

Winny Lang to be allowed the sum of 5 pds. a year for the maintinace of a Bastard Child begot on her Body by William Boyce decd. until the said Child should arrive to the age of 6 years.

David Watson Admr. of the Estate of William Boyce decd. to sell so much of the Estate of the said decd. as will pay debts.

Joseph Riddick and Jethro Ballard Esqrs. and Joseph Hurdle and Benjamin Gordon or any three of them to Audit State and Settle the Accounts of the Extrs. of Colo. Jesse Eason decd.

Inventory of the Estate of Edward Warren decd. was exhibited by John Warren and William Warren Extrs.

Hardy Griffin orphan of Joseph Griffin about 16 years of age bound as an apprentice to Jonathan Rogers to learn the business of a Blacksmith.

Mary Griffin orphan of Joseph Griffin about the age of 13 years bound as an apprentice to William Boyce to learn House Business.

Richard Bond appointed Guardian to Elisha Bond orphan of Demsey Bond decd. He to give Security in the sum of 1000 pds. John B. Walton and David Harrell Securities.

Deed of land Abraham Eason to James Gregory proved by the oath of Thos. Hunter.

August 18, 1789. Tuesday morning.

Present: James Gregory, John Baker, Joseph Riddick, William Baker, Jethro Sumner, Christopher Riddick, Jethro Ballard, Justices.

James Gregory, Joseph Riddick, Jethro Sumner and Josiah Granbery or any three of them to Audit State and Settle the Account of Abraham Sumner Admr. of Jacob Sumner decd. and make report.

Deed of Gift of land Joshua Small to John Small proved by the oath of Jethro Ballard.

Deed of Gift Joshua Small to John Small for Goods & Chattels proved by the oath of Jethro Ballard.

Samuel Harrell Extr. of Thomas Walton decd. exhibited his Accounts with Miles Walton orphan of the decd.

Stephen Copeland orphan of William Copeland decd. came into Court and made choice of Whitson Jones as his Guardian. Whitson Jones to give Security in the sum of 600 pds. William Goodman and Demsey Odom Securities.

Kedar Hinton to be exempt from paying a Tax on a certain Negro

Murriah Dilday daughter of Lettice Dilday about the age of 3 years bound as an apprentice to William Brooks to learn the business of Spinning and Weaving.

Deed of Gift Jethro Benton to Miles Benton proved by the oath of Moses Benton.

James Gregory, David Rice and Joseph Riddick Esqrs. or any two of them to take the private examination of Mary Scott Wife of Joseph Scott of the County of Southampton Virginia for her free consent in his executing a Deed of conveyance made to Josiah Granbery by said Joseph Scott and his Wife Mary.

James Gregory, David Rice and Joseph Riddick Esqrs. or any two of them to take the private examination of Peggy Rice Wife of John Rice of this County her free consent in his executing a Deed of Conveyance to Josiah Granbery.

Thomas Iredell Esqr. State Atto. for this County allowed the sum of 12 pds. for his Services for one year.

The Collector of the Public Tax in this County to be allowed in the settlement of his accounts for the following persons tax as listed in this County: Thomas Trotman, Junr., Andrew Matthews, Samuel Thomas, Evin Jones, Demsey Hinton, Simon Faulk, John Ellis, Wright Ellis, George Lassiter, Sr., David Kelly, Kedar Benton, Elisha Parker, Charles Rooks, Major Phillips, Thomas Green, Robert Wood, Benjamin Eure, Timothy Rogers, Abraham Sumner, Edward Drake, Hezekiah Jones, Josiah Brinkley, James Skinner, James P. Arline, Edward Kelly, Robert Moore, Fullington Speight, Matthew Thomas, Jacob Howard, Benjamin Odom, John Fountain, James Fountain and John Cowpers lands in Virginia.

David Rice Esqr. to be allowed in the settlement with the Public Treasurer for the sum of 5 pds. 10 sh. 4 pc. and half penny in money and 4 pds. 14 sh. and 7 pc. certificates the amount of Richard Mitchells Tax for the year 1787 which was then paid by the Extrs. of James Sumners and also listed by the said Richard Mitchell.

A Sec. Fa. to issue against Luke Sumner to show cause why he did not appear as a Juryman to this Court.

Nov. 16, 1789. Third Monday in Nov.

Present: Thomas Hunter, Christopher Riddick, Jethro Sumner, William Goodman, Justices.

Deed of land James Skinner to Cyprian Cross proved by the oath of John Odom.

Last Will and Testament of Jacob Spivey exhibited by Simon Stalling one of the Extrs. therein appointed and proved by the oath of Thomas White one of the witnesses.

Inventory of the Goods & etc. of the Estate of Jacob Spivey was exhibited by Simon Stallings Extrs.

Deed of Sale Job Umfleet to Israel Beeman proved by the oath of John Parker.

Account of Sales of the Estate of William Boyce decd. exhibited by David Watson Admr.

Accounts of David Watson with the Estate of William Boyce decd. was exhibited.

William Baker, Christopher Riddick and John Baker Esqrs. who were summoned to attend at the Goal of the County to discharge out of Prison John Cuff an insolvent imprisoned Debter made report.

David Cross, Benjamin Barnes, James Landing and William Odom or any three of them to divide the Estate of William Boyce decd.

Inventory of the Goods & etc. of the Estate of Joseph Parker decd. was exhibited by John Robbins, Sr.

Deed of Gift Thomas Green to Hugh and Parnell King proved by the oath of Thomas Piland.

Samuel Phelps an Illegitimate Child Son of Susanna Phelps about the age of 6 years and 3 months bound as an apprentice to Thomas Piland to learn Plantation business.

Account of Sales of the Estate of John Randolph Wilkinson decd. exhibited by Seth Eason Sheriff.

Last Will of Thomas Piland decd. exhibited by Thomas Piland and Willis Piland Extrs. therein appointed and proved by the oaths of William Davidson and William Fryer and David Piland Witnesses.

Deed of Sale Elisha Hiatt to Thomas Hiatt proved by the oath of Henry Goodman.

Deed of Sale Jesse Brown to Robert Parker proved by the oath of Moor Carter.

Deed of Lease John Robbins and James Bennett to Edward Brisco proved by the oath of Robert Taylor.

Deed of Sale Isaac Hunter Sheriff to Moor Carter proved by the oaths of Robert Parker and Edward Gatling.

Bill of Sale Willaby McCoy to John A. Manion proved by the oath of Samuel Cross.

Bill of Sale Jacob Carter (?) to John Atkinson proved by the oath of Hardy Cross.

Bill of Sale John Powell to Eliza. Chansey Mironey proved by the oath of Kedar Ballard.

The Surveyer in complience with Joseph Riddick, David Rice, Thomas Trotman and Samuel Harrell, Freeholders, to lay out the bounds of disputed lands between Thomas Hoffler, Henry Hill and John B. Walton. The said Hill and Hoffler refusing to have their land processioned as they formerly were. And also between John Robbins, Junr. and Thomas Marshall.

James Gregory, Joseph Riddick, Thomas Trotman and Simon Stallings or any three of them Audit State and Settle the Accounts of Charles Rountree with the Estate of Thos. Rountree decd.

Jethro Ballard and Jethro Sumner Esqrs. and Mr. James Norfleet and Bray Gordon Audit State and Settle the Accounts of Judith Wilkinson Admr. of Jas. R. Wilkinson decd.

Thomas Hunter Esqr., Mr. James Freeman, Thomas Trotman and John B. Walton or any three of them to make a division of the Estate of Jacob Spivey decd.

The Sheriff to summon the following persons as Jurymen: James Walton, John B. Walton, Richd. Bond, Thomas Trotman, Amos Trotman, Abraham Hurdle, Aaron Lassiter, Isaac Hunter, Jacob Gordon, Abraham Spivey, Abraham Eason, John Powell, John Darden, Joseph Hase, Henry Forrest, Jesse Benton, Peter Parker, Philip Rogers, Lewis Walters, Micajah Riddick, James Pruden, Thomas Barnes, Benjamin Barnes, David Cross, William Warren, Sr., Abraham Saunders, Elisha Ellis, Charles Eure, William Harriss and Levi Lee.

Tuesday morning. Present: Christopher Riddick, James Gregory, Jethro Sumner, Justices.

David Rice and Joseph Riddick Esqrs. two of the Gentl. who were appointed to take the examination of Ann Granbery Wife of Josiah Granbery reported in the following words: - - - she the said Ann Granbery did Sign, Seal and etc. a certain Deed of Sale for a Certain tract or tracts of land to Josiah Collins - - - the said Ann Granbery did ack. that she the said Ann Granbery did sign, seal and deliver the Deed of Sale to Josiah Collins freely of her own accord without any compulsion or fear of Josiah Granbery, her husband.

James Gregory, Josiah Granbery and David Rice to divide and lay off Milly Riddicks part of her Fathers Estate agreeable to the Will of the decd.

Deed of Sale Clement Hill to James Freeman proved by the oath of James Walton.

The private examination of Judith Morris Wife of William Morris respecting her free concent - - - relinquished her right of Dower in a certain tract of land sold by her husband Wm. Morris to Henry Goodman bearing date the 18th. May 1787.

Deed of Sale Willis Hughes to Thomas Vann proved by the oath of Kedar Odom.

Wednesday morning. Present: Christopher Riddick, James Gregory, William Goodman, William Baker, Justices.

John Odom, David Cross, Henry Goodman and John Bethey attend with the Surveyor to settle the dispute in lines returned by the prosessioners, between Joseph Speight and Benjamin Barnes, and that

James Landing, Demsey Barnes, Jesse Vann and Thomas Barnes also attend with the Surveyor to settle dispute in the lines between James Crafford and Abel Cross, and that Able Cross, Cyprian Cross, Benjamin Barnes and Isaac Langston attend with the Surveyor to the disputed lines between John Gatling and Henry Copeland.

William Bond, Reubin Lassiter, Robert McCullock and Amos Lassiter attend with the Surveyor in settling dispute in lines returned by William Booth and Timothy Lassiter Prosessioners between Aaron Blanshard and Joseph Alphin and that Abraham Spivey, James Costen, Isaac Costen and Job Riddick attend with the Surveyor in settling a dispute in lines of Wm. Lewis and Jonathan Lassiter also that Jonathan Roberts, James Freeman, William Freeman and William Hinton attend the Surveyor in settling disputed lines between the Extrs. of Demsey Bond and Extrs. of Joseph Parker decd.

Henry Forrest, William Cleaves, Humphry Hudgins and Joseph Figg attend with the Surveyor in settling dispute in lines returned by Samuel Smith and Thomas Smith Prosessioners between Isaac Miller and Anthony Matthews and also they settle the dispute between Jeremiah Speight and Timothy Hunter and also they settle the dispute in the lines between Capt. Wm. Harris and Jeremiah Speight. George Williams, James Brown, Robert Parker and Willis Brown attend with the Surveyor to settle a dispute in lines returned by William Brooks and Bond Minshew Prosessioners between Aaron Harrell and James Piland.

William Hunter, James Norfleet, Jacob Gordon and John Riddick attend with the Surveyor in settling the disputes in the following lines: Disputed lines between the Extrs. of Jacob Powell and David Jones and between the Guardian of William Webb and Elisha Benton.

Seth Eason, Jacob Gordon and James Norfleet to divide the lands of Jacob Powell between his sons agreeable to the Will.

John Robins Extr. of Joseph Parker decd. to sell the perishable Estate of the decd. agreeable to the Will.

Willis Brown Goaler to be allowed the sum of 1 pd. 18 sh. 4 pc. for Imprisoning and finding diat for John Cuff an Insolvent Debter.

<u>Third Monday in February, 1790.</u>

Present: Christopher Riddick, John Baker, David Rice, Justices.

Reuben Sparkman appointed Overseer of the Road instead of Asa Harrell resigned.

Deed of land Abram Hill to Kedah Hill proved by the oath of Thomas Hunter.

Deed of land John Harrell & Ux. to Saml. Thomas proved as to John Harrell by William Thomas.

Deed of land Mills Skinner to William Crafford proved by the oath of Demsey Harrell.

Shadrack Ellis to be exempt from the payment of his taxes until he becomes more able to pay them.

Deed of Sale Willis Sparkman to Reuben Sparkman proved by the oath of Jesse Harrell.

Deed of Sale Mary Harrell and Asiah Harrell to Demsey Harrell proved by the oath of David Harrell.

Deed of Sale Elisha Copeland to Watson Stott proved by the oath of James Thorburn (to wit: that the said James Thorburn heard the said Elisha Copeland ack. the signature thereof to be his hand and Seal and that he heard George Sparling a witness ack. that he had assigned the same as witness.

Account of Sales of the Estate of Jacob Spivey decd. exhibited by Simon Stallings Extr.

George Outlaw Guardian to Richard Freeman orphan of Demsey Freeman exhibited his accounts.

John White Guardian to (page torn) Spivey and Sinath Spivey orphans of William Spivey decd. exhibited his account.

Henry Goodman and William Gatling who were appointed to procession the bounds they were appointed to made report.

Bill of Sale for one Feather Bed, one pach Flax and one Trunk and Furniture John Parnell to Aaron Hobbs proved by the oath of Moses Hill.

Moses Hobbs Guardian to William Hobbs and Jesse Hobbs orphans of Guy Hobbs decd. exhibited his accounts.

Samuel Eure Guardian to Nancy Eure orphan of Enos Eure decd. made report.

Joseph Riddick, Thomas Trotman and Simon Stallings who were appointed to audit state and settle the accounts of Moses Hobbs Extr. of Guy Hobbs decd. made report

Deed of Land Henry Delday to Ebron Sears proved by the oath of James Brady Senr.

Deed of Land Jesse Jones & Ux. to Ebron Sears proved by the oath of James Braddy Jr.

Deed of Gift of Land James Brady Senr. to Ebron Sears ackd.

Selah Hill moved for Administration on the Estate of Kedar Hill decd. - granted. She to give Bond in the sum of 5000 pds. Thomas Hunter and Amos Trotman Securities.

Inventory of the Goods & ect. of the Estate of Kedar Hill decd. exhibited by Selah Hill Admr.

Deed of Sale William Williams to James Brown proved by the oath of William Brown.

William Hunter Guardian to Theopholes Hunter orphan of John Hunter decd. made return of his account current.

Jonathan Williams appointed Overseer of the Road instead of Moses Kittrell decd.

Cyprian Cross Guardian to Joseph Smith orphan of James Smith decd. made return of his account current.

Selah Hill appointed Guardian to Docton Bagley, Henry Bagley and Trotman Bagley orphans of Jacob Bagley decd. She to give Security in the sum of 1000 pds. for each with Amos Trotman and Thomas Trotman Securities.

Liddey Spivey Guardian to Jacob Spivey and Sarah Spivey orphans of Thomas Spivey decd. exhibited her accounts current.

Thomas Trotman appointed Guardian to Noah Hill orphan of Kedar Hill decd. He to give Security in the sum of 1000 pds. Joseph Riddick and Amos Trotman Securities.

John Duke to be exempt from the payment of a Tax on a Negro Man, Marcus, belonging to Wm. Edwards Webb he having listed him by mistake.

Deed of Land John Odom & Ux. to Henry Copeland proved by the oath of Jesse Vann.

Deed of Sale Ann Carter to Isaac Carter proved by the oaths of Jesse Vann and William Warren.

Bond - Israel Beeman to James Braddy proved by the oath of Mills Lewis.

Deed of Gift Joshua Small to Mary Gwinn proved by the oath of James Small.

Deed of Gift Joshua Small to Mary Gwin proved by the oath of James Small.

Deed of Sale Edward Brisco to Henry Hill proved by the oath of Willis Parker.

Thomas Hunter, Thomas Trotman, James Freeman and Moses Hill or any three of them to make a division of the Estate of Kedar Hill decd.

Selah Hill Admr. of the Estate of Kedar Hill decd. to sell so much of the perishable Estate of the decd. as will pay his just debts.

Sarah Varden a Mulatto about the age of 9 years bound to Jethro Benton, Junr., to learn to Knitt, Spin and House Business.

Tuesday Feb. 16. Present: Thomas Hunter, James Gregory,

Christopher Riddick, John Baker and David Rice, Justices.

William Goodman Esqr. moved for administration on the Estate of Moses Kittrell decd. - granted. He to give Security in the sum of 4000 pds. John Pipkin and Benjamin Barnes Securities.

Mary Rountree Guardian to Mary Rountree returned her account current.

Inventory of the Goods & etc. of the Estate of Moses Kittrell decd. was exhibited by William Goodman Admr.

William Goodman Admr. of Moses Kittrell decd. to sell so much of the perishable Estate of the decd. as will pay his just debts.

Benjamin Barnes, James Landing and David Cross three Gentm. who were appointed to make a division of the Estate of William Boyce decd. made report.

James Gregory, Jacob Gordon and Samuel Harrell three of the Gentlm. who were appointed to audit, state and settle the accounts of Thomas Hunter and Joseph Riddick Esqrs. Extrs. of Elisha Hunter decd. made report.

Josiah Granbery, James Gregory and Joseph Riddick three of the Gentlm. who were appointed to audit, state and settle the accounts of Abraham Sumner Admr. of Jacob Sumner Jr. decd. made report.

Henry King & Ux Deed of Land to Thomas Smith of Nansemond Co., Virginia proved by the oath of Elisha Cross.

Thomas Hunter, James Freeman and John B. Walton three of the Gentlm. who were appointed to make a division of the Estate of Jacob Spivey decd. made report.

Deed of Land William Boyce to Timothy Lassiter ackd.

Samuel Cross moved for administration on the Estate of William Davidson decd. - granted. He to give Security in the sum of 200 pds. David Cross Security.

Inventory of the Goods & etc. of the Estate of William Davidson decd. was exhibited by Samuel Cross admr.

Inventory of the Goods & etc. of the Estate of Thomas Piland decd. exhibited by Thomas Piland and Willis Piland Admrs.

Samuel Cross Admr. of William Davidson decd. to sell so much of the Estate of the decd. as will pay debts.

William Harris, Henry Forrest, William Cleaves and Joseph Figg to attend with the Surveyor and settle disputed lines between Anthony Matthews and Isaac Miller.

On Petition of Robert McCulloh for building a water Grist Mill across the Ready Branch adjoining his own land on one side and the lands of Maxn. Minshew on the other side. Ordered that Bond Minshew be summoned & etc.

Henry Harrell moved for Administration on the Estate of Jane Hill decd. - granted. He to give Security in the sum of 300 pds. Samuel Harrell and Jesse Spivey Securities.

Inventory of the Goods 7 etc. of the Estate of Jane Hill decd. exhibited by Henry Harrell Admr.

Deed of Land Robert Parker & Ux. to William Boyce. Private Exm. taken by John Pipkin.

Joseph Riddick, Thomas Trotman, Simon Stallings & John B. Walton to make a division of the Estate of Jane Hill decd.

Richard Bond Guardian to John Hill and Elizabeth Hill orphans of Guy Hill decd. exhibited his accounts.

Deed of Land Henry Hill to Edward Brisco proven by the oath of Willis Parker.

Account of Sales of the Estate of Joseph Parker decd. exhibited by John Robbins.

Deed of Land Seth Riddick Shff. to Patrick Hegerty proved by the oath of William Harriss.

Jesse Spivey Guardian to Frederick Blanshard, William Blanshard, Sarah Blanshard and Mary Blanshard orphans of Absolom Blanshard decd. exhibited his accounts.

John B. Walton appointed Guardian to Guy Hill orphan of Kedar Hill decd. He to give Bond of 1000 pds. Thomas Hunter and Richard Bond Securities.

Joseph Riddick, Thomas Trotman and Simon Stallings who were appointed to audit and settle the accounts of Charles Rountree with the Estate of Thomas Rountree decd. made report.

Humphry Hudgins, Henry Forrent, William Cleaves and Timothy Lassiter to attend with the Surveyor to settle the disputed line between William Harriss and Jeremiah Speight.

Wright Wiggins and Illegitimate child of Ruth Wiggins about five years old bound as an apprentice to Noah Felton to learn the Business of a Hatter.

Miles Parker to be exempt from payment of a tax on a Negro Woman Milly she having been subject to fitts.

Seth Riddick late Sheriff is Dead. Seth Eason appointed Sheriff untill May Court next. He to give bond with Jethro Sumner and Edwin Sumner Securities.

Thomas Hurdle appointed Constable in the lower end of Capt. Isaac Hunter's Captaincy.

Wednesday morning.

Thomas Boon orphan of James Boon decd. about 12 years of age bound to Thomas Marshall to learn the Business of a Shoemaker.

Thomas Piland and Willis Piland Extrs. of Thomas Piland decd. to sell so much of the Estate of the decd. as will pay his just debts.

John Baker, Charles Eure, Israel Beeman and George Williams to make a division of the Estate of Thomas Piland decd.

James Baker Sumner appointed Entrytaker of Vacant Lands. He to give Bond with Jethro Sumner and William Walters Securities.

A Tax of 1 shill. 6 pence to be levied on each Poll and a Tax of 6 pence on each Hundred Acres of Land in this County for 1790.

Kedar Ballard, John Powell, James Outlaw and Demsey Barnes to be summoned as Jurymen for the Supr. Court to be held at Edenton on 3 May next.

Israel Beeman, Moses Hill, Samuel Eure, Richard Mitchell, Wm. Crafford, Aaron Hobbs, James Landing, James Norfleet, Abraham Eason, George Williams, Francis Speight, Henry Goodman, John Riddick, William Ellis, William Daughty, Elisha Cross, James Bethey, William Boyce, Richard Briggs, William Hurdle, Amos Lasseter, Henry Harrell, William Matthias, John Weatherly, Solomon King, Job Riddick, Jeremiah Speight, William Cleaves, Jonathan Smith and Demsey Odom to be summoned as Jurymen for next term.

Henry Hall Admr. of Jane Hill decd. to sell as much of her Estate as will pay her debts.

Reuben Riddick to collect the Public and County Tax for the year 1789 in the Company of Capt. Isaac Hunter and that William Walters collect the Tax in the Company of Capt. Jethro Sumner and Capt. Jesse Benton and that Edward Gatling collect the Tax in the Captaincy of Capt. William Goodman and Capt. Charles Eure and that Isaac Miller collect the Tax in the Captaincy of Capt. William Harriss and that James Walton collect the Tax in the Captaincy of Capt. Jonathan Roberts.

William Hunter appointed Guardian to Robert Hill and Whitmell Hill orphans of Kedar Hill, decd. and that he give Bond in the sum of 1000 pds. each. Thomas Hunter and John B. Walton Securities.

Seth Rountree Guardian to Rachel Rountree, Priscilla Rountree and Penny Rountree exhibited his accounts.

Richard Arnold granted administration on the Estate of Henry Hunter Benton. He to give Bond of 2000 pds. Miles Benton and Lewis Walters Securities.

Inventory of the Goods & etc. of Henry Hunter Benton was exhibited by Richard Arnold admr.

Richard Arnold admr. of Henry Hunter Benton to sell so much of the Estate as will pay his debts.

Lawrence Baker Clerk of this Court to be allowed 20 pds. for extra services to this Court for the year passed.

Jonathan Roberts appointed Guardian to Joseph Parker orphan of Joseph Parker decd. He to give bond of 1000 pds. William Booth and Willis Baker Securities.

James Gregory, Joseph Riddick, William Hinton and Thomas Hunter to make a division of the Estate of Docton Riddick decd.

The Road leading over Seth Eason's Mill to be a Public Road and that said Seth Eason to keep the Road in Order without being exempt from working on other Roads.

Abraham Eason, Aaron Lasseter and Abraham Spivey and John Darden fined 5 pds. each for their non attendance as Jurymen.

Thursday. Present Joseph Riddick, John Baker, Justices.

Court Adjourned.

Third Monday in May in the Fourteenth year of American Indenpendence, the Year of Our Lord One Thousand Seven Hundred and Ninety. (May, 1790)

Present: John Baker, William Goodman, Jethro Sumner and Thomas Hunter, Justices.

Deed of Land Thomas Young to Elisha Benton proved by the oath of Mills Benton.

Deed of Land James Cole to John Rochell acknowledged.

Deed of Land Jethro Ballard, David Rice and Timothy Hunter, Extrs. of James Sumner decd. to Joshua Small proved by the oath of James Norfleet.

Deed of Land Henry Copeland to John Odom proved by the oath of Jesse Vann.

Deed of land James Robins, Benjamin Robins, George Bennett and Joseph Bennett to William Lewis and Samuel Harrell proved by the oath of Thomas Mashall who declares he did not see Benjamin Robins sign the said deed but that James Robins signed for him.

Deed of sale John Rochel & Ux. to Matthew Wills acknowledged.

Deed of sale William Green to Stephen Harrell proved by the oaths of John Felton and Thomas Felton.

John Odom, son of William, appointed Overseer of the Road in the room of Abraham Saunders.

William Walters and William Daughtee Processioners have made return of their Proceedings in the District; and returned a line disputed between Noah Felton and William Matthews disputed by Noah Felton. Isaac Miller, Wm. Harriss, Edwin Sumner and Humphry Hudgins to attend with the Surveyor and settle the disputed line.

William Berryman to pay Milley Bowen the sum of 5 pds. per year for the term of 5 years for the Maintenance of a Bastard Child begot on the body of the said Bowen by the said Berryman.

Deed of Gift Isaac Harrell to Noah Harrell proved by the oath of Samuel Harrell.

Deed of Gift Thomas Langston to Luke Langston and Demsey Langston proved by the oath of John Parker.

Deed of Trust Solomon King to David Darden, John Lee and Jethro Sumner proved by the oath of Uriah Odom.

Account of sale of the Estate of Thomas Piland decd. was exhibited by Thomas Piland and Willis Piland Extrs.

Deed of sale of Land Abraham Saunders and Charity Saunders to Jesse Saunders proved by the oath of Bray Saunders.

Leah Riddick and Isaac Hunter granted administration on the Estate of Seth Riddick decd. They to give Bond in the amount of 5000 pds with Joseph Riddick and Christopher Riddick Securities.

Jethro Miller Constable to be allowed 3 pds. 12 shill. for warning the inhabitants of Capt. Jonathan Roberts Captaincy to give a list of Taxables and for services attending this Court six days as Constable.

Joseph Riddick granted the administration on the Estate of Spencer Brinkley decd. He to give Bond of 400 pds. Thomas Hurdle and William Baker Securities.

Seth Eason Guardian to Josiah Rountree orphan of Charles Rountree decd. exhibited his account with said orphan.

Seth Eason, Jacob Gordon and James Norfleet who were appointed to make a division of the Lands of Jacob Powell between his three Sons James Powell, John Powell and Robert Powell viz. James Powell to have the part of the Premisses where he now resides adjoining William Ellis and the main Road that leads from the Folly to Josiah Granbery's. John Powell to have that part whereon the Houses and Orchard stands adjoining the run of the Loosing Swamp and the aforesaid James Powells line. Robert Powell to have the part of the Premisses next to William Ellis adjoining the run of the Loosing Swamp, John Powell's line and James Powell's line.

Deed of land Zadock Hinton and Ux. to Henry Forrest acknowledged. William Baker took the private examination of Leah Hinton who relinquished her right of Dower.

Deed of land Henry Forrest and UX. to Zadock Hinton acknowledged. William Baker examined Anna Forrest who relinquished her right of Dower.

Deed of sale Richard Bond and UX. to Demsey Jones proved by the oath of William Bristow.

Matthias Green to be exempt from the payment of Poll Tax for the year 1789.

Moses Hare Constable to be allowed 48 Shill. for Summoning the inhabitants of the Captaincy of Capt. Jethro Sumner to give a list of Taxables and attending this Court.

Joseph Speight Guardian to the orphans of Solo. Freeman to be exempt from payment of Tax on Negro Girl named Philis belonging to the Orphans of Solomon Freeman decd. for the year 1789.

Richard Arnold Admr. of Henry Hunter Benton returned account of Sales of the said Estate.

William Bond to be exempt from paying Tax on two Taxables which was put down to him through mistake.

Deed of land Miles Benton to Abraham Morgan acknowledged.

William Baker County Trustee returned his Account with this County.

Tuesday morning May 18, 1790

Present: Christopher Riddick, John Baker, Joseph Riddick, James Gregory, David Rice, Justices.

Samuel Harrell and Jacob Gordon who were appointed to Procession the lines of lands on the east side of Edenton Road in Capt. Isaac Hunters Captaincy made report. A line between the Orphans of Mills Riddick and Moses Brigs disputed by said Briggs. Joseph Hurdle, Isaac Hunter, Abraham Harrell and Thos. Hurdle to attend with the Surveyor and settle the dispute.

James Davis Guardian to James Hodges orphan of James Hodges decd. made return of his account.

Account of Sales of the Estate of Kedar Hill decd. was exhibited by Seth Eason on oath.

Account of Sales of the Estate of Moses Kittrell decd. was exhibited by Wm. Goodman Admr.

Deed of land Aaron Lassiter to Isaac Harrell proved by oath of David Rice.

James Gregory exhibited a Bond of Charity Lilly and Joseph Brinkley for maintainance of a Bastard Child.

Henry Lee Admr. of Sarah Drury decd. exhibited his accounts against the said Estate.

A Commission to Issue to the County of Southampton, Virginia to take the private examination of Judith Rochell Wife of John Rochell her free consent in conveying certain Lands by Deed from the said John Rochell and Judith Rochell to Matthew Wills.

Deed of Land Zachariah Menshew to Robert McCollock proved by the oath of Willefred Hocton.

James Walton Taxgatherer in Capt. Jonathan Robert's Captaincy be allowed in the settlement of his account with the County Treasurer the Tax of Clement Hill, Nathaniel Spivey and Richard Ward.

Luke Langston granted the Administration on the Estate of Thomas Langston decd. He to give Bond in the amount of 200 pds. Henry Copeland and John Gatling Securities.

Robert McCullock to have Leave to build a Water Grist Mill across the Ready Branch adjoining on his own land on both sides of the said Branch.

The Entry taker having returned a Caveat Bond wherein Elizabeth Norfleet, in behalf of her Son, Caveated an'Entry No. 21 made by Edward Daughtee for 50 acres of land lying on the Mare Branch. The Sheriff to Summon a Jury and go on the Premisses.

Deed of Gift for Goods & ect. Priscilla Lasseter the Elder to Aaron Blanshard Junr., Abselah Blanshard and Rachel Lasseter proved by the oath of Aaron Blanshard.

The Entry taker returned a Caveat Bond wherein Edward Brisco and Jonathan Roberts Caveated an Entry No. 15 made by Jethro Meltear. The Sheriff to summon a Jury and go on the Premisses.

The Hands of Nathaniel Riddick to work on the new Road where Jacob Gordon is Overseer.

William Booth, James Freeman, William Freeman, William Hinton to attend with the Surveyor to settle a disputed line between the Extrs. of Demsey Bond and Joseph Parker.

Jethro Sumner, Jethro Ballard, Kedar Ballard and James Norfleet made a division of the Estate of Jno. R. Wilkenson.

James Jones of Lewis, to pay to the Wardens of the poor the sum of 12 Shill. for his full Tax for the year 1789.

Joseph Riddick Admr. of the Estate of Spencer Brinkley decd. exhibited the inventory of the Goods & ect. of the decd.

Joseph Riddick Admr. of the Estate of Spencer Brinkley decd. to sell so much of the Estate as will pay his just Debts.

Wednesday morning. Present: Christopher Riddick, John Baker, James Gregory, Jethro Sumner, David Rice, William Goodman, John Pipkin, Justices.

Thomas Hunter elected as Sheriff for the present year. He to give Bond. James Gregory and David Rice Securities.

Philip Lewis and Francis Speight who were appointed by the Wardens of the Poor for the purpose of Processioning the Lands in the District they were appointed to made return.

Lewis Walters to be appointed Overseer of the Road instead of Josiah Benton.

The Following persons to attend this Court next Term as Petit and Grand Jurymen viz. Jonathan Roberts, William Booth, Kedar Hinton, Simon Stallings, Demsey Jones Junr., John B. Walton, James Walton, Willis Parker, James Piland, William Brooks, Willis Brown, Stephen Eure, William Crafford, Isaac Langston, Cyprean Cross, John Odom, William Warren Jr., Abel Cross, James Brady, Ebron Sears, Hillery Willey, Edward Daughty, Jesse Benton, James Bristow, Humphry Hudgins, Miles Benton, Simeon Brinkley, James Small, Robert Riddick and William Harriss.

The following Justices to be appointed to take a list of Taxables and Taxable property in the County viz. James Gregory to take a list in Capt. Isaac Hunters Captaincy. Joseph Riddick in Capt. Jonathan Roberts's Captaincy. David Rice in Capt. Jethro Summers Captaincy. William in the Captaincy where he is Capt. John Pipkin in Capt. Charles Eures Captaincy. Jethro Sumner in Capt. Jesse Benton's Captaincy. Christopher Riddick in Capt. William Harriss' Captaincy.

James Landing, Thomas Barnes and Jesse Vann Freehoulders with the Surveyor Patrick Hegerty who were appointed to settle a disputed line between Abel Cross and James Crafford made report (viz) March 8, 1790. It appeared the disputed land belonged to said Crafford and processioned the same, and whereas Demsey Barnes did not appear agreeable to the above Orders, the contending parties agreed that one should decide the Cause Certified by us. James Landing, Thomas Barnes, Patrick Hegerty, Surv., Jesse Vann.

William Cleaves, William Harriss, Joseph Figg, Freehoulders with Patrick Hegerty Surveyor who were appointed to settle a Dispute between Anthony Matthews and Isaac Miller, made report, viz. April 5, 1790 it was agreed by said Miller and said Matthews to establish a new line between them adjoining William Powells line. Said Miller should pay all Costs. William Cleaves, William Harriss, Joseph (X) Figg, Patrick Hegerty.

Will of Amos Trotman decd. was exhibited by Thomas Trotman Extr. therein appointed and proved by the oath of Thomas Hunter one of the Witnesses.

Inventory of the Goods and etc. of the Estate of Amos Trotman decd. was exhibited by Thomas Trotman Extr.

Thomas Trotman Extr. of Thomas Trotman to sell as much of the Estate as will pay his just debts.

Joseph Reddick, Thomas Trotman and John B. Walton who were appointed to make a Division of the Estate of Jane Hill decd. made report.

David Rice, Samuel Harrell, Thomas Trotman, Joseph Riddick,

Freehoulders and Patrick Hegerty Surveyor who were appointed to
settle disputed lines between John Benbury Walton and Henry Hill
and Thomas Hoffler made report, viz. Henry Hill, John B. Walton
and Thomas Hoffler agreed and settled the Bounds of each themselves, towit, Henry Hill's and John B. Walton's line adjoining
Richard Freeman's Corner and Capt. Blanshard decd. old Pattent
line agreed on. Said Hill to have the Northwestwardly side and
said Walton the Southeasterly side. The said John B. Walton and
Thomas Hoffler agreed to the line adjoining Capt. Blanshard decd.
old Patent line, the School House Branch, William Hintons path
and Miery Branch. Land lying Southeasterly of said line and path
to be to said Hoffler and the land lying Northwesterly of said
line to be to said Walton. March 15, 1790. David Rice, Samuel
Harrell, Thomas Trotman, Jo. Riddick, Patrick Hegerty Surv.

Benjamin Barnes, Cyprean Cross, Isaac Langston Freehoulders and
Patrick Hagerty Surveyor who were appointed to settle disputed
lines between John Gatling and Henry Copeland made report (to
wit) May 14, 1790. Line was Processioned in favour to said
Gatling (to wit) line adjoining Francis Brinkley and said Cope-
land, said Brinkley, Cyprean Cross, John Gatling and Rogers's
Branch. Henry Copeland to pay all Costs. Benjamin Barnes,
Cyprean Cross, Isaac Langston, Patrick Hegerty.

Jacob Gordon, James Norfleet, John Reddick, William Hinton Senr.,
Freehoulders and Patrick Hegarty Surveyor who were appointed to
settle disputed lines between the Estate of Jacob Powell and
David Jones and between the Guardian of William Webb and Elisha
Benton made report (to wit) February 25, 1790 - it appeared to
us that the Land in dispute did belong unto said Powell decd.
and Processioned the line (to wit) adjoining William Ellis,
Moses Hare and said Powell decd. Jacob Gordon, James Norfleet,
John Reddick, William Hinton, Patrick Hegerty. April 27, 1790
the disputed Land between Elisha Benton and William Webb orphan
appeared to belong to said orphan wherefore Elisha Benton and
William Harriss for William Webb agreed between themselves and
line was Processioned. The line adjoining Miles Benton's line
it appearing to be the Bounds of Pughs Patent. Jo. Riddick,
John Riddick, Patrick Hegerty, Surv.

William Walters Constable to be allowed 6 pds. for Services
attending this Court and warning the Inhabitants of Capt.
Bentons Captaincy to give a list of Taxables.

Thursday, May 20, 1790

Present: Christopher Riddick, John Baker, Jethro Sumner, Joseph
Riddick, William Goodman, Justices.

Thomas Finney moved for his Tavern License being Contd. James
Baker Sumner his Security.

Willis Brown Guardian to Nancy Garrett orphan of James Garrett
exhibited his account with said Orphan.

Isaac Benton to be exempt from payment of Tax on two Hundred Acres
Land and one Tithable - his last Taxables being twice intered.

William Ellis to have Licence to keep a Tavern at the Folly in this County. Jethro Sumner his Security.

Edward Gatling Taxgatherer in the District of Capt. William Goodman and Capt. Charles Eure to be allowed in the Settlement of his account with the County Treasurer for the Poll Tax on John Lewis Clozel, Miles Skinner, Joseph Rooks and Charles Carter.

Samuel Harrell Constable to be allowed 4 pds. for his Services to this Court 8 days and two days warning the Inhabitants in Capt. I. Hunters Captaincy to return a list of their Taxable property. Christo. Riddick, Jo. Riddick, Wm. Goodman.

Third Monday in August, 1790.

Present: James Gregory, David Rice, William Goodman, Justices.

The Sheriff of this County to sell as much of the Real Estate of Abraham Sumner to pay and Satisfie a Judgment obtained by Seth Rountree Guardian to the Orphans of Thos. Rountree decd. for 10 pds. 1 shill and 5 pence with Interest from May 23, 1789.

Additional Inventory of the Goods & etc. of the Estate of Amos Trotman decd. was exhibited by Thomas Trotman, Exr.

Account of Sales of part of the Estate of Amos Trotman was exhibited by Thomas Trotman, Extr.

Deed of Sale of Land Benjamin Harrell to William Crafford proved by the oath of Willis Stallings.

Deed of Land John Hunter to Thomas Hunter proved by the oath of Simon Stallings.

Deed of Land Henry Hill and Ux. to John White Acknowledged. Private examination taken by Christo. Reddick.

Deed of Land Joseph Norfleet to Thomas Robertson proved by the oath of Edward Piland.

Emilia Harrell granted Administration on the Estate of Henry Harrell decd. She to give bond in the amount of 800 pds. Samuel Harrell and John B. Walton Securities.

Inventory of the Goods and etc. of the Estate of Henry Harrell decd. exhibited by Emila Harrell Admx.

Emila Harrell Admx. of Henry Harrell to sell so much of the Estate as will pay his Debts.

Division of the Estate of Charles Rountree decd. was exhibited by Thomas Hunter, Seth Eason and Thomas Trotman who were appointed to make said division.

James Gregory and David Rice, Henry Walton and John Hoffler to make a Division of the Estate of Henry Harrell decd.

James Small and John Powell Processioners made report.

Deed of Land John Hunter and Uxor to William Hunter proved by the oath of Riddick Trotman.

Deed of Gift William Powell to Micajah Riddick proved by the oath of Noah Felton.

Deed of Land Luke Sumner to William Ellis Acknowledged.

Deed of Sale Humphry Hudgins to Easther Matthews Acknowledged.

Deed of Land Samuel Green to David Lewis Acknowledged.

Inventory of the Goods & etc. of the Estate of Thomas Langston decd. was exhibited by Luke Langston Admr.

Deed of Land Thomas Hunter to John Hoffler proved by the oath of Samuel Smith.

Noah Harrell appointed Overseer of the Road instead of Timothy Lassiter.

Deed of Land Seth Eason Sheriff to William Freeman Acknowledged.

Inventory of the Goods & etc. of the Estate of Seth Riddick decd. exhibited by Isaac Hunter one of the Admrs.

Benjamin Gordon to be exempt from paying a Poll Tax on a Negro Woman Rose she being away.

John Walton orphan of Thomas Walton about the age of 11 years to be bound to Americas Blanshard to learn the business of a Cooper.

The Lands of Abraham Sumner to be sold at Public Sale to pay a Judgment obtained against him by Joseph Riddick returned by Thos. Hurdle Constable.

Seth Eason late Sheriff of this County to be allowed 20 lbs. for extra Services for the year passed.

James Outlaw and Aaron Hobbs Processioners made report wherein they returned a disputed line between William Hurdle and Jacob Eason, Jacob Eason refusing to have the line processioned. The Surveyor with William Kelly, Mordicai Perry and Seth Rountree, and Simon Stallings Freehoulders attend on the premisses and settle the disputed lines.

John Powell and James Small who were appointed to Procession the lands in certain bounds made report.

William Goodman and Jethro Sumner who were appointed to take Lists of Taxables and Taxable Property in Capt. William Goodman's and Capt. Jesse Benton's Captaincy made report.

Tuesday, Aug. 17, 1790.

Present: Christopher Riddick, David Rice, Joseph Riddick, John Baker, Justices.

Isaac Hinton, Miles Benton, John B. Walton and Micajah Riddick, Junr. to be summoned to attend at Edenton as Jurymen for the Superior Court to be held Nov. 3 next.

Christopher Riddick who was appointed to take a list of Taxables in Capt. William Harriss' Captaincy made report.

The Sheriff returned the panel of a Jury with the Verdict in a Certain Caveat made by Elizabeth Norfleet in behalf of her Son against an Entry of Edward Daughty. It appears that part of the Entry made by said Daughty is Vacant. The said Daughty to pay the Cost & etc. July 26, 1790. K. Ballard, Edwin Sumner, James Smith, Moses Davis, Henry Griffin, Moses Hines, James Jones, Jeremiah Speight, Demsey Odom, Moses Boyce, Robert Riddick, William Ellis. Thomas Hunter, Shff.

Jonathan Roberts, Thomas Marshal, Wm. Booth and William Lewis to Audit and Settle the Accounts of Kedah Hinton Admr. of the Estate of Richard Freeman decd.

The following persons to attend this Court next Term as Jurymen viz. Job Riddick, Isaac Costin, Jacob Eason, Moses Hill, William Hunter, Abraham Eason, Henry Hobbs, John Powell, Thos. Parker, William Arnold, Alexander Eason, Seth Eason, Joshua Small, William Ellis, George Williams, Aaron Harrell, Jr., Asa Harrell, Samuel Eure, Israel Beeman, David Lewis, Thomas Marshall, Willis Parker, William Boyce, Demsey Odom, Henry Goodman, John Gatling, Jeremiah Speight, William Odom, William Warren, Senr., and Cyprian Cross.

Joseph Riddick who was appointed to take a list of Taxables in Capt. Jonathan Roberts' Captaincy made report.

John Pipkin and David Rice who were appointed to take the List of Taxables in Capt. Charles Eure and Capt. Jethro Sumner's Captaincy made return.

Thomas Hunter, James Gregory and Simon Stallings who were appointed to Audit State and Settle the Accounts of Mary Rountree Admrx. and John Rountree and James Norfleet Admrs. of Charles Rountree decd. made report.

Robert McCullock, William Bond, Amos Lassiter, Reuben Lassiter, Freehoulders and Patrick Hegerty, Surveyor, who were appointed to settle a dispute in lines returned by the Prosessioners made report as follows (to wit) Feb. 24, 1790. The disputed line between Joseph Alphin and Aaron Blanshard was prosessioned in behalf of said Blanshard. Said line joined Reuben Lassiter's corner. Robert McCullock, William Bond, Amos Lassiter, Reubin Lassiter, Patrick Hegerty, Surv.

August 16, 1790.

This may certify that the Subscribers to the above proceedings have this day made oath that the above report is their opinion as there stated. Joseph Riddick, JP.

Henry Forrest, William Cleaves, Humphry Hudgins and Timothy Lassiter with Patrick Hegerty Surveyor who were appointed to settle disputed lines between Jeremiah Speight and William Harris made report (to wit) August 10, 1790. It appeared unto us that the land in dispute did belong to said Speight and processioned the line accordingly. Henry Forrest, William Cleaves, Humphry Hudgins, Timothy Lassiter, Patrick Hegerty, Surv.

William Harris, Edwin Sumner, Humphry Hudgins and Isaac Miller, Freehoulders with Patrick Hegerty Surveyor, who were appointed to settle a disputed line between Noah Felton and William Matthews made report (to wit) August 4, 1790. It appeared that the land in dispute did belong to said Matthews and processioned the line which joined Moses Kittrell and Samuel Baker. William Harris, Edwin Sumner, Humphrey Hudgins, Isaac Miller, Patrick Hagerty, Sur.

Benjamin Gordon appointed Entry Taker instead of James B. Sumner, resigned.

On the Petition of the Inhabitants of the Fort Island and Inhabitants that live adjacant thereto the Sheriff Summons a Jury and lay off a Public Road from the main road that leads to Winton from Law. Bakers Mill and thence by Israel Beemans and John Eures to the Cypress Bridge near Samuel Taylors from thence along by Elisha Harrells to the Fort Island Bridge across the Bridge and the most convenient way from thence to Cuba Swamp across the said Swamp to the Lower end of Cuba Island and that the Hands that work on the Road under William Crafford, David Lewis and Reuben Sparkman assist in cuting open and clearing the said Road to the Cuba Swamp and Israel Beeman be appointed Overseer.

William Baker, Christopher Riddick and Lawrence Baker who were appointed to Audit State and Settle the accounts of William Harvy (?) Admr. of Docton Riddick decd. in right of his Wife made report.

William Goodman, John Pipkin, Francis Speight and Jesse Vann made a Division of the Estate of John Lewis decd.

The Road that leads from Bennetts Creek near Capt. Harriss's to the Main Road that leads by Jethro Benton Senr. to remain as it is at this time opened.

Lawrence Baker, Micajah Riddick, Robert Parker, Senr., and Christopher Riddick made a Division of the Estate of Seth Riddick decd.

The Admrx. and Admr. of the Estate of Seth Riddick decd. to sell all the personal Estate of the Orphans of said deceased except Negroes and Silver Plate.

James Brady, Israel Beeman, John Pipkin and Cyprian Cross to Audit State and Settle the accounts of Kedar Odom Admr. of Sarah Odom decd.

Wednesday Morning. Present: Joseph Riddick, Christopher Riddick, William Goodman, Justices.

William Walters appointed Deputy Sheriff of this County.

Josiah Granbery, David Rice, James Baker and Thomas Hunter to Audit State and Settle the Accounts of James Gregory Admr. of John Gregory decd.

Nelson Burket a Molatto Child son of Elizabeth Burket about five years of age bound to Edward Brisco to learn the Business of a Shoemaker. Signed: Christo. Riddick, James Gregory, Jo. Reddick.

Third Monday in November 1790.

Present: William Baker, Jethro Ballard, William Goodman, Justices.

Deed of Gift Solomon King to Martha Sumner proved by the oath of David Darden.

Deed of Trust Solomon King, Abigal Volentine and Joseph Voluntine to David Darden, John Lee and Jethro Sumner proved by the oath of Isaac Weatherly.

The Will of Joshua Small decd. was exhibited by James Small and Jacob Gordon Extrs. therein appointed and was proved by the oaths of Jacob Gordon and William Ellis witnesses.

The Inventory of the Goods & etc. of the Estate of Joshua Small decd. was exhibited by James Small and Jacob Gordon Extrs.

Deed of Land William Ellis & Uxor to William Hinton acknowledged.

Deed of Land Alse Owens to Henry Goodman proved by the oath of William Gatling.

Deed of Land Luke Sumner to Jethro Ballard proved by the oath of William Ellis.

Deed of Land Thomas Robertson & Uxor. to John Parker proved by the oath of Cyprean Cross.

John Pipkin, Israel Beeman, James Brady and Cyprean Cross who were appointed to Audit State and Settle the Amounts of Kedar Odom Admr. of Sarah Odom decd. made report.

Lewis g.parkman and William Ritter who were appointed to procession the Lands in the Fort Island retruned a disputed line between Samuel Eure Guardian to Nancy Eure orphan of Enos Eure decd. and Henry Goodman. John Odom, Cyrpean Cross, Jesse Vann and Philip Lewis with Patrick Hagarty Surveyor to settle the disputed lines.

Deed of Land Job Umfleet to Stephen Eure Acknowledged.

Deed of Land Demsey Phelps to Henry Forrest proved by the oath of Ephraim Morris.

John Warren and William Warren Extrs. of Alexander Carter decd. to sell the perishable Estate of the decd. in order to make a division.

Philip Lewis, Benjamin Barnes, Francis Speight and John Odom made a division of the Estate of Alexander Carter decd.

Thomas Hunter, Joseph Riddick, Thomas Trotman and John B. Walton to Audit State and Settle the Accounts of Selah Hill Admr. of Kedar Hill decd.

Chanady Curle orphan of Richard Curle decd. about fifteen years of age to be bound to Demsey Langston to learn the business of a Hatter.

Hardy Eason orphan of William Eason deceased made choice of Frederick Eason as his Guardian. Said Frederick Eason to give Bond of 500 lbs. with Moses Briggs and Abraham Hurdle Securities.

Solomon Eason orphan of William Eason decd. made choice of Frederick Eason as his Guardian. Said Frederick Eason to give Bond of 500 lbs. with Moses Briggs and Abraham Hurdle as Securities.

Tuesday, Nove. 16.

Present: Jethro Ballard, David Rice, William Goodman, Justices.

James Jones Admr. of Jonathan Boyce decd. to sell the perishable Estate of the decd.

John Odom, Jesse Vann, Benjamin Barnes and Henry Copeland to make a Division of the Estate of Jonathan Boyce decd.

Humphry Hudgins to be appointed Constable in the stead of Isaac Miller resigned.

Joseph Delday to be appointed Guardian to Jesse Odom and Jacob Odon Orphans of Elisha Odom. Said Delday to give Bond of 500 lbs. with Thomas Vann and Edward Gatling Securities.

Deed of Land Watson Stott to Luke Sumner proved by the oath of Jethro Ballard.

Deed of Land Isaac Hunter to Samuel Harrell proved by the oath of William Harriss and Benjamin Gordon.

Richard Baker vs Lewis Walters on the Case. Jury Empannelled as follows: William Ellis, Job Riddick, William Harriss, Jeremiah Speight, John Gatling, Thomas Marshall, Thomas Parker, Isaac Costen, Moses Hill, William Hunter, Abraham Eason and Willis Brown.

Leah Riddick appointed Guardian to Julia Riddick, Sarah Riddick and Elizabeth Riddick minor orphans of Seth Riddick decd. She to give Bond of 3000 lbs. with William Baker and Isaac Hunter Securities.

Isaac Hunter appointed Guardian to John Hunter Reddick minor orphan of Seth Riddick decd. Said Hunter to give Bond of 3000 lbs. with Benjamin Gordon and Thomas Parker Securities.

Josiah Granbery, Jethro Ballard, David Rice and James Gregory made a Division of the Estate of Mills Riddick decd.

Joseph Reddick, Thomas Trotman, Simon Stallings and Joseph Hurdle made a Division of the Estate of John Hobbs decd.

Thomas Iredell Attorney for this State in this County allowed 1200 lbs. for his services from August Term 1789 to August Term, 1790.

Samuel Smith Coroner of this County allowed 1 lb. 12 shill. for taking Inquisition on the Body of a Child born of Milley Beasly and summoning a Jury.

Wednesday Nov. 16, 1790.

Present: William Baker, David Rice, William Goodman, Justices.

Jeremiah Benton granted Administration on the Estate of Samuel Benton decd. He to give Bond of 400 lbs. with Samuel Smith and Demsey Odom Securities.

Thomas Parker granted the Administration on the Estate of Elizabeth Norfleet decd. He to give Bond of 2000 lbs. with William Harriss and William Ellis Securities.

Jeremiah Benton Admr. of the Estate of Samuel Benton decd. to sell the Estate of the decd.

Thomas Parker Admr. of the Estate of Elizabeth Norfleet decd. to sell so much of the Estate for ready money as will pay a Judgment obtained against the said decd. by the Extrs. of James Sumner and he to sell as much of the balance of the said Estate as will pay debts.

Abel Cross, David Cross, Thomas Barnes, William Warren, Junr., Henry Lee, Jonathan Rogers, Elisha Cross, Hillory Willey, Enos Rogers, Jesse Benton, Kedar Parker, Isaac Langston, John Parker Gatling, Mills Lewis, Bond Menshew, William Cleaves, Michael Lawrence, William Brooks, Kedar Ballard, John Riddick, Richard Briggs, Robert Riddick, Timothy Lassiter, Abraham Hurdle, Reuben Riddick, Simon Stallings, James Freeman, Henry Forrist, James Piland and James Walker summoned as Jurymen.

Thomas Marshall, Jonathan Roberts and William Booth who were appointed to Audit State and Settle the Accounts of Kedar Hinton Admr. of Richard Freeman made report. (this all marked out.)

Isam Curle an illegitimate child about Eight years of age bound to David Watson to learn the business of a Planter or Farmer.

The Sheriff returned the pannel of a Jury with the verdict for the purpose of laying off a New Road from the Road that leads to Winton to the Cuba Swamp. Elisha Harrell, Mills Eure, Elisha Ellis, Levi Lee, Edward Lee, John Eure, Elijah Harrell, John Harrell, Frederick Farrow, William Ritter, Claiborn Ostin, Eli Morriss, Noah Morriss, Hezekiah Jones, Samuel Harrell, Peter Harrell, Isaac Green, Samuel Taylor, Stephen Eure, Blake Eure, Jesse Taylor, Thomas Norris, Samuel Green, Willis Sparkman, Nathan Cullins and Thomas Cullins to work on the said New Road under Israil Beeman Overseer.

Petition of Elizabeth Harvey who was the widow or Relict of Docton Riddick decd. A Jury to be summoned to Lay off the Dower of the said Petitioner.

Moses Hare appointed Overseer of the Road instead of Jethro Benton, Junr.

Third Monday in Feb. 1791.

Present: James Gregory, David Rice, William Goodman, Justices.

Deed of Land John Wallis to David Cross proved by the oath of Cyprian Cross.

Inventory of the Estate of Elizabeth Norfleet decd. was exhibited by Thomas Parker Admr. on oath.

Deed of Land James Arline to Robert Napper proved by oaths of James Russel and Mills Odom.

Deed of Land Abraham Eason and Thos. Hunter Shff. to Joseph Hurdle proved by the oath of Abraham Hurdle.

Will of Edward Daughtee decd. was exhibited by William Daughtee Extr. therein appointed and proved by the oath of Edwin Sumner one of the Witnesses.

Inventory of the Estate of Edward Daughtee decd. was exhibited by William Daughtee Extr. on oath.

Deed of Sale David Goodman to Isaac Darden proved by the oath of Hy. Goodman.

Deed of Land James Brown to Miles Parker proved by the oath of Lewis Sparkman.

Will of Benjamin Berriman decd. was exhibited by William Berriman Etr. therein appointed and was proved by the oaths of Joseph Riddick and Orson Nixon Witnesses.

Inventory of the Goods & etc. of the Estate of Benjamin Berriman was exhibited by William Berriman on oath.

Deed of Land Ebron Sears to Henry Dilday proved by the oath of James Brady.

George Outlaw Guardian to Richard Freeman Orphan of Demsey Freeman decd. returned his Account Current with said Orphan.

John White Guardian to Seth Spivey and Smith Spivey Orphans of William Spivey decd. exhibited his Account Current with said Orphans.

Deed of Land Joseph Riddick to James Baker proved by the oath of Jethro Meltear.

Deed of Land Randal Moor to Abel Cross proved by the oath of Henry Goodman.

Deed of Land Zacharia Copeland and William Faulk to Abel Cross proved by the oath of James Rawls.

Deed of Land Jesse Saunders to Henry and Zacharia Copeland Acknowledged.

Inventory of the Goods & etc. of the Estate of Samuel Benton decd. was exhibited by Jeremiah Benton Admr.

Account of Sales of the Estate of Samuel Benton decd. was exhibited by Jeremiah Benton on oath.

Deed of Sale William Wallis to John Wallis Acknowledged.

Deed of Land Moses Jones to William Wallis proved by oath of Cyprean Cross.

Deed of Land Robert McCullock to Jethro Meltear proved by the oath of William Gooden.

The Will of Saml. Williams decd. was exhibited by Samuel Williams and Halan Williams Extrs. therein appointed and proved by the oath of Jonathan Williams one of the Witnesses.

James Russel granted Administration on the Estate of George Russel decd. He to give Bond of 150 lbs. with Demsey Odom and Abel Cross Securities.

Inventory of the Goods & etc. of the Estate of George Russel decd. was exhibited by James Russell Admr.

James Russel Admr. of George Russel decd. to sell as much of the Estate of the deceased as will pay his Debts.

William Goodman, Elisha Cross, Jonathan Rogers and Enos Rogers made a Division of the Estate of George Russell decd.

James Small granted Administration on the Estate of Daniel Gwinn decd. He to give Bond of 600 lbs. with Jethro Ballard and James Norfleet Securities.

Inventory of the Goods & etc. of the Estate of Daniel Gwinn decd. was exhibited by James Small Admr.

James Davis Guardian to James Hodges exhibited his Account Current with the said Orphan.

James Small Admr. of Daniel Gwinn decd. to sell so much of the Estate as will pay his Debts.

Jethro Ballard, Kedar Ballard, James Norfleet and Seth Eason to make a Division of the Estate of Daniel Gwinn decd.

Susanna Baker granted Administration on the Estate of Samuel Baker decd. She to give Bond of 3000 lb.s with Jonathan Williams and Patrick Hegarty Securities.

Susanna Baker Admrx. of Samuel Baker decd. to sell so much of the Estate of the decd. as will pay his Debts.

Inventory of the Goods & etc. of the Estate of Samuel Baker decd. was exhibited by Susanna Baker Admrx. on oath.

Jethro Ballard, James Norfleet, Benjamin Gordon, William Ellis to make a Division of the Estate of Joshua Small decd.

The Will of Isaac Benton decd. was exhibited by David Benton and Benton Jones Extrs. therein appointed and was proved by the oath of Miles Benton one of the Witnesses.

Jethro Sumner, Edwin Sumner, Micajah Riddick and Jesse Benton to make a Division of the Estate of Samuel Baker decd.

Inventory of the Goods & etc. of the Estate of Isaac Benton decd. was exhibited by David Benton and Benton Jones Extrs.

Deed of Land Lewis Jones to Hugh Griffin proved by oath of Robert Riddick.

Deed of Land Moses Hare Senior to Elisha Hare proved by the oath of William Arnold.

Jethro Sumner, Jethro Ballard, Kedar Ballard and William Arnold to make a Division of the Estate of Elizabeth Norfleet decd.

Lidia Spivey Guardian to Jacob Spivey and Sallah Spivey Orphans of Thomas Spivey decd. returned her Account Current with said Orphans.

Mary Rountree Guardian to Mary Rountree Orphan of Charles Rountree decd. exhibited her account current with said Orphan.

Samuel Harrell Guardian to Thomas Walton, John Walton, Milicent Walton, Emelia Walton and William Walton Orphans of Thomas Walton decd. exhibited his Account Current with said Orphans.

Deed of Land Pasco Turner Extr. of the Revd. John Reed to Henry Goodman proved by the oath of Jonathan Roberts.

William Hunter Guardian to Theopholus Hunter Orphan of John Hunter decd. exhibited his Account Current with said Orphan.

Moses Hill Guardian of Miles Hill Orphan of Kedar Hill decd. exhibited his Account Current with said Orphan.

Moses Hobbs Guardian to William Hobbs and Jesse Hobbs Orphans of Guy Hobbs decd. exhibited his Account.

Jethro Sumner, Kedar Ballard, Miles Benton and Thomas Parker made a Division of the Estate of Isaac Benton decd.

Tuesday morning. Present: David Rice, Jethro Ballard and John Sumner, Justices.

John Gatling Guardian to John Rogers, William Rogers and Priscilla Rogers Orphans of Stephen Rogers decd. exhibited his Accounts Current.

Samuel Hobbs Orphan of John Hobbs, Junr. decd. made choice of George Eason, Junr. as his Guardian. The said George Eason to give Bond of 350 pds. with Ostin Nixon and Jacob Eason Securities.

Thomas Trotman, Thomas Hunter and Moses Hill who were appointed to make a Division of the Estate of Kedar Hill decd. made report.

William Volentine appointed Guardian to Miles Hill and Sally Hill Orphans of Kedar Hill decd. He to give Bond of 1000 pds. with William Harriss and Simon Stallings Securities.

The Will of William Gatling the Elder decd. was exhibited by John Gatling one of the Extrs. therein appointed and was proved by the oaths of Joseph Speight and Henry Speight two of the Witnesses.

Inventory of the Goods and Etc. of the Estate of William Gatling decd. (the Elder) was exhibited by John Gatling Extr.

Marriage Articles between Rachal Moor and Thomas Trotman to Stasky Sharp proved by the oath of Wm. Moore one of the Witnesses.

Thomas Trotman Guardian to Noah Hill orphan of Kedar Hill decd. exhibited his Account Current with the said Orphan.

William Goodman, Henry Goodman, Francis Speight and Isaac Pipkin to make a Division of the Estate of William Gatling the Elder decd.

Account of Sales of the Estate of Alexander Carter decd. was exhibited by John Warren and William Warren Extrs.

William Volentine Guardian to Docton Bagley, Henry Bagley and Trotman Bagley Orphans of Jacob Bagley decd. and Sally Hill Orphan of Kedar Hill decd. exhibited his Accounts Current. The Accounts of the said Docton and Henry Bagley are balanced and a balance due Trotman Bagley and Sally Hill.

The Sheriff to Summons a Jury and lay off the dower of Leah Riddick Relict of Seth Riddick decd.

Joseph Delday Guardian to Jacob Odom and Jesse Odom orphans of Elisha Odom decd. exhibted his Account with said Orphans.

Joseph Riddick, Thomas Trotman, John B. Walton and James Walton to Audit State and Settle the Accounts of Simon Stallings Extr. of Jacob Spivey decd.

Deed of Gift Joseph Riddick to Reuben Riddick acknowledged.

Jesse Spivey Guardian to Frederick Blanshard, William Blanshard, Sarah Blanshard and Mary Blanshard Orphans of Absolom Blanshard decd. exhibited his Account Current with said Orphans.

County Trustee to pay Samuel Smith Coroner 8 pds. for his services taking Inquisition on the Body of Patrick Kelly.

Jonathan Roberts, William Lewis and Thomas Marshal and John B. Walton to Audit State and Settle the Accounts of John Robbins Extr. of Joseph Parker decd.

William Lassiter son of Michel Lassiter about thirteen years of age bound to Timothy Lassiter to learn the business of a Cooper.

Joseph Riddick, Thomas Hunter, Thomas Trotman and John B. Walton who were appointed to Audit State and Settle the Accounts of the Admr. of Kedar Hill decd. made report.

Joel Williams Orphan of Isaac Williams of Bertie County about Fifteen years of age in August Last bound to Richard Baker to learn the business of House Carpenter.

Wed. morning, 23 Feby. 1791.

Present: James Gregory, David Rice, William Baker, Simon Stallings, Justices.

Account of sales of the Estate of Spencer Brinkley decd. was exhibited by Joseph Riddick Admr.

Deed of Land Abraham Sumner to Joseph Riddick proved by the oath of Reuben Riddick.

William Brooks appointed Overseer of the Road instead of Thomas Finney resigned.

James Hodges made choice of William Lewis to be his Guardian. Said Lewis to give Bond of 600 pds. with William Harriss and Samuel Harrell Securities.

Richard Bond Guardian to Elisha Bond Orphan of Demsey Bond decd. exhibited his Account Current with said Orphan.

James Rawls granted Administration on the Estate of William Booth decd. He to give Bond of 1000 pds. with Demsey Odom and Elisha Cross Securities.

Inventory of the Estate of William Booth decd. was exhibited by James Rawls Admr.

James Rawls Admr. of William Booth decd. to sell all the perishable Estate of the deceased Negros excepted for the payment of Debts and for the benefit of the Orphans.

The following persons to attend this Court next term as Jurymen (to wit) John Arnold, James Pruden, Abraham Morgan, Robert Parker (of Demsey), Henry Goodman, John Vann, Demsey Barnes, Stephen Eure, Isaac Miller, William Warren, Willis Parker, Charles Eure, Demsey Langston, Jesse Vann, Moses Hill, Richd. Bond, David Lewis, Demsey Jones Virga., James Freeman, Richard Mitchell, Isaac Costen, William Goodman, Zacharias Minshew, Kedar Hilton, John Powell, Alexander Eason, Abraham Hurdle, Aaron Hobbs, Jeremiah Speight and Robert Parker, Junr.

The following persons to attend as Jurymen at the next Supr. Court to be held for the District of Edenton at Edenton the 6th. day of April next (to wit) Edwin Sumner, James Walton, James Small and Cyprean Cross.

The following persons to gather or Collect the Public and County Tax (to wit) James Walton in Capt. Robert's District, Samuel

Harrell in Capt. Isaac Hunter's Captaincy, John Riddick in Capt. Jethro Sumner's Captaincy, Humphry Hudgins in Capt. Wm. Harriss's and Capt. Bentons Captaincys, and that Edward Gatling to collect the Tax in Capt. William Goodman's and Capt. Charles Eure's Captaincy.

A Tax of one Shilling and Six pence on each Poll and Six pence on each hundred Acres Land be Levied for County Tax.

Francis Speight, Henry Speight, Phillip Lewis and Miles Benton made a Division of the Estate of Henry Benton decd.

Isaac Costen and James Costen, Jr. appointed Guardian to Thomas Costen, Nathaniel Costen, Benjamin Costen, Demsey Costen and Polly Costen. They to give Bond of 1000 pds. with William Gordon and Timothy Lassiter Securities.

Jethro Sumner, Edwin Sumner, William Daughtee and William Walters to Audit State and Settle the accounts of Jeremiah Benton Admr. of Samuel Benton decd. and make a Division of the Estate of the decd.

John B. Walton Guardian to Guy Hill Orphan of Kedar Hill decd. exhibited his Account Current with said Orphan.

Willis Brown Guarian to Nancy Garrett Orphan of James Garrett decd. exhibited his account current with said Orphan.

Bill of Sale for a Negro Woman named Cherry and Child named Patt from Josiah Rogerson to Noah Felton proved by the oath of Shadrack Felton.

Thomas Marshall, Wm. Lewis and Jonathan Roberts who were appointed to Audit and Settle the Accounts of Kedar Hinton Admr. of Richard Freeman decd. made report.

William Harriss appointed Overseer of the Road instead of Humphry Hudgins resigned.

William Goodman, Jesse Vann and Francis Speight who were appointed to make a Division of the Estate of John Lewis decd. made report.

Richard Bond Guardian to John Hill and Elizabeth Hill Orphans of Guy Hill decd. exhibited his Account Current with said Orphans.

James Robbins an Indian Boy about Eleven Years of age bound to William Gordon to learn the business of Turner.

Mills Ellis granted Administration of the Estate of James Ellis decd. He to give Bond of 100 pds. with Moses Hare and David Rice Securities.

Inventory of the Goods & etc. of the Estate of James Ellis decd. was exhibited by Mills Ellis Admr.

Lawrence Baker Clerk of this Court allowed 20 pds. for Extra services for the year passes.

Mills Ellis Admr. of James Ellis decd. to sell so much of the Estate of the decd. as will pay his debts.

Thomas Hurdle, Abraham Hurdle, Joseph Riddick and Thomas Trotman made a Division of the Estate of Benjamin Berriman decd.

The Executor of Benjamin Berriman to sell perishable part of the Legacy given Benjn. Bennett by the said Benjamin Berriman.

Third Mon. in May, 1791.

Present: Christopher Riddick, James Gregory, David Rice, Justices.

Jonathan Williams and Demsey Williams two of the Gentlemen who were appointed to make the Division of the Estate of Arthur Willey decd. made report.

Deed of Land Josiah Lassiter to Samuel Harrell proved by the oath of Joseph Riddick.

Account Current by James Brady with Estate of Arthur Willey decd. was exhibited by the said James Brady Extr.

William Ellis appointed Overseer of the Road instead of James Small resigned.

Thomas Trotman, Thomas Hurdle and Joseph Reddick who were appointed to make a Division of the Estate of Benjamin Berriman decd. made report.

Deed of Land Luke Sumner to John Powell proved by the oath of Jethro Ballard.

Deed of Sale William Freeman & Ux. to Daniel Eure proved by the oath of Moses Blanshard.

Easther Hall granted Administration of the Estate of John Hall decd. She go give Bond of 200 pds. with Ebron Sears and Willis Hewes as Securities.

Inventory of the Goods & etc. of the Estate of John Hall decd. was exhibited by Easther Hall Admx.

Thomas Piland a very Lame Infirm Man to be exempt from payment of a Poll Tax for the year 1790.

Deed of Sale Cadar Raby & Ux. to Samuel Rabey proved by the oath of John Powell.

Deed of Land John Pipkin & Ux. to Isaac Pipkin proved by the oath of Isaac Pipkin Junr.

Charity Piland granted Administration on the Estate of Peter Piland decd. She to give Bond of 200 pds. with Ebron Sears and William Polson Securities.

Inventory of the Goods and Etc. of the Estate of Peter Piland decd. was exhibited by Charity Piland Admx.

Bill of Sale for a Negro Woman named Philes- James Bristow to William Daughtee proved by the oath of William Boyce.

Bill of Sale from Josiah Collins and Josiah Granbery for a Negro Boy named Jim to Moses Davis acknowledged by Josiah Granbery.

William Daughtee Extr. of Edward Daughtee decd. exhibited Account of sales of the decd. Estate.

An agreement between William King and Joseph Speight proved by the oath of Thomas Hunter.

Account of sale of the Estate of Isaac Benton decd. was exhibited by David Benton Extr.

Deed of Land Wright Hayes and Ux. to William Hayes acknowledged by said Wright Hayes.

The Will of Robert Taylor was exhibited by Elisha Perry and Ephraim Morris and James Freeman Extrs. therein appointed by the oath of Demsey Phelps one of the Witnesses thereto.

Inventory of the Goods & etc. of the Estate of Robert Taylor decd. was exhibited by Elisha Perry, Ephraim Morris and James Freeman.

Petition of Susanna Baker Relict of Samuel Baker decd., the Sheriff to summon a Jury and lay off the Dower of the Petitioner.

Bill of Sale for a Negro Girl Philis. George Eason, John Eason and Isaac Eason to Isaac Langston proved by the oath of Lawrence Baker.

Deed of Land Solo. King & Ux. to John Gatling proved by the oath of Edward Gatling and William Warren.

Thomas Hurdle Constable allowed 24 Shill. for his Services 3 days warning Inhabitants in Capt. Isaac Hunter's Captaincy to give list of Taxables.

Inventory of the Goods & etc. of the Estate of Samuel Williams Sen. decd. was exhibited by Samuel Williams, Jr., Extr.

James Freeman, William Hinton, Jonathan Roberts and Henry Forrest to make a Division of the lands of Henry Hill decd.

A Road leading from the Court House of this County to the Honey Pott Bridge as the path now goes by Robert Parkers to be layed out by a Jury.

Kinchen Norfleet about Sixteen years of age bound to William Lewis to learn the business of a House Carpenter and Joiner.

Cyprean Cross appointed Guardian to Parthena Boyce and Jonathan Boyce Orphans of Jonathan Boyce decd. He to give Bond of 500 pds.

with Aaron Ellis and Henry Goodman Securities.

Thomas Parker appointed Guardian to Kinchen Norfleet Orphan of Jacob Norfleet decd. He to give Bond of 1000 pds. with Jethro Ballard and Abraham Morgan Securities.

Deed of Land Abraham Sumner to Jethro Ballard proved by the oath of Miles Benton.

Moses Hare Constable to be allowed 2 pds. 8 Shill. for Summoning the Inhabitants of Capt. Jethro Sumner's Captaincy to return a list of Taxables for the two last years.

Joseph Speight Guardian to the Orphans of Solomon Freeman decd. to be exempt from payment of a Tax on a Negro Girl who is very infirm.

Elizabeth Kittrell appointed Guardian to John Kittrell, Mary Kittrell, William Kittrell, Sarah Kittrell, Charity Kittrell, Elizabeth Kittrell, George Kittrell and Moses Kittrell. She to give Bond of 2000 pds. with William Goodman and Henry Goodman Securities.

William Baker, Enos Rogers, Jonathan Rogers and Philip Rogers to Audit State and Settle the Accounts of Hardy Cross Admr. of William Davidson decd.

Henry Goodman, Jonathan Williams, Demsey Williams and Patrick Hagarty to Audit State and Settle the Accounts of William Goodman Admr. of Moses Kittrell.

Accounts of Sales of the Estate of Benjamin Bennett exhibited by Thomas Hunter Sheriff.

Elisha Hare appointed Overseer of the Road instead of Hezekiah Jones.

Hillory Willey & Matthias Willey still continue to work on the road under Jonathan Williams Overseer.

Jethro Sumner, Jesse Benton, Edwin Sumner and William Walters to make a Division of the Estate of Edward Daughtee decd.

Bryant Curle and Illegitimate Child a Molatto Son of Nancy Curl about four years of age bound to Aaron Ellis to learn the business of a Planter.

Henry Forrest, William Cleaves, Humphry Hudgins and Joseph Figg with Patrick Hagarty Surveyor who were appointed to settle a disputed line between Timothy Hunter and Jeremiah Speight made report. April 30, 1791 line found and processioned. Henry Forrest, William Cleaves, Humphry Hudgins, Joseph (X) Figg, Pa. Hagerty C. Surveyor.

Joseph Hurdle, Isaac Hunter, Abraham Harrell and Thomas Hurdle with Patrick Hagerty Surv. who were appointed to settle a disputed line between the Hairs of Mills Riddick decd. and Moses Briggs made report. Said line did not belong to said Briggs. Joseph Hurdle, Isaac Hunter, Abraham Harrell, Thomas Hurdle, Patrick Hegerty Surveyor.

William Kelly, Mordecai Perry, Simon Stallings and Seth Rountree with Patrick Hagerty Surv. who were appointed to settle disputed lands between Jacob Eason and William Hurdle made report. It appears said land belongs to said Hurdle. 9 May, 1791. William Kelly, Mordicai Perry, Simon Stallings, Seth Rountree, Pa. Hagerty.

Tuesday morning. Present: Joseph Riddick, Jethro Sumner and David Rice, Justices.

Bill of Sale Josiah Granbery and Josiah Collins to Isaac Eason for Negro Merreck proved by the oath of Thomas Granbery.

Deed of Land Henry Forrest to Lawrence Baker proved by the oath of Jonathan Roberts.

William Goodman, Henry Goodman and Isaac Pipkin who were appointed to make a Division of the Estate of William Gatling Senr. decd. made report.

Deed of Land John Powell to Luke Sumner proved by the oath of Jethro Ballard.

Deed of Land Luke Sumner to Jethro Ballard acknowledged.

Bill of Sale for a Negro Woman June. Josiah Granbery and Josiah Collins to Lawrence Baker acknowledged by said Josiah Granbery.

John Bethy, John Odom, David Cross and Henry Goodman with Patrick Hegerty Surv. who were appointed to settle a disputed line between Joseph Speight and Benjamin Barnes made report. It appears the said land is the property of said Barnes and joins Demsey Barnes' line. 11 Oct. 1790. John Bethey, John Odom, David Cross, Henry Goodman, Patrick Hegerty Surveyor.

John Odom, Philip Lewis, Jesse Vann and Cyprean Cross with Patrick Hegerty Surv. who were appointed to settle a disputed line between Henry Goodman and Saml. Eure Guardian of Nancy Eure Orphan of Enos Eure decd. made report. April 28, 1791. It appears the said land should be the property of said Goodman. John Odom, Philip Lewis, Jesse Vann, Cyprian Cross, Patrick Hegerty Surveyor.

Joseph Riddick, William Lewis, Samuel Harrell, David Rice with Patrick Hegerty Surv. who were appointed to settle a disputed line between John Robbins and Thomas Marshall made report. 8 April 1790. Jo. Riddick refused to report untill he made a Survey of Robbins patent which did not cover the land in Dispute. Oct. 25, 1790.

The following appointed to receive Tax Lists for the present year, viz. Simon Stallings in Capt. Robert's Captaincy, James Gregory in Capt. Isaac Hunter's Captaincy, Jethro Sumner where he commands as Capt. and in Capt. Jesse Benton's Captaincy, William Goodman in Captaincy where he commands, William Goodman in the Captaincy where he commands, Christopher Riddick in Capt. William Harrisses Captaincy and John Baker in Capt. Charly Eure's Captaincy.

William Ellis appointed Constable in room of Moses Hare.

Sheriff to summons a Jury with the Surveyor to make a Division of the lands of Samuel Baker decd. who died Intestate.

Thomas Marshall, Jonathan Roberts and William Lewis who were appointed to Audit State and Settle the Accounts of John Robbins decd. ("with the Estate of Jos. Parker decd.") made report.

The Will of John Rice decd. was exhibited by Peggy Rice Extrx. and was proved by the oath of William Harris one of the Witnesses.

Inventory of the Goods & etc. of the Estate of John Rice decd. was exhibited by Peggy Rice Extrx.

James Walton, Taxgatherer in Capt. Jonathan Robert's Captaincy allowed in the Settlement of his Account with the County for the Tax on Ephraim Griffin, David Small, Hardy Robbins and John Roberts, Insolvants.

The Sheriff returned the pannel of a Jury with the Verdict for laying off the Dower of Leah Riddick widow of Seth Riddick decd. towit, land joining Christopher Riddick, Seth Riddick decd., Kedar Riddick decd. and Colo. Lawrence Baker, containing 50 acres. 17 March, 1791. John B. Walton, James Freeman, James Jones, John Powell, Wm. Hunter, Jas. B. Sumner, Jesse Spivey, Richard Briggs, Michael Lawrence, James Costen, Zadok Hinton, Amariah Blanshard, Thomas Hunter Shff.

Edward Gatling Taxgatherer allowed in the Settlement of his accounts for the Tax on Jacob Howard. Josiah Stallings with 76 acres land and Robert Douglas.

Edward Gatling Constable allowed 4 pds. for Summoning the Inhabitants of Capt. Wm. Goodmans and Capt. Charles Eures Captaincy to give their Tax list.

Account of Sales of the Estate of Demsey Bond decd. was exhibited by Richd. Bond Extr.

Humphry Hudgins Taxgatherer allowed in the Settlement of his Account the Tax on John Geo. Garlock and Mills Parker in Capt. Jesse Pentons Captaincy and on James Brown with 13 acres land in Capt. William Harriss's Captaincy.

Deed of Land Henry Blanshard to Palatiah Blanshard proved by the oath of Demsey Blanshard.

Simon Stallings, James Walton, James Freeman and Thomas Trotman to Audit State and Settle the Accounts of the Extrs. of Demsey Bond decd.

Account of Sales of the Estate of William Booth decd. exhibited by Thomas Hunter Sheriff and James Rawles, Admr.

Additional Inventory of the Estate of William Booth decd. was exhibited by James Rawls Admr.

Count adjourned until tomorrow.

Wednesday morning, May 18, 1791.

Present: Jethro Sumner, David Rice, Joseph Riddick, Justices.

Jethro Meltear allowed 4 pds. 16 Shill. for 3 days services warning Inhabitants of Capt. Jonathan Robert's Capty. to give in their Tax list and for 9 days attendance as Constable.

The Extrs. of Robert Taylor decd. to sell so much of the Estate as will pay his Debts.

Jonathan Roberts, Henry Forrest, William Hinton and Simon Stallings to make a division of the Estate of Robert Taylor decd.

William Walters allowed 2 pds. 8 Shill. for 3 days service warning the Inhabitants in Capt. Jesse Bentons Capty. to give in Tax list and for 3 days attendance as Constable.

Willis Brown, Thomas Marshall and William Lewis appointed Commission to let to the Lowest Bidder the building of Bennetts Creek Bridge.

William Powell Orphan of Jacob Powell about 17 years of age bound to Henry Lee to Learn the business of a House Carpenter.

Bill of Sale for a Negro Girl named Venus - Moses Hare Senr. to Moses Hare Junr. proved by the oath of Jethro Sumner.

Jonathan Roberts, Thomas Marshall, William Lewis and John Bunbery Walton to make a Division of the Estate of Joseph Parker decd.

The following persons to attend this Court at next Term as Grand and Petit Jurors (towit) William Berryman, Henry Hobbs, William Hurdle, James Outlaw, Seth Rountree, Abraham Eason, William Hunter, Demsey Blanshard, Reuben Lassiter, Noah Harrell, Moses Davis, Robert Riddick, William Matthias, Miles Benton, Thomas Parker, Peter Parker, Jesse Benton, Elisha Cross, Demsey Odom, Noah Felton, Jonathan Smith, Robert Parker Senr., George Williams, William Boyce, John Gatling, John Odom, Henry Lee, Benjamin Barnes, Philip Lewis and Asa Harrell.

Bill of Sale Katherine Parker to Jonathan Roberts for Goods & etc. proved by the oath of David Harrell.

John Riddick Taxgatherer in Capt. Jethro Sumners Capty. allowed in the Settlement of his Accounts the Tax on Josiah Brinkley and John Jones of Lewis and William Taylor.

Thomas Hunter appointed Sheriff for the present Year. David Rice, Jethro Sumner and Joseph Riddick were on the Bench. Said Thomas Hunter to give Bond with Jethro Sumner and James Baker Sumner as Securities.

Thursday morning.
Present: John Baker, Jethro Sumner, Joseph Riddick, Justices.

Demsey Barnes, Jesse Vann, David Lewis, Richard Mitchell and Alex. Eason to appear at next term to shew cause & etc. Fined each 5 pds.

Richard Baker vs. Lewis Walters. Jurors: Robert Parker, Kedar Hinton, Jethro Meltear, Jesse Benton, Miles Benton, Daniel Powell, Demsey Parker, Isaac Parker, Abraham Morgan, John Vann, Zachariah Menshew, James B. Sumner.

Lawrence Baker allowed 4 pds. for finding plank and puting it on Bennetts Creek Bridge and puting Steps to the Court House Door.

Richard Bond Extr. of Guy Hill decd. to take under his care the Orphans of said Guy Hill until next setting.

William Walters appointed Deputy Sheriff.

Humphry Hudgins allowed 2 pds. 16 Shill. for attendance on Court 7 days.

Joseph Riddick appointed Guardian to Jesse Eason Orphan of Jesse Eason decd.

Jeremiah Speight summoned to appear next setting to shew cause why Wm. Harriss should not have a patent line between them surveyed.

Samuel Harrell Constable allowed 1 pd. 12 Shill. for attending Court 4 days as Constable.

Third Monday in August, 1791.

Present: James Gregory, Joseph Riddick, Simon Stallings, Justices.

Deed of Land Cyprian Cross to James Landing acknowledged.

William Berryman granted Administration on the Estate of Benjamin Bennit Minor Orphan of Benjamin Bennett. He to give Bond of 50 pds. with Thomas Hurdle and William Hurdle as Securities.

Deed of Land Josiah Stallings to William Crafford proved by the oath of David Harrell.

Deed of Land Benjamin Harrell to Demsey Harrell proved by the oath of William Crafford.

Inventory of the Goods & etc. of the Estate of Benjamin Bennett decd. was exhibited by William Berryman Admr.

Deed of Land Jesse Benton to Moses Hines acknowledged.

Deed of Land William Pierce to Abner Pierce proved by the oath of Moses Lassiter.

Bill of Sale for a Negro Girl named Venus - Moses Hare to John Darden acknowledged.

Deed of Land Jethro Sumner to Moses Hare acknowledged.

Jethro Sumner who was appointed to take a List of Taxables in the Captaincy where he commands as Capt. and in the Captaincy of Capt. Jesse Benton made report.

Deed of Land Henry Copeland to Josiah Harrell proved by the oath of John Odom.

William Goodman who was sppointed to take a List of Taxables in the Captaincy where he commands made return.

Deed of Land Jacob Darden Jr. to Elisha Norfleet proved by the oath of Jethro Ballard.

Bill of Sale for a Negro Woman named Jinney - Miles Turner to William Ritter proved by the oath of Moor Carter.

Noah Curle an Illegitimate Child Son of Nancy Curle about 8 years of age bound to Michael Lawrence to learn the business of a Farmer.

Henry Goodman granted Administration of the Estate of James Arline decd. He to give Bond of 500 pds. with William Goodman and Cyprean Cross Securities.

Account of Sales of the Estate of Samuel Baker decd. was exhibited by William Walters Depty Sheriff.

Jonathan Williams, Henry Goodman, Demsey Williams and Patrick Hegerty who were appointed to Audit State and Settle the Accounts of William Goodman Admr. of Moses Kittrell decd. made report.

Petition of the Habitants of Gates County for cuting and clearing a Road from Gates Court House across Sarum Creek at or near the Foot way into Sarum Creek Road the nearest way to Browns Ferry. David Lewis, Charles Eure, Isreal Beeman, Mills Eure, Peter Harrell, Reuben Sparkman, Uriah Eure, John Piland, Willis Barnes, George Williams, John Baker and Edward Piland summoned to lay off the said Road and the hands that work on the Roads under William Brooks and Reuben Sparkman cut the said Road with the Compy. under David Lewis.

The Will of James Costen decd. was exhibited by David Rice and Isaac Costen two of the Extrs. therein appointed and proved by the oath of James Gregory one of the Witnesses thereto.

Inventory of the Goods & etc. of the Estate of James Costen decd. was exhibited by David Rice and Isaac Costen Extrs.

Bill of Sale for two Negroe Men Will and Farly - Josiah Granbery and Josiah Collins to William Harriss acknowledged.

Petition of Elizabeth Costen Relict of James Costen decd. A Jury to lay off the Dower of the said Elizabeth Costen out of the Lands of the decd.

The Will of Thomas Trotman decd. with a Noncupative Will of the said deceased was exhibited by Joseph Riddick one of the Extrs. and proved by the oath of Wm. Volentine.

Deed of Land James Gregory to Thomas Trotman proved by the oath of James Baker.

Demsey Trotman appointed Guardian to Joseph and Sarah Scott Children of James Scott which was left them by their Grandfather Edward Trotman. He to give Bond of 200 pds. with Thomas Hunter and Seth Eason Securities.

Jonathan Roberts, John B. Walton and Thomas Marshall who were appointed to make a Division of the Estate of Joseph Parker decd. made report.

Deed of Land Timothy Walton to Josiah Parker Acknowledged.

Deed of Land Joseph Norfleet to Thomas Robertson proved by the oath of Edward Piland.

Bill of Sale Joseph Norfleet to Thomas Robertson proved by the oath of Edward Piland.

Jonathan Williams, Jesse Benton, Edwin Sumner and Jethro Sumner to make a Division of the Estate of Moses Kittrell decd. and that Jethro Sumner, Edwin Sumner, Jonathan Williams, William Doughtie and Demsey Williams with the County Surveyor divide the Lands of Moses Kitrell decd. between the Heirs of said decd.

a Jury to be summoned to Lay off and alot to Elizabeth Kittrell Relict of Moses Kittrell decd. her Dower.

Deed of Land Thomas Lewis to David Harrell proved by the oath of Jonathan Roberts.

Account of Sales of the Estate of Robert Taylor decd. was exhibited by Thomas Hunter Sheriff.

Jethro Sumner, Jesse Benton, Elisha Cross and Enos Rogers to make a Divison of certain Negroes formerly in the Possession of James Arline agreeable to his Will.

Account of Sales of the Estate of Seth Riddick decd. was exhibited by Thomas Hunter Sheriff.

Account of Sales of the Estate of Jesse Eason decd. was exhibited by Alexander Eason.

Tuesday August 16, 1791.

Present: William Baker, James Gregory, Jethro Sumner, Justices.

Bill of Sale for a Negro Girl named Hannah - John Carter to James Carter acknowledged.

William Baker County Trustee exhibited his Account with this County. Balance due him 1 Shll. and 1 penny farthing.

Present: William Goodman, Jethro Ballard and Simon Stallings.

Thomas Hunter Sheriff allowed 20 pds. for extra Services for 1790.

Peggy Rice, Extrx. of John Rice decd. to sell as much of the Estate as will pay the Debts.

Jonathan Roberts against Jethro Meltear. Jury as follows: James Outlaw, Moses Davis, Henry Hobbs, William Hunter, Robert Riddick, Miles Benton, Thos. Parker, Peter Parker, Jesse Benton, George Williams, John Odom and Ebron Sears.

Verdict of a Jury which was to alott and lay off the Dower of Susanna Baker Widow and Relict of Samuel Baker decd. (towit) her Thirds of the Lands and Tennements – adjoining Parkers path, Isaac Walters, Moses Boyce and Merryhill Pocosion so as to include the new pattent of 55 acres and Plantation House. 24 June 1791. Edwin Sumner, Miles Benton, Jesse Benton, John Arnold, Micajah Riddick, Jonathan Williams, Isaac Miller, Jeremiah Speight, Thomas Smith, Henry Griffin, William Matthews, Abraham Morgan. Wm. Walters Sheriff.

Verdict of a Jury which were to make a Division of the Lands of Samuel Baker who died Intestate, towit, Allotted to Samuel Baker Tract No. 1 joining Odom's pattent, Kittrell's line, Parker's path and including the mansion Plantation; Wm. Baker Tract No. 2 joining Demsey Williams, Isaac Walters including Plantation where Thomas Baker formerly lived with 55 acres; Bray Baker Tract No. 3 joining Isaac Walters and Moses Boyce including 17 acres being his part of an entry made by him and Moses Kittrell; Richard Baker Tract No. 4 joining James Matthews, William Arnold and Noah Felton known as Bakers old fields; Blake Baker Tract No. 5 joining Timothy Lassiter, Lewis Walters and William Matthews known as the Middle Swamp; Benjamin Baker Tract No. 6 joining Timothy Lassiter, William Vann, Anthony Matthews, Junr. and Edwin Sumner. 2 August 1791, Miles Benton, Samuel Smith, Micajah Riddick, Enos Rogers, Jonathan Rogers, Timothy Lassiter, William Matthews, Henry Griffin, Hillery Willey, Elisha Cross, Jonathan Williams, Abraham Morgan, Pa. Hegerty. Wm. Walters Sheriff.

The Will of Francis Parker decd. exhibited by Fereby Parker, Extrx. therein appointed and proved by oath of John Sumner one of the witnesses thereto.

Inventory of the Goods & etc. of the Estate of Francis Parker decd. exhibited by Fereby Parker Admx.

Henry Goodman Admr. of James Arline decd. to sell as much of the Estate as will pay his Debts.

Account of Sales of the Estate of Maximilion Minchew decd. was exhibited by Zacheriah Minchew.

Thomas Hurdle, Abraham Hurdle, Moses Hill and Joseph Riddick to make a Division of the Estate of Benjamin Bennett decd.

Jonathan Roberts appointed Guardian to Elizabeth Parker, John Parker, Kadar Parker, James Parker, Nancy Parker and Christian Parker orphans of Joseph Parker decd. He to give Bond of 400 pds. with Timothy Lassiter and William Harriss Securitys.

Bill of Sale for a Negro Woman named Aggy and Child named Peg – Josiah Granbery and Josiah Collins to William Baker Acknowledged.

Jonathan Roberts, Henry Forrest and Simon Stallings who were appointed to make a Division of the Estate of Robert Taylor decd. made report.

Jacob Gordon, Benjamin Gordon, Jethro Ballard and Joseph Riddick to Auduit State and Settle the Accounts of Alexander Eason and James Jones Extrs. of Jesse Eason decd.

Wednesday August 17, 1791

Present: Christopher Riddick, David Rice, Jethro Sumner, John Baker and Joseph Riddick, Justices.

Timothy Lassiter, Job Riddick, Samuel Harrell and John Riddick to make a Division of the Estate of James Costen decd.

David Cross appointed Overseer of the Road in the Room of Demsey Barnes.

Willis Hughes and Sarah Hughes moved by William Blair their Attorney for Administration on the Estate of Ahn Carter decd. They to give Bond of 400 pds. with Demsey Barnes and Ebron Sears Securitys.

Simon Stallings, James Gregory, Moses Hill and William King to Auduit State and Settle the Accounts of Thomas Trotman decd. Extrs. of Amos Trotman decd. with the said Amos Trotman Estate

A Jury summoned to lay off the Road which is to begin at the Public Road that leads by Timothy Lassiters across the Creek at Timothy Lassiters Bridge and so into the main road that leads by Thomas Smiths.

Seth Rountree to appear at this Court to shew cause why James Walton should not build a Water Grist Mill across Katherine Creek where Thos. Walton formerly built a Mill.

Thos. Iredell Attorney for the State in this Coty. be allowed 12 pds. for his services for the year passed.

Henry Goodman, Jesse Benton, Richard Bond and Noah Harrell to appear as Jurymen at the Superior Court to be held at Edenton for the District of Edenton on 6 Oct., 1791.

William Doughtie, Moses Boyce, Hillory Willey, Demsey Williams, James Wright, William Arnold, John Powell, Benjamin Gordon, William King (of Henry), David Cross, William Warren, Jr., Thomas Barnes, John Lewis, Demsey Langston, Isaac Langston, William Crafford, William Brooks, Moor Carter, Thomas Smith, Zadock Hinton, William Lewis, Amos Lassiter, Thomas Hoffler, David Harrell, Jacob Outlaw, William Hinton, Kedar Hinton, Demsey Jones, Jr., Aaron Hobbs and John Hoffler to be Jurymen at the next Court to be held the third Monday in November next.

The hands of George Outlaw to work on the old town Road under James Outlaw Overseer.

Daniel Rogers orphan of Daniel Rogers about Sixteen years old bound to Benjamin Barnes to learn the Business of Blacksmith.

<u>Third Monday in November 1791.</u>

Present: Christopher Riddick, William Goodman and David Rice, Justices.

Deed of Land - Hardy Wills to Isaac Pipkin proved by oaths of Henry Goodman and James Ransom.

Deed of Land - Jethro Ballard and David Rice as Extrs. of James Sumner decd. to George Outlaw proved by the oath of James Outlaw.

Deed of Land - Jacob Pierce to William Pierce proved by the oath of John Hofler.

William Goodman, Elisha Cross, Jonathan Rogers and Enos Rogers who were appointed to Auditt, State and Settle the accounts of James Russell Admr. of George Russel decd. made report.

Jonathan Roberts, Henry Forrest, James Outlaw and William Hinton to Audit and Settle the Accounts of Elisha Perry, James Freeman and Ephraim Morriss Extrs. of Robert Taylor, decd.

Thomas Parker Admr. of Jacob and Elizabeth Norfleet decd. returned an account of Sales of the Perishable part of the Estates.

Abraham Phelps orphan of about the age of eighteen years bound to Jethro Haslet to learn the business of Carpenter.

Isaac Pipkin Guardian of Elizabeth Rogers orphan of Stephen Rogers decd. exhibited his Account Current for said orphan.

Isaac Pipkin Guardian to Stephen Rogers orphan of Stephen Rogers decd. exhibited his account current for the said orphan.

Isaac Pipkin Guardian to Sarah Rogers orphan of Stephen Rogers decd. exhibited his Account Current for the said orphan.

Inventory of the Goods and etc. of the Estate of Thomas Trotman decd. exhibited by Joseph Riddick Extr.

Bill of Sale from Demsey Rooks and Edith Rooks to James Brady, Jr. proved by the oath of Thomas Vann.

Deed of Land - Francis Speight to William Crafford Acknowledged.

John Hare appointed Overseer of the road in room of Jethro Meltear resigned.

John Lang to be Admr. of the Estate of James Lang decd. He to give Bond of 1000 pds. Philip Rogers and Enos Rogers Securities.

Deed of Land - Seth Eason to James Norfleet proved by the oath of John Cowper.

Inventory of the Goods & etc. of the Estate of James Lang decd. was exhibited by John Lang Admr.

Willis Parker appointed Overseer of the Road from the uper end of Majr. John Bakers plantation by Robt. Parker to the road that leads over the Honey Pot Swamp and that the following hands work on the said road. Viz. James B. Sumner's hands, Robert Parker, Miles Boyce, Bond Menshew, William Hays, William Polson and Willis Mores hands.

Elisha H. Bond orphan of Demsey Bond decd. about the age of 17 years bound to Jethro Haslet to learn the Business of house Carpenter.

Inventory of the goods & etc. of the Estate of Ann Carter decd. exhibited by Willis Hughs Admr.

George Williams, Edward Piland, George Piland, Willis Sparkman, Isaac Green, John Felton, Thomas Felton, William Felton, Richard Felton, Jesse Green, Jonathan Cullins, Uriah Eure, James Eure, Wright Eure, and Majr. Baker's hands appointed to work on the new road leading from the Court house into Sarum Creek road and Majr. John Baker be Overseer.

Deed of land - William King, Joseph Speight, Joseph Parker, Elizabeth Dwire and Sarah Saunders to Henry Speight proved by the oath of Jesse Saunders.

Deed of Land - William King, Joseph Speight, Joseph Parker, Elizabeth Dwire and Sarah Saunders to Jesse Saunders proved by the oath of Henry Speight.

Fereby Parker Admx. to the Estate of Francis Parker decd. returned an Account of Sales of part of the Estate.

Christopher Riddick made return of the List of Taxable property he had taken for 1791.

<u>Tuesday, November 22</u>

Present: Jethro Ballard, Jethro Sumner and William Goodman, Justices.

Elisha Cross, Philip Rogers, Hillory Willy, Demsy Barns and Jonathan Rogers with the County Surveyor to make a Division of the Lands of James Arline decd.

John Lang to sell so much of the perishable part of the Estate of James Lang decd. as will pay his debts.

William Vallentine Guardian of Sally Hill lately decd. Majr. Joseph Riddick, Kedar Ballard and James Gregory to Audit State and Settle accounts as Guardian.

Bill of Sale for Negroes Aggy and Peg from Josiah Granbery and Josiah Collins to William Baker proved by the oath of Alexander Miller.

Bill of Sale for a Negro Man named Pompy from Jacob Raby to Samuel Harrell proved by the oath of Jethro Ballard.

Inventory of the Goods & etc. of the Estate of James Arline decd. exhibited by Henry Goodman Admr.

Account of Sales of the Estate of James Arline decd. exhibited by Henry Goodman Admr.

Elisha Hare appointed Guardian to Mourning Norfleet orphan of Jacob Norfleet decd. He to give Bond of 500 pds. with Jesse Benton and James Small Securities.

William Cumming appointed States Attorney for the County of Gates.

William King, Moses Hill and Simon Stallings who were appointed to Audit State and Settle the Accounts of Thomas Trotman Extr. of Amos Trotman decd. exhibited their account.

Joseph Riddick, Thomas Hurdle and Moses Hill who were appointed to make a Division of the Estate of Benja. Bennett decd. exhibited an Acct. in which Elizabeth Bennett and Milicent Bennett were due 5 pds. 13 Shill each as their part of the Estate.

Isaac Miller, James Phelps, Jethro Meltear, Jacob Hayes, Micajah Riddick, Junr., Noah Felton, Micajah Riddick Junr., Moses Boyce, James B. Sumner, Samuel Smith, Demsey Williams and Wm. Matthews who were to lay off a Road from Bennetts Creek road to the Honey Pott Road have laid off said Road as follows: Beginning at the main road near the Corner of Majr. Jno. Baker's fence, thence running by a line of Blas'd Trees near by as the old path runs to the road that leads across the Honey Pott Swamp.

James Gregory, Joseph Hurdle, Henry Walton and Thos. Hurdle to divide a parcel of Negroes of Joseph Riddick Junr. decd.

Wm. Brooks, Uriah Ellis, John Pyland, Willis Brown, Ewd. Pyland, George Williams, David Lewis, Charles Eure, Peter Harrell, Stephen Eure and Reubin Sparkman who were to lay off a Public Road from the Court House a Cross Sarum Creek or near the foot way into the Sarum Creek road to Brown's Ferry and the hands under Wm. Brooks, Reubin Sparkman and David Lewis Overseers should cut and clear said Road have proceeded as follows: Beginning at Bennetts Creek Road near the Court House thence running through Jno. Bakers plantation thence by Geo. Williams's, thence a Cross Coles Creek thence Sarum Creek Road between Wm. Green's and Richard Green's.

Nansy Hall orphan of John Hall decd. aged about eight years bound to Miles Boyce to learn the business of a weaver.

Demsey Odom, Demsey Williams, James Knight, Jonathan Rogers, Wm. Barr, Lewis Walters, Wm. Matthews, Micajah Riddick, Noah Felton, Elisha Hare, John Parker and James Parker who were to lay off the Dower of Eliza. Kittrell widow and relick of Moses Kittrell decd. exhibited proceedings. She to get 532 acres joining Saml. Williams, Edwin Sumner, Wm. Matthews, Richd. Baker and Samuel Baker.

Moses Boyce, Demsey Williams, Lewis Walters, Noah Felton, Micajah Riddick, James Filps Sr., Micajah Riddick Jr., James Pruden, Thos. Smith, Saml. Smith and Henry Forest who were to lay off a Public

Road from the Main Road near Timothy Lassiters across Bennetts Creek at the sd. Lassiters bridge and from thence into the Main Road leading by Thos. Smiths plantation exhibited proceedings as follows: beginning at the Main Road which leads from Hunter's Mill to Bennetts Creek bridge thence by a row of Blas'd Trees across Bennett's Creek at Timothy Lassiters bridge thence by the sd. row of Trees near Jeremiah Speights House thence into the Main Road leading to the Honey Pott near Thos. Smith's.

A Negro Boy named Jacob belonging to Abner Blanshard exempted from paying taxes for 1791.

Reuben Lassiter appointed Overseer of the Road instead of Kedar Hinton resigned.

Trustees to pay the builders of Bennett's Creek bridge 60 pds.

Simon Stalling made return of the Taxable property taken by him in Capt. Roberts's Capty.

William Goodman to take the private examination of Mary Scott wife of Joseph Scott concerning relinquishing her Dower to certain land sold by Joseph Scott and his Wife Mary and George Wynns and his Wife Judith to Leven Dure.

Patrick Hegerty, Jonathan Williams, Demsey Williams and Hellory Willy to Audit, State and Settle the Accts. of Susanna Baker Admx. of the Estate of Saml. Baker decd.

John B. Walton appointed Guardian to Noah Hill orphan of Kedar Hill decd. He to give Bond of 1000 pds. Thomas Hunter and Jeremiah Speight Securities.

Wednesday, November 23

Present: David Rice, Jethro Sumner and Jethro Ballard, Justices.

James Rawls Admr. of Wm. Booth decd. to sell as much of the Estate as will pay his Debts.

Deed of Land - William Harriss, Amelia Harriss, Samuel H. Jameson, and Peggy Jameson to John Odom proved by the oath of Humphrey Hudgins.

A Jury summoned to lay off the Dower of Calea Valentine and James Walton, Henry Walton, Moses Hill and Ezekial Trotman to divide the Estate of the Infant Kidar Hill between the Petitioner Calia and the Children of Kedar Hill decd.

Wm. Goodman, Enos Rogers, Henry Goodman and John Van to divide the Estate of Elish Odom decd.

Humphrey Hudgins appointed Overseer of the Road instead of William Harriss.

A Jury to lay off the Dower of land of Eliza. Wills relict of Saml. Wills decd.

James Gregory returned a Tax list taken by him in Capt. Isaac Hunter's Capty.

John Hofler, Moses Hill, Jonathan Roberts and Thomas Hofler appointed to value and lay off one acre of land at the end of the old Mill Dam formerly belonging to Thomas Walton decd.

Thursday, November. Present: David Rice, Wm. Baker and John Baker, Justices.

Deed of Land - Joseph Scott, Junr., Mary Scott and George Wynns to Leven Dure proved by the oath of William Jordan.

Moses Hill, James Walton, Thomas Brickell, John Roundtree, Reuben Riddick, Wm. Freeman, David Harrell, Jonathan Roberts, William Gordon, Henry Forest, Zachariah Menchew, Amos Lassiter, James Pruden, Micajah Riddick, Junr., Robert Riddick, Isaac Hunter, Job Riddick, Isaac Costen, David Lewis, Charles Eure, Kedar Ballard, Thomas Parker, Henry Goodman, Willis Pyland, Willis Parker, Willis Moore, George Williams, John Gatling, John Odom and Asa Harrell to appear as Jurymen at next Court on the Third Monday in Feb. next.

George Williams, Charles Eure and John Baker appointed Commissioners to let out the building of a Bridge across Coles Creek.

Hunphrey Hudgins, Bond Minchew and Jonathan Smith, Pattroll Capt. Harriss muster bounds.

Isaac Coston, David Harrell (son of Abraham) and Timothy Lassiter to pattroll Capt. Isaac Hunter's muster bounds.

The Hands of Jeremiah Speight, Timothy Lassiter and Zadoc Hinton to work on the new road from Thomas Smith's across Bennetts Creek to the road leading to Mr. Granberys and Jeremiah Speight to be Overseer.

Thomas Barnes, Edward Gatling, William Warren, Junr., John Vann, Junr., and John Warren to pattroll Capt. Goodman's muster bounds.

Alexander Eason to appear next Court to shew Cause why he has not had his Accts. as Extr. to Jesse Eason's Estate laid before the Auditors.

Noah Felton, Hellory Willy and Elisha Cross to pattroll Capt. Jesse Benton's muster bounds.

William Ellis, James Jones and Jethro Benton to pattroll Capt. Jethro Sumner's muster bounds.

Third Monday in February, 1792.

Present: Christopher Reddick, James Gregory, Jethro Sumner, William Goodman and Simon Stallings, Justices.

Deed of Land - John Robbins and Ux. to Thomas Travis proved by the oath of Jonathan Nichols.

Deed of Land - Abraham Pierce to William Pierce proved by the oath of Jonathan Nichols.

Deed of Land - William Walters to William Daughtie Acknowledged.

Deed of Land - Isaac Darden & Ux. to William Goodman proved by the oath of Joel Goodman.

Deed of Land - Mordicai Perry to Levi Eason Acknowledged.

The Will of Rachel Lawrence decd. was exhibited by Christopher Reddick Extr. therein appointed and proved by the oath of Mary Raby.

Deed of Land - Jacob Gordon to Seth Eason Acknowledged.

Bill of Sale for a Negro Man Merica - Isaac Eason to Seth Eason Acknowledged.

Deed of Land - William King, Joseph Speight, Joseph Parker, Elizabeth Dwyre to Sarah Saunders proved by the oath of Jesse Saunders.

Release: Wm. King, Joseph Speight, Joseph Parker and Elizabeth Dwyre to Sarah Saunders proved by the oath of Jesse Saunders.

Deed of Land - George Gatling & Ux. to Jesse Saunders proved by the oath of Edward Gatling.

Deed of Land - Richard Baker to James Phelps Acknowledged.

Bill of Sale for a Negro Boy Child Jim - Richard Baker to Joseph Rogers junr. Acknowledged.

Jethro Sumner, Miles Benton and Thomas Parker who were appointed to make a Division of the Estate of Isaac Benton decd. made report.

George Outlaw Guardian to Richard Freeman orphan of Demsey Freeman decd. exhibited his account.

William Valentine Guardian to Docton Bagley, Henry Bagley, Trotman Bagley and Sally Hill orphans of Jacob Bagley and Kedar Hill exhibited his accounts.

Account of Sales of the Estate of James Lang decd. was exhibited by John Lang Extr.

William Volentine Guardian to Miles Hill orphan of Kedar Hill exhibited his account.

Deed of Land - William Sumner to George Eason proved by the oath of Isaac Coston.

Account of Sales of the Estate of Amos Trotman decd. exhibited by Amos Trotman Extr.

Deed of Land - George Eason to Timothy Lassiter proved by the oath of Josiah Granbery.

John Gatling Guardian to William Rogers orphan of Stephen Rogers decd. exhibited his account.

John Gatling Guardian to John Rogers orphan of Stephen Rogers decd. exhibited his account.

John Gatling Guardian to Priscilla Rogers orphan of Stephen Rogers decd. exhibited his account.

Deed of Sale James Bristow to James Tugwell proved by the oath of Wm. H. Boyce.

Deed of Land - Cyprian Cross to John Landing Acknowledged.

William Odom granted Administration on the Estate of Hardy Howard decd. He to give Bond of 600 pds. Jesse Saunders and Henry Speight Securitys.

Inventory of the Goods & etc. of the Estate of Hardy Howard decd. exhibited by William Odom.

Priscilla Rogers minor orphan of Stephen Rogers decd. made choice of James Goodman as her Guardian. He to give Bond of 500 pds. Henry Goodman Security.

Henry Goodman qualified for the office of Commission of the peace.

Deed of Land - Isaac Pepkin to Richd. Barnes proved by the oath of Isaac Pipkin Junr.

John White Guardian to Seth Spivey exhibited his account.

Joseph Taylor Guardian to Sarah Spivey orphan of Thomas Spivey decd. exhibited his account.

William Odom to sell the perishable Estate of Hardy Howard decd. to pay his Debts.

Moses Hobbs Guardian to Jesse Hobbs and William Hobbs orphans of Guy Hobbs decd. exhibited his account.

Colo. William Baker to take the private examination of Mrs. Judith Wynns to a deed to Levin Dure.

Geo. Wynns vs Isaac Hunter. Stay of Execution Six Mo.

Tuesday. Present: Christopher Riddick, James Gregory, Jethro Sumner, William Goodman, David Rice and Henry Goodman, Justices.

Deed of Land - Elisha Ellis to Charles Eure proved by the oath of Wm. H. Boyce.

Timothy Lassiter, Job Riddick, Samuel Harrell and John Riddick who were appointed to make a Division of the Estate of James Coston decd. made report.

Deed of Land - Thomas Trotman to James Baker proved by the oath of Joseph Riddick.

Account of Sales of the Estate of Daniel Gwinn decd. exhibited by James Small.

Account of Sale of the Estate of Joshua Small decd. exhibited by James Small Extr.

James Gregory, Henry Walton and Joseph Hurdle who were appointed to make a Division of the Estate of Joseph Riddick decd. (Senr. of _____ Coty.) made report.

William Hunter Guardian to Theopholus Hunter exhibited his account.

Deed of Land - James Lassiter to Samuel Harrell proved by the oath of Henry Goodman.

Deed of Land - Amos Lassiter &. James Gregory to Saml. Harrell proved by the oath of Henry Goodman.

Isaac Pipkin Junr. appointed Overseer of the Road where Mills Lewis was Overseer.

Deed of Land - Jesse Benton to William Barr Acknowledged.

Philip Rogers, Enos Rogers and Jonathan Rogers who were appointed to Audit State and Settle the accounts of Hardy Cross Admr. of William Davidson decd. made report.

Henry Goodman and William Goodman, Enos Rogers and John Vann who were appointed to make a Division of the Estate of Elisha Odom decd. made report.

Bill of Sale for a Negro Man Ben - Alexander Eason to Mourning Sumner Acknowledged.

Richard Bond Guardian to Elisha Bond orphan of Demsey Bond and John Hill and Elizabeth Hill orphans of Guy Hill exhibited his accounts.

Deed of Land - Abraham Sumner and Abraham Eason to James Gregory proved by the oath of Jonathan Roberts.

Samuel Smith, Jeremiah Speight, Richard Bond Junr. and James Baker Sumner to Auduit State and Settle the accounts of Zacheriah Minshew Extr. of Maxamilion Minshew decd. with the orphans of the decd.

John B. Walton Guardian to Guy Hill orphan of Kedar Hill decd. exhibited his account.

Jethro Ballard, Kedar Ballard, Jacob Gordon and Benjamin Gordon to Auduit State and Settle the accounts of Alex Eason and Jas. Jones Extrs. to the Estate of Jesse Eason.

Mary Rountree Guardian to Mary Rountree orphan of Charles Rountree decd. exhibited her account.

Jesse Spivey Guardian to Frederick Blanshard, Sarah Blanshard,

William Blanshard and Mary Blanshard orphans of Absolom Blanshard exhibited his accounts.

Bill of Sale for a Negro Girl philes - Humphry Hudgins to Joel Foster proved by the oath of Isaac Miller.

Deed of Sale Timothy Walton to John B. Walton proved by the oath of Seth Rountree.

John White granted Administration on the Estate of Smith Spivey minor orphan of William Spivey decd. He to give Bond of 200 pds. James Walton and Samuel Harrell Securities.

Thomas Hurdle Constable allowed 2 pds. 5 shill. for services attending Court and summoning Inhabitants of Capt. Isaac Hunter's Capty. to give a tax list.

Inventory of the Goods & etc. of the Estate of Smith Spivey decd. exhibited by John White Admr.

Simon Stallings, James Walton, George Outlaw and James Outlaw to make a Division of the Estate of Smith Spivey decd.

Aaron Hobbs Overseer of the New Road and the hands that work under him to work on the road that James Walton is Overseer of and James Walton to keep the road in order that Aron Hobbs is now Overseer of.

Wednesday. Present: Christopher Riddick, Jethro Sumner, James Gregory and William Goodman, Justices.

William Hinton Guardian to Whitmell Hill and Robert Hill orphans of Kedar Hill decd. exhibited his accounts.

Petition of Timothy Lassiter for Building a Water Grist Mill on the Watry Swamp granted.

Deed of Land - Willis Parker to Jonathan Roberts Acknowledged.

John Hamelton to procure a Stove for this Court.

William Volentine granted Administration of the Estate of Sally Hill decd. He to give Bond of 600 pds. Moses Hill and James Walton Securitys.

Inventory of the Goods & etc. of the Estate of Sally Hill decd. exhibited by Wm. Volentine Admr.

Deed of Land - Henry Copeland to Isaac Williams Acknowledged.

Joseph Riddick and Thomas Hunter and James Gregory and James Walton to make a Division of the Estate of Sally Hill decd.

Moses Hill, William Volintine, Thomas Hurdle and Simon Stallings to Divide the Estate of Spencer Brinkley decd. and settle the accounts of the Admr.

Jacob Gordon, Nathaniel Riddick, Abraham Hurdle and Joseph Hurdle to divide the Negroes of the Estate of William Eason decd.

Sheriff to sell the Estate of Sally Hill decd. orphan of Kedar Hill, that an equal Division of said Estate may be made.

Levied on each poll 1 Shill. 6 pence and 6 pence for each hundred Acres Land for the year 1791.

William Lewis Guardian of James Hodges orphan of James Hodges decd. exhibited his account.

Willis Brown Guardian to Nancy Garrett orphan of James Garrett decd. exhibited his account.

Moor Carter appointed Overseer of the road instead of Reuben Sparkman resigned.

John Vann to be allowed 33 Shill. for his Services for serving a Warrant on Bryant Walters in behalf of the State.

Hillery Willey, Elisha Cross, Demsey Odom and Jonathan Rogers and Philip Rogers with Patrick Hagerty Surveyor who were appointed to make a Division of the Estate of Jas. Arline decd. made report.

William Doughtee appointed Guardian to Benjamin Baker. He to give Bond of 550 Pds. William Walters and Isaac Walters Securitys.

Jonathan Williams appointed Guardian to Blake Baker orphan of Samuel Baker decd. He to give Bond of 550 pds. Thomas Parker and John Hare Securitys.

Susanna Baker appointed Guardian to Peggy Baker orphan of Samuel Baker decd. She to give Bond of 550 pds. Jethro Sumner and William Walters Securitys.

William Walters appointed Guardian to Bray Baker orphan of Samuel Baker decd. He to give Bond of 550 pds. with William Doughtie and Humphry Hudgins Securitys.

Thursday, Feby. 23, 1792.

Present: Joseph Riddick, Simon Stallings and Henry Goodman.

Deed of Confermation signed by the Governor to Wm. Lewis and Samuel Harrell proved by the oath of Jos. Riddick.

John Hamilton to procure one of Judge Iredels revisal of the Laws of this State.

Edward Gatling granted Guardianship of Jacob Odom and Jesse Odom orphans of Elisha Odom decd. He to give Bond of 700 pds. Willis Brown and William Warren Securitys.

Philip Lewis, Benjamin Barnes, Francis Speight and John Odom made a Division of the Estate of Alexander Carter decd.

Demsey Williams appointed Guardian to Samuel Baker orphan of Samuel Baker decd. He to give Bond of 550 pds. William Doughtie and George Williams Securitys.

Demsey Trotman take into his own possession for the safe keeping the Estate of William Scott decd. until Admn.

Jas. Walton, Wm. Volentine, Demsey Barnes and John Odom to appear at Edenton on 6 April next as Jurors for the Supr. Court.

Miles Rountree, Timothy Walton, William Hurdle, Philip Lewis, Robert Riddick, William Gatling, Benjamin Barnes, Jesse Vann, Demsey Blanshard, Jacob Eason, John Powell, James Jones of David, Edwin Sumner, Thomas Smith, George Dunn, Moses Briggs, Kedar Hinton, Demsey Jones (Virga.), Robert Parker of Demsey, Robert Parker sen., John Hare, Henry Lee, Israel Beeman, Peter Harrell, Uriah Eure, William Ritter, William King of Hy., Miles Benton, James Costen and Samuel Green to appear at next Term as Jurors.

Thomas Piland of Jas. a very lame infirm Man to be exempt from paying Tax for 1791.

Monday, 21 May, 1792.

Present: Jethro Ballard, David Rice, William Goodman, Justices.

Deed of Land - John Lewis Atto. for George Washington and John Lewis Extr. of Fielding Lewis proved by oath of Reddick Hunter.

Deed of Mortgage - John Cowper to John Lewis proved by the oath of Riddick Hunter.

Account of Sales of the Estate of Sally Hill decd. exhibited by Thomas Hunter Extr. Sheriff.

Deed of Land - John Robbins & Ux. to John Jones proved by the oath of James Brown.

Will of Moses Spivey decd. exhibited by Jesse Spivey one of the Extrs. therein appointed and proved by the oath of Christopher Riddick one of the Witnesses.

Inventory of the Goods & etc. of the Estate of Moses Spivey decd. exhibited by Jesse Spivey Extr.

Joseph Speight Guardian to John Freeman, David Freeman, Joseph Freeman and Anne Freeman orphans of Solomon Freeman decd. exhibited his account.

The Will of John White decd. was exhibited by Joshua White and Elizabeth White Extrx and Extr. therein appointed and proved by the oath of James Outlaw one of the witnesses thereto.

John Odom, Benjamin Barnes and Philip Lewis who were appointed to make a Division of the Estate of Alexander Carter decd. made report.

Deed of Land - Henry Dilda to Amos Delday proved by the oath of Tiberias Purvis.

Thomas Dunn by John Hamilton his Attoryney moved for and was granted Administration on the Estate of George Dunn decd. He to give Bond of 4000 pds. Jesse Saunders and Miles Benton Securitys.

Deed of Sale - Richard Green & Ux. to Jonathan Cullins proved by the oath of Samuel Eure.

Bill of Sale for a Negro Boy Ben - Benjamin Parker to Caleb Savage proved by the oath of Samuel Eure.

Isaac Costen and James Costen Guardians to Thomas, Nathaniel, Benjamin, Demsey, Elizabeth and Polly Costen orphans of Demsey Costen decd. exhibited their account.

Inventory of the Goods & etc. of the Estate of George Dunn decd. exhibited by Thos. Dunn Admr.

Deed of Sale Jonathan Cullins & Ux. to Samuel Eure acknowledged and private examination taken by James Gregory.

Jethro Sumner, Jesse Benton and Micajah Riddick who were appointed to make a Division of the Estate of Samuel Baker decd. made report.

Thomas Dunn Admr. of the Estate of George Dunn decd. to sell the perishable Estate.

Samuel Smith, Richard Bond and James B. Sumner who were appointed to auduit State and settle the accounts of Zacheriah Menshew Extr. of Mazimelian Menshew decd. made report.

John Small appointed Overseer of the Road instead of Wm. Ellis resigned.

Demsey Trotman granted Administration on the Estate of William Scott decd. He to give Bond of 100 pds. Jas. Freeman and William Volentine securitys.

Inventory of the Goods & etc. of the Estate of William Scott decd. exhibited by Demsey Trotman Admr.

Joseph Speight appointed Guardian to Susanna Dunn minor orphan of George Dunn decd. He to give Bond of 400 pds. Francis Speight and Henry Speight Securitys.

Hardy Reid granted Administration on the Estate of James Reid decd. He to give Bond of 100 pds. Samuel Smith and Charles Eure Securitys.

A Jury summoned to lay off the Dower of Jemima Lang relict of James Lang decd.

Henry Goodman, James Bethey, Philip Rogers, Jonathan Rogers and Enos Rogers appointed Commissioners who with the Sheriff are to make a Division of the Estate of James Lang decd.

Jethro Sumner, Jesse Benton and Jonathan Williams who were appointed to make a Division of the Estate of Moses Kittrell decd. made report.

Accounts of Sale of the Estate of Thomas Trotman decd. exhibited by Joseph Riddick Extr.

Winnifred Taylor appointed Guardian of Isaac Taylor, Robert Taylor, and Hillory Taylor orphans of William Taylor decd. She to give Bond of 100 pds. James Freeman and William Valentine Securitys.

Jesse Spivey Extr. of Moses Spivey decd. to sell so much of the personal Estate as will pay his debts.

Timothy Lassiter at this Court at Feby Term obtained an order for Building a Water Grist Mill a Cross the Watery Swamp. Proceedings to be continued next setting.

James Gregory and Joseph Riddick who were appointed to Audit, State and Settle the accounts of William Volentine Admr. of Sally Hill decd. made report.

Jonathan Boyce orphan of Jonathan Boyce about twelve years of age bound to Abel Cross to learn the business of a Farmer.

Joseph Hurdle, Abraham Hurdle, Reuben Riddick and Joseph Riddick to make a Division of the Estate of William Scott decd.

Thomas Walton orphan of Thomas Walton decd. about Sixteen years of age bound to David Harrell to learn the Business of Shoemaker.

Isaac Reid granted Administration on the Estate of Jacob Reid. He to give Bond of 100 pds. with Samuel Smith and William Carter Securitys.

Lewis Sparkman Constable allowed 16 Shill. for 2 days service summoning the inhabitants of Capt. Chas. Eure's Capty. to give Tax list.

Tuesday. Present: Jethro Ballard, Jas. Gregory, David Rice and Jethro Sumner.

James Gregory, Joseph Riddick and Thomas Hunter who were appointed to make a Division of the Estate of Sally Hill decd. made report.

Present: John Baker, Christo. Riddick, Joseph Riddick and Henry Goodman.

Lawrence Baker Clerk of this Court allowed 18 pds. 10 Shill. for Extra Services for the year ending August Term last.

The following to receive lists of the Taxable property (towit) Simon Stallings in Capt. Roberts's Capty., Joseph Riddick in Capt. Isaac Hunters Capty., Jethro Ballard in Capt. Jethro Summers Capty., Christo. Riddick in Capt. William Harriss's Capty., Jethro Sumner in Capt. Jesse Benton's Capty., Henry Goodman in Capt. John Bethey's Capty. and William Baker in Capt. Eure's Capty.

John Powell and Moses Briggs who were summoned as Jurors to this Term failed to appear. They to be fined 5 pds. each.

Christo. Riddick allowed 8 pds. for Extra Services when he acted as Sheriff.

Jesse Arline orphan of James Arline decd. about (left blank) years of age bound to Jethro Haslet to learn the business of a House Carpenter and Joiner.

Henry Goodman Extr. of Solomon Hiatt decd. returned accounts of Sales of the Estate.

Bill of Sale for a Mare - John Lee to Rebecca King Volentine proved by the oath of Uriah Odom.

Deed of Trust - Solomon King to David Darden, John Lee and Jethro Sumner for the Benefit of Abegail King Volentine and Rebecca King Volentine proved by the oath of John Odom.

James Freeman, Jesse Spivey, Richard Mitchell, Aaron Hobbs, William Hinton Sn., Henry Hobbs, Isaac Hunter, William Hunter, Abraham Green, John Hoffler, Noah Harrell, Reuben Riddick, James Small, Richard Briggs, David Brinkley, James Knight, Amos Parker, Matthew Willey, Enos Rogers, Jonathan Rogers, William Daughtie, Peter Parker, Richard Barnes, James Bethey, Abel Cross, Francis Speight, Henry Speight, William Cleaves, Bond Menshew and William Brooks to appear at Court next Term as Petit and Grand Jurors.

Thomas Hunter allowed 18 pds. 10 Shill for Extra Services as Sheriff for the year passed.

George Eason granted Administration of the Estate of Susanna Hobbs decd. He to give Bond of 500 pds. Jacob Eason and William Hurdle Securitys.

Wm. Goodman Sheriff to give Bond of 200 pds. for the faithful collection of Tax in the District of Edenton with Saml. Smith as Security.

Commissioners to let the building of a Bridge across Coles Creek to Willis Brown who was paid 28 pds. 19 Shill.

Rachel Reid granted Administration on the Estate of Jacob Reid Senr. decd. She to give Bond of 100 pds. John Shepherd and David Small securitys.

Willis Sparkman granted Administration on the Estate of Abraham Harrell decd. He to give Bond of 100 pds. Saml. Smith and Daniel Eure Securitys.

Jonathan Roberts, Henry Forrest and William Hinton who were appointed to Audit State and Settle the accounts of Elisha Perry and Ephraim Morris Extrs. of Robert Taylor decd. made report.

William Goodman Elected Sheriff for the present year. He to give Bond with William Baker and Henry Goodman as Securitys.

Jonathan Roberts Guardian to Joseph Parker orphan of Jno. Parker decd. exhibited his account.

Humphry Hudgins Constable allowed 5 pds. 5 Shill. for Services.

William Ellis Constable allowed 2 pds. 8 Shill for Services.

Samuel Harrell Constable allowed 2 pds. for Services

Isaac Pierce appointed Overseer of the Road that Abraham Eason was formerly Overseer of and that Seth Eason put the Bridge a Cross his Millpond in good order and keep it so.

Demsey Trotman Admr. of William Scott decd. to sell as much of the personal Estate as will pay his Debts.

Alexr. Eason and James Jones Extrs. to Colo. Jesse Eason decd. to be summonsed to appear at next Court to shew cause why they have not settled the Estate.

Third Monday in August, 20 Aug., 1792.

Present: Christopher Riddick, James Gregory, Henry Goodman, Justices.

Account of Sales of part of the Estate of Moses Spivey decd. exhibited by Jesse Spivey Extr.

Deed of Land - Amos Smith to George Brooks proved by the oath of William Brooks.

Deed of Land - Samuel Thomas to James Thomas proved by the oath of Wm. H. Boyce.

Present: Thomas Hunter.

Deed of Land - William Wallis to James Outlaw proved by the oath of James Trevathan.

Demsey Harrell granted Administration on the Estate of John Harrell decd. He to give Bond of 1000 pds. with Jesse Vann and James Thomas Securitys.

Inventory of the Goods & etc. of the Estate of John Harrell decd. exhibited by Demsey Harrell Admr.

Inventory of the Estate of Rachel Laurence decd. exhibited by Christopher Riddick Admr.

William King moved by John Hamilton Attorney at Law for Administration on the Estate of Charlotte King minor orphan of Henry King decd. He to give Bond of 500 pds. John Kittrell and Jesse Saunders securitys.

George Outlaw, James Outlaw and Simon Stallings who were appointed to make a Division of the Estate of Smith Spivey made report.

Nancy Blanshard granted Administration on the Estate of Abner Blanshard decd. She to give Bond of 1500 pds. Richard Bond and Jesse Spivey securitys.

Inventory of the Goods & etc. of the Estate of Abner Blanshard decd. exhibited by Nancy Blanshard Admx.

On Petition of sundry People of this County an order of this Court passed at Feb. Term last to Timothy Lassiter for Building a Water Grist Mill a Cross the Watery Swamp be done away with.

Deed of Land - John Hunter to James Gregory proved by the oath of William Hunter.

Thomas Hunter Sheriff and William Walters Deputy Sheriff exhibited an account of Insolvants for the year 1791.

Nancy Blanshard Admx. of Abner Blanshard decd. to sell so much of the Estate as will pay his debts.

John Odom, Cyprean Cross, Jesse Vann and Benjamin Barnes to make a Division of the Estate of John Harrell decd.

William Goodman, Francis Speight, Solomon King and Laurence Baker to Audit, State and Settle the Accounts of Abel Cross Guardian of the orphans of Henry King decd.

Simon Stallings, James Walton and James Freeman who were appointed to Audit State and Settle the Accounts of Richard Bond and John B. Walton Extrs. of Demsey Bond decd. made report.

Deed of Sale of Land Sarah Spivey, Parscilla Spivey and Jesse Spivey to Willis Brown proved by the oath of John Polson.

Deed of Land - Elisha Parker to John Kittrell acknowledged.

Deed of Land - Luke Sumner to William Matthias proved by the oath of Jethro Benton.

Bill of Sale - Noah Harrell to William Lewis acknowledged.

Inventory of the Goods & etc. of the Estate of John White decd. was exhibited by Joshua White Extr.

Mrs. Judith Wynns relict of Colo. Geo. Wynns acknowledged deed by Jos. Scott and Mrs. George Wynns and herself to Leven Dure and was privately examined by James Gregory.

Bill of Sale for a Negro - James Freeman to William Lewis Ackd.

Jethro Benton granted Administration on the Estate of William Scott decd. He to give Bond of 500 pds.- Kadar Ballard and Miles Benton Securitys.

Bill of Sale for three Negros - William Harriss and Samuel Heath Jameson to Charles Powell proved by the oath of Samuel Harrell.

Deed of Land - Abisha Lassiter and Ux. to James Davis proved by the oath of Jonathan Lassiter.

Will of Joseph Speight decd. was exhibited by Francis Speight and Henry Speight Extrs. therein appointed and proved by the oath of Thomas Barnes and William Goodman two of the witnessess thereto.

Account of Sales of the Estate of George Dunn decd. exhibited by Needham Jernagan Sheriff of Hertford County and John Crutchlow Admrs.

Inventory of the Goods & etc. of the Estate of Joseph Speight decd. exhibited by Francis Speight and Henry Speight Extrs.

Account of Sales of a Negro Girl belonging to the Estate of William Booth decd. was exhibited by James Rawls Admr.

The Sheriff to sell the perishable part of the Estate of Henry Harrell decd.

Deed of Land - Sarah Saunders to Francis Speight proved by the oath of Henry Speight.

Deed of Land - Bond Menshew to Jeremiah Lassiter proved by the oath of William Gordon.

Henry Goodman, Patrick Hegerty, John Baker and Willis Brown to Audit State and Settle the Accounts of James Rawls Admr. of the Estate of William Booth decd.

<u>Tuesday</u>. Present: John Baker, Jethro Sumner, David Cross, Justices.

Levin Dure to be Licensed to keep a public House at the Place he now lives called the Brick House. He to give Bond of 1000 pds. Jeremiah Speight and Samuel Smith Securitys.

James Gregory and David Rice and John Hoffler who were appointed to Audit State and Settle the Accounts of Amilia Rountree Admx. of Henry Harrell decd. made report.

Seth Eason, James Norfleet, Jesse Vann and William Brooks to attend next Superior Court as Jurymen.

Benjamin Williams, Charles Eure, David Lewis, Asa Harrell, Benjamin Barnes, William King, David Cross, Henry Lee, William Crawford, John Lewis, Luten Lewis, Jesse Benton, William Harriss, Elisha Cross, Enos Rogers, James Tugwell, Hillary Willey, Thomas Smith, Jeremiah Speight, Miles Benton, Thomas Parker, John Powell, Moses Hare, Benjamin Gordon, Isaac Costen, Job Riddick, Jacob Hobbs, Henry Forrest, Kedar Hinton and Reuben Lassiter to appear at next County Court as Jury men.

William Baker made return of the List of Taxables in the District of Capt. Charles Eure.

Jethro Sumner made return of the List of Taxables in the Capty. of Capt. Jesse Benton.

Sophia Curle an Illegitimate Child of Milley Curle about 5 years old bound to Jesse Benton to learn House hold Business.

John Parker Extr. of Francis Saunders decd. exhibited the Account of the Sales of part of the Estate of Francis Saunders decd.

Deed of Land - Edward Coffield, Job Coffield and Mary Coffield to John Hunter proved by the oath of Abraham Reddick.

John Crutchlow appointed Guardian to Susanna Dunn orphan of George Dunn decd. He to give Bond of 5000 pds. Needham Jarnigan of Hertford County and Abel Cross of this County Securitys.

Account of Sales of the Estate of Christian Scott exhibited by Demsey Trotman and proved by the oath of Jos. Riddick.

John Lang appointed Guardian to James Lang (the said James first came into Court and choose said John as such). He to give Bond of 500 pds. with Robert Parker (of Demsey) and Enos Rogers Securitys.

Inventory of the Estate of James Reid exhibited by Hardy Reid.

Inventory of the Estate of Jacob Reid decd. exhibited by Isaac Reid Admr.

Deed of Gift. William Harriss to William Pugh Jameson his Grandson acknowledged.

William Goodman Sheriff exhibited the Accounts of Sales of the Estate of George Dunn decd.

Deed of Land - Willis Moor to Benjamin Williams proved by the oath of George Williams.

Joseph Riddick, Abraham Hurdle, Reuben Riddick and Joseph Hurdle who were appointed to make a Division of the Estate of William Scott decd. made report.

Patrick Hagerty Surveyor made avedavit that he surveyed Lands for William Warren and found that there is no vacant land within the bounds of said Warrant as directed to him by the entry Taker.

The Sheriff to summons a Jury and view the Roads that leads by Seth Easons Mill and make report whether the Road shall be continued as it now goes or the one below the said Mill.

Wednesday. Present: James Gregory, John Baker, Joseph Riddick, Jethro Ballard, Henry Goodman, Christopher Riddick, Justices.

Henry Goodman, James Bethey, Jonathan Rogers, Philip Rogers, Philip Rogers (shown twice in the original book) and Enos Rogers who were appointed to make a Division of the Estate of James Lang decd. with Patrick Hegerty Surveyor made report.

William Baker, John Baker, Henry Goodman and William Goodman to Audit State and Settle the accounts of Willis Riddick Admr. of James Riddick decd. and make a Division of said State.

William Glover granted License to keep an Ordinary at Gates Court House. He go give Bond with William Lewis and Willis Brown as Securitys.

John Kittrell appointed Deputy Sheriff.

James Jones to take Jesse Eason minor orphan of Jesse Eason decd. under his care with his Estate until next Term.

The Sheriff to sell the Estate of Charles King decd. minor orphan of Henry King decd. in order that a Divsion be made.

19 November 1792.

Present: Christopher Riddick, James Gregory, David Rice, Simon

Stallings, Justices.

Deed of Land - David Cross to Abel Cross acknowledged.

Deed of Land - William Crafford to Claiborn Osten acknowledged.

Jethro Ballard, Kedar Ballard, Jethro Sumner and Benjamin Gordon to Audit State and Settle the Accounts of William Arnold Extr. of the Estate of Joseph Jones decd.

Bill of Sale for a Negro Cloe - William Evans to Cyprian Cross proved by the oath of Priscilla Cross.

Deed of Sale Abraham Eason & Ux. to Thomas Hunter proved by the oath of Easther Harriss.

Thomas Hurdle and Abraham Hurdle granted Administration on the Estate of Joseph Hurdle decd. They to give Bond of 2500 pds. Reuben Riddick and John Riddick Securitys.

Inventory of the Estate of Joseph Hurdle decd. was exhibited by Thomas Hurdle and Abraham Hurdle Admrs.

Deed of Land - William Green to John Piland proved by the oath of Asa Harrell.

Deed of Gift of Land - Joseph Riddick to Jesse Rogerson proved by the oath of Reuben Riddick.

Thomas Hunter and Simon Stallings, John B. Walton and Moses Hill to Audit State and Settle the Accounts of Amos Trotman Extr. of Amos Trotman decd.

James Gregory, David Rice, Thomas Hunter and William King to make a Division of the Estate of Joseph Hurdle decd.

James Gatling granted Administration of the Estate of Edward Gatling decd. He to give Bond of 1000 pds. William Baker and William Goodman Securitys.

Inventory of the Goods & etc. of the Estate of Edward Gatling decd. exhibited by James Gatling.

Deed of Land - Joseph Holland & Ux. to Mills Lewis acknowledged.

Deed of Land - James Phelps & Ux. to John Arnold acknowledged by Jas. Phelps and Terentha his Wife. Private examination of Terentha by James Gregory.

Accounts of Sales of the Estate of John Harrell decd. exhibited by Demsey Harrell Admr.

Benjamin Barnes, Cyprean Cross and Jesse Vann who were appointed to make a Division of the Estate of John Harrell decd. made report.

Deed of Land - John Arnold & Ux. to John Simons acknowledged.

Deed of Mortgage - Mordicai Perry to Frederick Eason proved by the oath of Isaiah Reddick.

85

Bill of Sale - Mordicai Perry to Frederick Eason proved by the oath of Thomas Twins.

James Brown appointed Overseer of the Road in the room of William Brooks.

The Public Road that leads over Seth Easons Mill Pond to be turned below the said Mill and said Eason to keep the said Road in good order.

Thomas Piland son of James to be exempt from paying Taxes until better able being a very infirm lame Man.

Deed of Land - Zachariah Menshew to Bond Menshew proved by the oath of William Gordon.

Deed of Land - Timothy Walton to James Walton acknowledged.

Tuesday. Present: Christopher Riddick, James Gregory and David Rice, Justices.

Account of Sales of part of the Estate of Abner Blanshard decd. exhibited by John Kittrell Deputy Sheriff.

Account of Sales of the Estate of John Harrell exhibited by John Kittrell Deputy Sheriff.

Israel Beeman granted Administration on the Estate of Hardy Brown decd. He to give Bond of 100 pds. Isaac Carter and Demsey Langston Securitys.

Inventory of the Goods & etc. of the Estate of Hardy Brown decd. exhibited by Israel Beeman Admr.

Account of Sales of the Estate of Charlotte King exhibited by William Goodman Sheriff.

Josiah Granbery, John Cowper, Richard Briggs, Jacob Gordon, Thomas Parker, William Matthias, Abraham Hurdle, Demsey Trotman, Reubin Riddick, Moses Hill, James Walton, John B. Walton, William Hinton, John Rountree, William Gordon, William Cleaves, William Daughtee, Abraham Morgan, John Arnold, John Gatling, Richard Barnes, John Odom, James Pruden, Micajah Riddick, Francis Speight, Robert Baker senr., Israel Beeman, James Landing, Timothy Lassiter and Henry Walton to appear at next Term as Jurors.

The hands of John Odom to work under William Crafford Overseer of the Road instead of working under Cyprean Cross and that Thomas Harrell and Levi Lee and their hands work on the Road under the said Crafford instead of Working under Israel Beeman.

Jesse Arline orphan of James Arline decd. made Choice of Jethro Haslett as his Guardian. He to give Bond of 300 pds. with Israel Beeman and Samuel Smith Securitys.

Moses Hill, John Hoffler, Jonathan Roberts and Thomas Hoffler who were appointed to lay off and value one Acre of Land the property of Seth Rountree made report.

Additional Inventoy of the Estate of John Benton decd. was exhibited by Jesse Benton Extr.

William Gordon appointed Overseer of the Road instead of Reubin Lassiter.

Israel Beeman to sell so much of the Estate of Hardy Brown decd. as will pay his debts.

Bill of Sale- Mordicai Perry to Frederick Eason proved by the oath of Harmon Hurdle.

James Gatling to sell the perishable part of the Estate of Edward Gatling decd.

James Gatling appointed Constable in the District where Edward Gatling decd. was formerly Constable. He to give Bond with Benjamin Barnes and Elisha Cross Securitys.

Bill of Sale - Anderson Stroud to Benjamin Gordon for a Stud Horse proved by the oath of William Ellis.

John B. Walton appointed Guardian to Selah, Demsey and Thomas Bond orphans of Demsey Bond decd. He to give Bond of 1000 pds. Jonathan Roberts and Timothy Walton Securitys.

Wednesday. Present: Christopher Riddick, James Gregory, David Rice, Justices.

Bill of Sale - John Arline to Henry Goodman proved by the oath of William Goodman.

Power of Sttorney- John Arline to Henry Goodman proved by the oath of William Goodman.

Deed of Sale - Henry Goodman to Elisha Cross acknowledged.

Lawrence Baker appointed Guardian to Jesse Odom and Jacob Odom orphans of Elisha Odom decd. He to give Bond of 800 pds. William Goodman and John Kittrell Securitys.

18 February 1793.

Present: Christopher Riddick, William Baker, David Rice, Justices.

William Griggs orphan of William Griggs about Fifteen years of age bound to Robert Pentell to learn the Business of a House Carpenter and Joiner.

Deed of Land - John Landing to James Landing acknowledged.

Deed of Land - James Landing to John Landing proved by the oath of Elisha Landing.

Deed of Land - Enos Rogers to Hardy Cross acknowledged.

Deed of Sale - Enos Rogers to Jonathan Rogers acknowledged.

The Will of John Davis exhibited and proved by the oath of Benjamin Gordon a Subscribing Witness thereto.

Sarah Davis relict of John Davis decd. granted Administration on the Estate of the decd. She to give Bond of 300 pds. Benjamin Gordon and Abraham Hurdle Securitys.

Deed of Land - Robert Parker of Demsey to James Goodman ack.

Deed of Land - William Doughtee to Elisha Parker acknowledged.

Moses Hobbs Guardian to William Hobbs and Jesse Hobbs orphans of Guy Hobbs decd. made his return of accounts.

Samuel Harrell Guardian to the orphans of Thomas Walton decd. exhibited his accounts.

Deed of Gift - William Odom to John Odom acknowledged.

Account of Sales of the Estate of Jacob Powell decd. exhibited by Daniel Powell Admr.

Account of Sales of the Estate of Jacob Powell decd. exhibited by William Goodman and Daniel Powell Extrs.

Deed of Land - Zadock Hinton to Thomas Smith proved by the oaths of Humphry Hudgins and Samuel Smith.

Deed of Land - John Piland to Elijah Harrell acknowledged.

George Outlaw Guardian to Richard Freeman orphan of Demsey Freeman exhibited his account.

Seth Rountree Guardian to Penny Rountree orphan of Thomas Rountree exhibited his account.

Deed of Land - Jethro Meltear to William Gordon proved by the oath of Edward Brisco.

Charles Powell appointed Guardian to Richard Freeman orphan of Demsey Freeman decd. He to give Bond of 100 pds. with James Outlaw and John B. Walton Securitys.

Bill Sale for a Negro Girl Celia - James Powell to Levin Dure proved by the oath of James Gregory.

John B. Walton Guardian to Noah Hill and Guy Hill orphans of Kedar Hill decd. exhibited his accounts.

Richard Bond Guardian to Guy Hill and Elizabeth Hill orphans of Guy Hill decd. and to Elisha Hanie Bond orphan of Demsey Bond decd. exhibited his accounts.

Deed of Land - John B. Walton and Esther Walton his wife to Thomas Hunter acknowledged. The said Esther Walton was privately examined by James Gregory.

David Powell orphan of Jacob Powell decd. about the age of Sixteen years Bound to William Carter to learn the Business of a House Carpenter.

John Gatling Guardian to John Rogers and William Rogers orphans of Stephen Rogers decd. exhibited his accounts.

Deed of Gift - Richard Bond to William Bond and Richard Bond, Jr. proved by the oath of David Rice.

Micajah Riddick, Timothy Lassiter and Reuben Riddick to be exempt from serving as Jurymen this term.

Account of Sales of the Estate of Abner Blanshard decd. exhibited by William Williams.

Deed of Land - William Gordon to Jethro Meltear acknowledged.

Jacob Gordon, Abraham Hurdle and Nathl. Riddick who were appointed to divide the Negroes belonging to the Estate of William Eason decd. made report.

Celia Bond orphan of Demsey Bond decd. made choice of Demsey Jones as her Guardian. He to give Bond of 400 pds. with Richard Bond and William Williams as Securitys.

John B. Walton, Richard Bond, Uriah Blanshard and Simon Stallings to divide the personal Estate of Abner Blanshard decd.

Deed of Land - Seasbook Hinton to Daniel Powell proved by the oath of Jonathan Roberts.

Polly Rountree and Miles Rountree granted Administration of the Estate of John Rountree decd. They to give Bond of 3000 pds. Joseph Riddick and Demsey Trotman Securitys.

Inventory of the Goods & etc. of the Estate of John Rountree was exhibited by Polly Rountree and Miles Rountree Admr. and Admx.

The Admr. and Admx. of John Rountree to sell so much of the personal Estate as will pay his Debts.

Joseph Riddick, Thomas Hunter and Simon Stallings and James Baker to make a Division of the Estate of John Rountree decd.

Isaac and James Costen Guardians to Thomas, Nathaniel, Benjamin, Demsey, Elizabeth and Polly Costen exhibited their accounts.

Tuesday. Present: William Baker, James Gregory. Joseph Riddick, Simon Stallings, Justices.

Solomon King, Henry Goodman, Francis Speight and Henry Speight to Audit, State and Settle the Accounts of William Odom Admr. of Hardy Howard decd.

Deed of Land - Patrick Garvey to Thomas Fitt proved by the oath of Joseph Nouris.

Account of Sales of the Estate of Thomas Trotman decd. exhibited by William Goodman Sheriff.

Account of Sales of the Estate of Henry Brown decd. exhibited by William Goodman Sheriff.

Account of Sales of the Estate of Joseph Speight decd. exhibited by William Goodman Sheriff.

Deed of Sale Thomas Robertson to Ebenezar Graham proved by the oath of Lemuel Lewis.

James Gregory and Simon Stallings, Moses Hill and Abraham Hurdle to Audit State and Settle the Accounts of Joseph Riddick Extr. of Thomas Trotman decd.

James Gregory and Simon Stallings, Moses Hill and Abraham Hurdle to Divide the Estate of Thomas Trotman decd.

Joseph Riddick appointed Guardian to Joseph Trotman, Lovey Trotman and Willis Trotman minor Orphans of Thomas Trotman decd. He to give Bond of 2500 pds. James Gregory and Simon Stallings Securitys.

Deed of Land - Robert Parker to Demsey Odom proved by the oath of Patrick Hegerty.

Joseph Riddick privately examine Rachel Stallings Wife of Seth Stallings relative to her signing a Deed of Sale of Land to Simon Stallings.

Deed of Gift - Zadock Hinton to Honour Hinton and Nancy Hinton, his Daughters, proved by oath of Humphry Hudgins.

Joseph Taylor Guardian to Sally Spivey Orphan of Thomas Spivey decd. exhibited his accounts.

Deed of Land - Israel Beeman Admr. of Hardy Brown decd. to Lodorick Brooks proved by the oath of William Brooks.

Elisha Hare Guardian to Mourning Norfleet Orphan of Jacob Norfleet decd. exhibited his account.

Bill of Sale for a Negro Girl Lidia - Seth Eason to John Darden proved by the oath of Jethro Sumner.

Bill of Sale - Pasco Turner Extr. of John Reid who was Extr. of Daniel Pugh for seven Negroes to Abraham Morgan proved by the oath of Jethro Sumner.

William Volentine Guardian to Docton Bagley, Henry Bagley, Trotman Bagley and Miles Hill orphans of Jacob Bagley and Kedar Hill exhibited his accounts.

Thomas Hobbs granted Administration on the Estate of William Hobbs decd. orphan of Amos Hobbs decd. He to give Bond of 100 pds. with Demsey Trotman and Miles Rountree Securitys.

William Hinton Guardian to Robert Hill and Whitmell Hill Orphans of Kedar Hill decd. exhibited his accounts.

Joseph Riddick granted Administration on the Estate of Mary Rountree decd. He to give Bond of 750 pds. Simon Stallings and Miles Rountree Securitys.

James Riddick granted Administration on the Estate of Edward Riddick minor Orphan of James Riddick decd. He to give Bond of 500 pds. John Gatling and Israel Beeman Securitys.

Saml. H. Jamison, William Harriss, James Pruden and Humphry Hudgins to make a Division of the Estate of Edward Riddick minor Orphan of James Riddick decd.

James Gregory, David Rice, Jacob Gordon and William Hunter to Audit State and Settle the Accounts of Thomas Hunter Extr. of Jacob Bagley.

Thomas Marshall appointed Guardian to John Hill Orphan of Guy Hill decd. He to give Bond of 500 pds. Israel Beeman and William Hinton Indian Neck as Securitys.

Thomas Trotman Orphan of Thomas Trotman decd. made choice of James Baker as his Guardian. He to give Bond of 2500 pds. William Baker and Thomas Hurdle Secys.

Joseph Rountree made Choice of Miles Rountree as his Guardian. He to give Bond of 1000 pds. John B. Walton and Charles Powell Securitys.

George Eason Guardian to Samuel Hobbs Orphan of John Hobbs decd. exhibited his account.

Simon Stallings and Joseph Riddick, Moses Hill and Aaron Hobbs to make a Division of the Estate of William Hobbs decd. Orphan of Amos Hobbs decd.

Abraham Hurdle appointed Guardian to Jacob Sumner son of Abraham Sumner on a certain Estate fell to him by his Grandfathers (Jos. Hurdle) Death. He to give Bond of 200 pds. Thomas Hurdle and Jeremiah Speight Securitys.

The Admr. of the Estate of Abner Blanshard decd. to sell the perishable part of the Estate of the decd. that may fall to the part of his Orphans after a Division is made.

Thomas Hunter late Sheriff to be allowed in settlement of his accounts the sum of 6 pds. 12 Shill. and Nine pence for insolvants, to wit, Thomas Felton, Ezekiel Ross, William Morris, Eley Morris, Thomas Smith, Isaac Darden, William Dilday, Timothy Rogers, Abraham Eason, Isaac Eason, Thomas Williams, Kedar Parker, Solomon Rountree and Benjamin Reid.

Jethro Ballard, Kedar Ballard and Jethro Sumner who were appointed to Audit State and Settle the Accounts of William Arnold Extr. of Joseph Jones made report.

Joseph Riddick Admr. of the Estate of Mary Rountree to sell so much of the Estate as will pay her debts.

William Volentine, Moses Hill, John B. Walton and Simon Stallings to Audit State and Settle the Accounts of Amelia Rountee who was Admx. of Henry Harrell decd.

Petition of Eliza. Hurdle relict of Joseph Hurdle decd. A Jury to be summoned by the Sheriff and lay off the Dower of the widow.

Willis Brown Guardian to Nancy Garrett orphan of James Garrett decd. exhibited his account.

Deed of Land - John Wills to Samuel Harrell proved by the oath of David Rice.

Bill of Sale - Jeremiah Speight to Zadock Hinton for a Negro Woman Hulday proved by the oath of Humphry Hudgins.

James Gregory, Thomas Hunter, William King and Joseph Riddick to Audit State and Settle the accounts of the Admr. of Joseph Hurdle decd.

John Gwinn about Nineteen years of age Bound to William Gordon to learn the Business of a Turner.

Demsey Jones appointed Guardian to Demsey and Thomas Bond Orphans of Demsey Bond decd. He to give Bond of 500 pds. Moses Hare and Demsey Trotman Securitys.

Bill of Sale for three Negroes - James B. Sumner to Jeremiah Benton acknowledged.

Thomas Parker Guardian to Kenchen Norfleet orphan of Jacob Norfleet decd. exhibited his account.

William Goodman Sheriff exhibited the Account of Sales of the Estate of Edward Gatling decd.

Richard Mitchell, William Harriss, John Powell and Henry Speight to attend the Superior Court on Apl. next as Jurymen.

John Cowper, James Knight, Miles Benton, Kedar Ballard, Robert Riddick, Leven Duke, Isaac Costen, William Valentine, James Walton, Aaron Hobbs, James Freeman, James Outlaw, David Harrell, William Lewis, Charles Eure, Isaac Langston, Stephen Eure, Asa Harrell, William Warren, Jr., Jesse Vann, David Cross, Jesse Benton, Elisha Cross, Peter Packer, Hillory Willey, Jeremiah Speight, Jonathan Smith, Micajah Riddick, Jr., and Willis Brown to attend this Court next Term as Jurymen.

Demsey Trotman granted Administration on the Estate of Miles, Ann and John Scott decd. who were Orphans of James Scott decd. He to give Bond of 50 pds. Miles Rountree and Demsey Jones Securitys.

Bill of Sale for a Negro Girl Venas - Moses Hare to David Rice acknowledged.

Account of Sales of the Estate of Henry Harrell decd. was exhibited by Miles Rountree and proved by the oath of Samuel Harrell.

Miles Rountree Admr. in right of his Wife exhibited an account of the Sales of the Estate of Thomas Harrell orphan of Henry Harrell decd.

Joseph Riddick, Abraham Hurdle, Thomas Hurdle and Reuben Riddick to Audit State and Settle the Accounts of Demsey Trotman with the heirs of Sarah Scott decd. and make a Division of the Estate.

David Jones an Illegitimate Child son of Mary Jones about Eighteen Years of age bound to James Parker to Learn the Business of a Farmer.

The Will of Rachel Trotman decd. was exhibited by Joseph Riddick Extr. therein appointed and was proved by the oath of James Baker.

A Tax of one Shill. 6 pence to be levied on each Taxable poll and 6 pence on each hundred Acres Land.

Joseph Riddick Extr. of Rachel Trotman decd. to sell so much of the Estate as is Perishable.

Lawrence Baker Clerk of this Court to be allowed 18. pds. 10 Shill. for Extra Services done in Augt. last.

20 May 1793.

Present: Christopher Riddick, James Gregory, David Rice, Justices.

Deed of Land - Joshua White to George Outlaw proved by the oath of James Freeman.

Deed of Sale - John Robbins to James Lassiter proved by the oath of Willis Brown.

Deed of Land - James Riddick to Henry Lee proved by the oath of Christopher Riddick.

Deed of Land - Luke Sumner to Elisha Brinkley proved by the oath of Henry Lee.

Deed of Land - Reuben Sparkman & Ux. to Samuel Green proved by the oath of David Lewis.

William King granted Administration on the Estate of John Parnell decd. He to give Bond of 200 pds. Thomas Brickett and Thomas Hurdle Securitys.

Bill of Sale - James Bristow to Isaac Pipkin proved by the oath of James Gatling.

Inventory of the Goods & etc. of the Estate of John Parnell decd. exhibited by William King Admr.

William King Admr. of the Estate of John Parnell decd. to sell all the Estate of the decd.

The Will of Jesse Spivey decd. was exhibited by Mary Spivey Extrx. and Amerias Blanshard Extr. and was proved by the oath of Thomas Hunter.

93

Inventory of the Goods & etc. of the Estate of Jesse Spivey decd. exhibited by Mary Spivey and Ameriah Blanshard Extrx. & Extr.

Division of the Estate of Thomas Trotman decd. made by James Gregory, Simon Stallings, Abraham Hurdle and Moses Hill was exhibited.

James Greogry and Simon Stallings, Mr. Abraham Hurdle and Moses Hill who were appointed to Audit State and Settle the Accounts of Joseph Riddick with the Estate of Thomas Trotman decd. made report.

Joseph Riddick Admr. of the Estate of Mary Rountree decd. exhibited an Inventory of the Goods & etc.

Inventory of the Goods and etc. of the Estate of William Hobbs decd. was exhibited by Thomas Hobbs Admr.

Elisha Hare's ear Mark - a Cross and a Slit in the left ear and a Slit in the right ear.

Joseph Riddick, Moses Hill and Aaron Hobbs who were appointed to Audit State and Settle the accounts of Thomas Hobbs Admr. of William Hobbs decd. and for making a Division of the Estate exhibited proceedings.

John Bird an Illegitimate Child son of Drucilla Bird about Eight years old Bound to Jonathan Lassiter to learn the Businexx of a Blacksmith.

John Howard Orphan of Hardy Howard decd. about eight years old Bound to Isaac Miller to learn the Business of a Farmer.

Joseph Riddick, Thomas Hurdle, Abraham Hurdle and Reuben Riddick who were appointed to Audit State and Settle the Accounts of Demsey Trotman Admr. of William, Noah and John Scott Heirs of Sarah Scott and for making a Division of the Estate made report.

Samuel Eure Guardian to Nancy Eure orphan of Enos Eure decd. exhibited his Account.

Simon Stallings, Ameriah Blanshard and Richard Bond who were appointed to make Division of Abner Blanshard decd. Estate made report.

Account of Sales of the Estate of Abner Blanshard decd. exhibited by Samuel Harrell.

Micajah Blanshard appointed Guardian to John, Kedar, James and Nancy Parker Orphans of Joseph Parker decd. and Ameriah Blanshard and William Williams to be Security on Bond.

Bill of Sale - Nancy D. Meroney to Patty Meroney proved by the oath of William Harriss.

Deed of Sale - Miles Parker to Willis Hughs proved by the oath of William H. Boyce.

Deed of Land - Saml. Williams to Halon Williams proved by the oath of Hezekiah Williams.

Mary Spivey appointed Guardian to Frederick, Sarah, William and Mary Blanshard Orphans of Absolom Blanshard decd. She to give Bond of 1000 pds. Ameriah Blanshard and Miles Rountree Securitys.

The Extrx. and Extr. of Jessey Spivey decd. to sell so much of the personal Estate as will pay his Debts.

William Berriman appointed Guardian to James Freeman Orphan of Richard Freeman. He to give Bond of 300 pds. Joseph Riddick and Reuben Riddick Securitys.

Inventory of the Goods & etc. of the Estate of Rachel Trotman decd. exhibited by Joseph Riddick Admr.

Deed of Land - Isaac Hunter to Thomas Hunter proved by the oath of William Valentine.

Jethro Meltear Constable allowed 48 Shill. for summoning the Inhabitants of Capt. Robert's Capty. to give List of Taxables for 1791 and 1792.

Kedar Hinton Guardian to James Freeman Orphan of Richd. Freeman decd. exhibited his Account.

Mills Eure appointed Overseer of the Road in the District and stead of Israel Beeman resigned.

Millory Willey appointed Overseer of the Road in the District and stead of Jonathan Williams resigned.

Tuesday. Present: William Baker, James Gregory, David Rice, Justices.

Kedar Ballard, Jethro Ballard, James Norfleet and Benjamin Gordon to Audit State and Settle the Accounts of James Small Extr. of Josehua Small.

Kedar Ballard, Jethro Ballard, James Norfleet and Benjamin Gordon to Audit State and Settle the Accounts of James Small Admr. of Daniel Gwinn decd.

Inventory of the Goods & etc. of the Estate of Miles Scott decd. exhibited by Demsey Trotman Admr.

Inventory of the Goods &etc. of the Estate of Noah Scott decd. exhibited by Demsey Trotman Admr.

Inventory of the Goods & etc. of the Estate of John Scott decd. exhibited by Demsey Trotman Admr.

George Williams appointed Overseer of the Road instead of John Baker.

Deed of Sale - Moses Hare to Demsey Odom acknowledged.

Humphry Hudgins allowed 2 pds. 8 Shill. for attending Court Six days as Constable at August & Nov. Courts last.

William Williams appointed Guardian to Polly, Abrella and Elizabeth Blanshard minor Orphans of Abner Blanshard decd. He to give Bond of 1500 pds. William Walters and Ebron Sears Securitys.

Wednesday. Present: Christopher Riddick, William Baker, Thomas Hunter, Justices.

Deed of Land - Thomas Smith to Micajah Phelps proved by the oath of Jonathan Smith.

Bill of Sale - John Darden to Moses Hare proved by the oath of David Rice.

The following to serve as Petit and Grand Jurors at August Term next, to wit, John Van son of Jesse, Benjn. Barnes, Francis Speight, John Odom, William Warren senr., William Crafford, Moses Carter, Edwin Sumner, Patrick Hegerty, Jonathan Roberts, Demsey Odom, Thomas Marshall, Timothy Walton, Miles Rountree, Jacob Eason, Jacob Thomas, Sam'l. Eure, Jesse Harrell, Jonathan Roberts, John B. Walton, Wm. Brooks, Henry Hobbs, John Hoffler, William Hunter, Abraham Hurdle, Nathaniel Riddick, William Hinton, Indian Neck, James B. Sumner, William Matthews and Michal Laurence.

The following Justices to take the Lists of Taxables and taxable property for the year 1795, to wit, Christopher Riddick in Capt. William Harress's Capty., Henry Goodman in Capt. John Bethey's Capty., William Goodman in Capt. Charles Eure's Captaincy, Simon Stallings in Capt. Jona. Robert's Capty., Joseph Riddick in Capt. Isaac Hunter's Capty., Jethro Sumner in Capty. where he commands as Capt., William Baker in Capt. Jesse Benton's Capty.

Henry Copeland, Ann Piland, John Hayes, Willis Hughs and Reuben Riddick to pay a single Tax for their Taxables instead of a double Tax for which they were liable for not giving in Lists of Taxables.

A Suit - Josiah Granbury against Seth Eason for Debt.

The Private examination of Rachel Stallings wife of Seth Stallings to be made by Joseph Riddick who made report.

Account of Sales of part of the Estate of Thomas Trotman decd. exhibited by Joseph Riddick Extr.

Deed of Land - Richard Baker to Patrick Hegerty proved by the oath of Demsey Williams.

Bill of Sale - Even Jones to Patrick Hegerty proved by the oath of Demsey Williams.

Account of Sales of the Estate of Mary Rountree exhibited by John Kittrell Deputy Sheriff.

Account of Sales of the Perishable property of the Estate of Rachel Trotman decd. by William Goodman

Joseph Riddick, James Walton and John B. Walton who were appointed to Audit State and Settle the accounts of Simon Stallings

Extr. of Jacob Spivey decd. made report.

Samuel Harrell to be allowed 4 pds. 8 Shill. for Services as pr. account exhibited.

John Baker appointed Sheriff for the present year. He to give Bond with William Goodman and Jethro Ballard Securitys.

James Gatling appointed Deputy Sheriff.

On the appointment and Qualifacation of the Sheriff Joseph Riddick, Simon Stallings, Jethro Ballard, David Rice and William Baker were present.

William Goodman late Shff. allowed 16.16 for extra Services.

William Walters allowed 3 pds. 12 Shill. for services as Constable.

Third Monday in August. 19 August 1793.

Present: William Baker, William Goodman and Henry Goodman, Justices.

Bill of Sale - Zadock Hinton to Aaron Lassiter for a Negro Woman Hulday proved by the oath of Samuel Harrell.

Deed of Sale - David Cross to James Crafford acknowledged by said Cross.

Deed of Land - William Wallis to James Crafford proved by the oath of Cyprean Cross.

The Will of Mary Cross decd. was exhibited by Abel Cross Extr. therein appointed and proved by the oath of Cyprean Cross one of the Witnesses thereto.

Deed of Land - George Brooks to William Brooks acknowledged.

Joseph Riddick, Simon Stallings, John B. Walton and Moses Hill to Audit State and Settle the accounts of the Extrs. of Amos Trotman decd.

A Petition of Isaac Pipkin and Sundry Inhabitants of this County. The said Isaac Pipkin Build a Water Grist Mill a cross Mill's Swamp where the land belongs to himself on one side and to the Heirs of John Gatling on the other side.

William Goodman, Francis Speight, Solomon King and Lawrence Baker to Audit State and Settle the accounts of Abel Cross Guardian of the Orphans of Henry King, decd.

Isaac Pipkin Guardian to Stephen Rogers orphan of Stephen Rogers decd. exhibited his account.

Isaac Pipkin Guardian to Sarah Rogers orphan of Stephen Rogers decd. exhibited his account.

Henry Goodman, William Gatling, Henry Lee and William Goodman to Lay off and value one Acre of Land on the West Side of Mills's Swamp where Isaac Pipkin has leave to Build a Water Grist Mill.

The Will of Daniel Doughtee was exhibited by William Doughtie Extr. therein appointed and proved by the oath of John Babb one of the Witnesses thereto.

A Petition of William Williams and Nancy Williams. The Sheriff to summons a Jury and lay off the Dower of Nancy Williams who was relict of Abner Blanshard decd. out of the lands said Abner Blanshard died possessed with.

Benjamin Weaver a Molatto Boy son of Lucy Weaver bound to James Weaver to learn the Business of a Shoemaker. The above orphan about fourteen years of age.

The Will of Moses Benton decd. was exhibited by Thomas Parker and Miles Benton Extrs. therein appointed and proved by the oath of David Benton.

Inventory of the Goods and Etc. of the Estate of Moses Benton decd. exhibited by Thomas Parker and Miles Benton Extrs.

Patrick Hegerty, Elisha Cross, William Walters and Jonathan Rogers to Audit State and Settle the accounts of Henry Goodman Admr. of James Arline decd.

John Baker, Jonathan Roberts, Willis Brown and Thomas Marshall to Audit State and Settle the accounts of James Rawls Admr. of William Booth decd.

The Court having issued an order for the purpose of laying off the dower of Elizabeth Hurdle relict of Joseph Hurdle decd. out of Certian Lands lying and being in Perquimans County the Sheriff having summoned a Jury who posponed acting there being a prior Petition for dower out of said lands by John Jones & Ux. of the County of Perquimans.

Miles Binton granted Administration on the Estate of John Morgan decd. He to give Bond of 200 pds. Francis Speight and Elisha Cross Securitys.

Inventory of the Goods and etc. of the Estate of John Morgan decd. was exhibited by Miles Benton Admr.

Henry Goodman, Jonathan Rogers, William Goodman and Philip Rogers to Audit State and Settle the Accounts of John Lang Admr. of James Lang decd.

Henry Goodman, Jonathan Rogers, William Goodman and Philip Rogers to make a Division of the Estate of James Lang decd.

<u>Friday</u>. Present: Joseph Riddick, Jethro Sumner, David Rice, James Gregory, William Baker and Simon Stallings, Justices.

Sarah Parker relict of William Parker decd. and Amos Parker granted Administration on the Estate of William Parkder decd. They to give Bond of 200 pds. Jethro Benton and James Jones Securitys.

John Baker Sheriff made a protest against the insufficiancy of

Jail of this County.

William Baker County Trustee exhibited his accounts for the years 1789, 1790 and 1791.

Deed of Sale - Daniel Eure to Uriah Eure proved by the oath of Luke Langston.

Henry Goodman who was appointed to take a List of Taxables in Capt. Bethey's Captaincy made report.

Christopher Riddick who was appointed to take a List of Taxables made report.

Jethro Sumner who was appointed to take a List of Taxables in the Capty. where he commands made report.

Inventory of the Goods & etc. of the Estate of William Parker decd. was exhibited by Sarah Parker Admx. and Amos Parker Admr.

Sarah Parker and Amos Parker Admx. and Admr. of William Parker decd. to sell so much as will pay his Debts.

Simon Stallings who was appointed to take a List of Taxables in the Capty. of Capt. Jonathan Roberts made report.

Solomon King, Henry Goodman, Francis Speight and Henry Speight who were appointed to Audit State and Settle the accounts of William Odom Admr. of Hardy Howard decd. made report.

William Arnold, Thomas Parker, James Knight and Jethro Benton to make a Division of the Estate of William Parker decd.

Sarah Parker Admx. and Amos Parker Admr. of William Parker decd. to sell the personal Estate of Orphan of William Parker decd.

Wednesday. Present: Christopher Riddick, Jethro Sumner and David Rice, Justices.

Account of Sales of part of the Estate of Jesse Spivey decd. was exhibited by James Gatling Deputy Sheriff.

The Sheriff summoned a Jury to lay off and alott to Elizabeth Hurdle relict of Joseph Hurdle decd. her Dower in certain Lands which said Jos. died possessed with. Return made as follows, to wit, We the jurors being Sworn to set off and allot to Elizabeth Hurdle widow of Joseph Hurdle senr., decd. one third part of the manse plantation and Land adjoining the same, Viz. land joining Reuben Riddick, the Swamp Field, the Land, the old Field, Priviledges of all Houses except the old Barn; priviledges of all appertanances except one Tarkiln that is already Built by Abraham Hurdle which she the said Elizabeth Hurdle is to have one fourth part of; one third part of all the Desert Lands. Signed: William King, Moses Hill, Miles Rountree, James Baker, Jacob Gordon, Benjamin Gordon, James Walton, James Small, Seth Rountree, Wm. Hunter, Samuel Green, Nathl. Riddick and James Gatling D. Shff.

Jethro Ballard, Kedar Ballard, Benjamin Gordon and James Norfleet to Audit State and Settle the accounts of Daniel Powell and James

Powell Extrs. of Jacob Powell decd.

James Gregory, Thomas Hunter, Job Riddick and Timothy Lassiter to Audit State and Settle the accounts of David Rice and Isaac Costen Extrs. of James Costen decd.

William Goodman and Henry Goodman appointed Guardians of John King, Eliza. King, Mary King and Sally King orphans of Henry King decd. They to give Bond of 4000 pds. John Odom and Francis Speight Securitys.

James Gregory, Joseph Riddick and Thomas Hunter who were appointed to Audit State and Settle the Accounts of Thomas Hurdle and Abraham Hurdle Admrs. of Joseph Hurdle decd. made report.

James Gregory, David Rice and Thomas Hunter who were appointed to make a Division of the Estate of Joseph Hurdle decd. made report.

David Rice, William Hunter and James Gregory who were appointed to Audit State and Settle the Accounts of Amos Trotman, Kedar Hill and Thomas Hunter Extrs. of Jacob Bagley decd. made report.

Joseph Riddick who was appointed to take a List of Taxables in the Capty. of Capt. Isaac Hunter made return.

Additional Inventory of the Estate of Rachel Trotman decd. was exhibited by Joseph Riddick Extr.

In a Suit brought by James Toye Hayes Guardian and next friend to James Hayes against James Hayes Ransom plea De_____(?) Jury impannelled and Sworn say the defendant does detain the Negroe Slaves following mentioned in the Plaintiffs declaration Viz. Negroe Man Harry valued to 125 pds., Negro Woman Bridget to 75 pds., Woman Chaney to 75 pds., Man Sam to 116.13.4, Man Harey to 83.6.8 pds., Woman Sillar to 66.13.4 pds., Girl Lucy to 38.6.8 pds., Girl Patiance to 20 pds., Girl Nan to 25 pds., Boy Charles to 16.12.4 pds.

Deed of Sale - Patrick Hegerty & Ux. to Evan Jones acknowledged by Patrick Hegerty.

Jethro Sumner, Jesse Benton, William Wallus and Peter Parker to Audit and Settle the accounts of William Doughtee Extr. of Edward Doughtee decd.

Deed of Land - Even Jones to William Ellis acknowledged.

Jesse Saunders appointed Guardian to Miles Parker orphan of Francis Parker decd. and that he give Bond of 600 pds. Benjamin Barnes and Francis Speight Securitys.

Thursday August 22nd., 1793.

Present: William Baker, James Gregory and Joseph Riddick, Justices.

The Sheriff summons a Jury and Lay off a public Road beginning at Sandyridge Road near William Kings Plantation or Hurdle's Mill path thence the most convenient way across to the Edenton Road between Seth Rountrees and Capt. Richard Mitchalls Plantation.

The Sheriff summons Asa Harrell, William Warren junr., Thomas Barnes, Abel Cross, Isaac Langston, Demsey Harrell, James Curle, Josiah Harrell, David Lewis, John Vann, Hillory Willey, Henry Speight, Richard Barnes, Micajah Riddick junr., Samuel Smith, Henry Smith, Isaac Costin, James Costin, Timothy Lassiter, Noah Harrell, Moses Hill, Benjamin Gordon, James Small, William Hurdle, Aaron Hobbs, Demsey Jones, James Outlaw, Levin Dure and Richard Mitchell and Simeon Brinkley - personally to appear at this Court next Term as Jurymen.

The Sheriff Summons James Walton, Seth Rountree, John B. Walton and Jesse Walton to personally appear at Edenton in October next as Jurymen at the Supr. Court.

Micajah Blanshard moved for Administration on the Estate of Priscilla Parker orphan of Joseph Parker decd. He to give Bond of 100 pds. John B. Walton and William Williams Securitys.

It having been represented to this Court that the County Lines between this County and the Countys of Pasquotank and Perquimans have not hitherto been run and that a considerable part of the County of Pasquotank will be cut off by the NEast line of the County and added to it, however inconveniantly actuated and as this Count are not desirous of acquiring any addition to their County more than was wished and expected which was to be bounded by the Pasquotank and Perquimans lines It is ordered that Joseph Riddick and Benjamin Jones of Pasquotank be requested to act in concert to have the lines of this County laid out bounded as aforesaid so that no dispute may in future take place either in respect of the Boundary of the County or of Private Property and that the Representatives of this County be requested to have the same affected by a Public Law at the next General Assembly under the direction of the said Joseph Riddick and Benjamin Jones Commissioners aforesaid.

William Goodman was appointed to take a List of Taxables and Tax.

Simon Stallings, James Freeman, John B. Walton and Timothy Walton to Audit and Settle the Accounts of Micajah Blanshard Admr. of Priscilla Parker decd. Minor Orphan of Joseph Parker decd.

Simon Stallings, James Freeman, John B. Walton and Timothy Walton to Divide the Estate of Priscilla Parker minor Orphan of Joseph Parker decd.

William Goodman, late Sheriff of this County, to be allowed in the Settlement of his Accounts for the Tax on the following persons to wit, John Delaney, John Harriss, John Wills, John Parnell, Joshua White, Christmas Perry, John Henderson, John Lewis Clozel, Randolph Moor and Charles Rooks.

Third Monday, 18 November, 1793.

Present: Christopher Riddick, David Rice and William Goodman Justices.

Henry Goodman, Philip Rogers and William Goodman three of the

Gentlemen who were appointed to Audit and Settle the Accounts of John Lang Admr. of James Lang decd. made report.

Henry Goodman, Philip Rogers and William Goodman who were appointed to make a Division of the Estate of James Lang decd. made report.

Inventory of the Goods & etc. which was of the Estate of Mary Cross decd. was exhibited by Abel Cross Admr.

Mary Parker and Robert Parker were granted Administration on the Estate of Willis Parker decd. They to give Bond of 1000 pds. John Vann and John Lewis Securitys.

Inventory of the Goods & etc. of the Estate of Daniel Doughtee was exhibited by William Doughtee Extr. (Note: All this entry marked out.)

Jethro Sumner, William Walters and Jesse Benton who were appointed to make a Division of the Estate of Edward Doughtee decd. made report.

Jethro Sumner, William Walters and Jesse Benton who were appointed to Audit and Settle the accounts of William Doughtee Admr. of Edward Doughtee decd. made report.

The Will of Dorcas Vann decd. was exhibited by Isaac Langston and Luke Langston Extrs. therein appointed and proved by the oath of Lewis Sparkman one of the Witnesses thereto.

Inventory of the Goods & etc. of the Estate of Dorcus Vann decd. was exhibited by Luke Langston and Isaac Langston Extrs.

Inventory of the Goods & etc. of the Estate of Daniel Doughtee decd. was exhibited by William Doughtee.

Elisha Landing appointed Overseer of the road instead of David Lewis resigned.

Lease for Land - Bray Warren to Sarah Winborn acknowledged.

Deed of Land - James B. Sumner to George Allen proved by the oath of Samuel Smith.

Deed of Land - Reuben Harrell and Ann Harrell to Elisha Harrell Proved by the oath of Lewis Sparkman.

Deed of Land - William Wallis & Ux. to David Cross proved by the oath of Abel Cross.

Deed of Land - Bray Warren & Ux. to Henry Copeland acknowledged and at the same time Priscilla Warren was privately examined by William Goodman.

Deed of Land - Clayborn Osten & Ux. to Henry Goodman acknowledged and at the same time Rachel Osten was privately examined by Wm. Goodman who reported she relinquished her right of Dower.

Deed of Land - John Wallis & Ux. to David Cross proved by the oath of Wat Phelps.

Deed of Land - Elisha Brinkley to John Brinkley proved by the oath of Pa. Hegerty.

Deed of Land - Luke Sumner to John Brinkley proved by the oath of Pa. Hagerty.

Deed of Land - Richard Bond & Ux. to Demsey Jones proved by the oath of Thomas Lodsom and at the same time Mary Bond was privately examined by William Goodman who reported that she relinquished her right to the said land.

Robert Parker junr. appointed Overseer of the Road in the Room of Willis Parker decd.

Tuesday. Present: Thomas Hunter, Christopher Riddick, David Rice and William Goodman, Justices.

Agreeable to a Writ of Dower directed to the Sheriff of this County for the purpose of laying off the Dower of Nancy Williams relict of Abner Blanshard decd. the Sheriff having summoned a Jury and they laid off the Dower of the said Nancy Williams in the manner following, towit, State of North Carolina Gates County. We the Jurors being summoned to Alot unto Nancy Williams one third part of the Lands that her decd. Husband died seized with & etc. - Land joining Jacob Spivey, plantation of Abner Blanshard decd.. James Lasiter, Moses Hill, Noah (X) Harrell, John Hare, Willis Brown, John Lewis, Joseph (X) Taylor, Josiah (X) Parker, Palatiah Blanshard, Richard Bond, Demsey (X) O. Jones, Samuel (B) Brown. Test, James Gatling.

Account of Sales of part of the Estate of William Parker junr. decd. was exhibited by James Gatling Depty Shff.

A Negro Boy named Jess belonging to the Estate of Abner Blanshard decd. to be sold by the Sheriff in order to be divided between the orphans of said Blanshard.

Account of Sales of the Estate of John Parnell decd. was exhibited by William King Admr.

Jos. Riddick, James Baker, Thomas Brickell and Thomas Hunter to Audit and Settle the accounts of William King Admr. of John Parnell decd.

Mary Parker and Robert Parker Admr. of Willis Parker decd. to sell so much of the Estate of the decd. as will pay his debts.

Inventory of the Goods & etc. of the Estate of Willis Parker decd. was exhibited by Mary Parker and Robert Parker Admx. and Admr.

Deed of Land - John Powell of Jacob and Ux. to James Jones proved by the oath of William Ellis.

The Sheriff to sell the Perishable Estate of the Orphans of John Duntree decd.

Deed of Land - Henry Forrest & Ux. to William Lewis proved by the oath of Jonathan Roberts.

Kedar Ballard, William Arnold, Jethro Sumner and Jethro Ballard to Audit and Settle the accounts of Thomas Parker with the Estate of Elizabeth Norfleet decd.

Thomas Marshall, Jonathan Roberts and Willis Brown who were appointed to Audit and Settle the accounts of James Rawls Admr. of William Booth decd. made report.

James Piland was granted Administration on the Estate of Thomas Piland his Brother decd. He to give Boud of 150 pds. John and Jesse Harrell Securitys.

Inventory of the Goods & etc. of the Estate of Thomas Piland decd. was exhibited by James Piland Admr.

The following Persons to be summoned where the Orphans live who are in a distresed situation, summoned to appear at this Court with the said Orphans to be bound out agreeabl to Law, viz. David Watson with Isam Curle, Benjamin Beasly and James Beasly at James Powell, Josse Rogers at Ann Hiatt, Isaac Gwinn at John Slaven's, Easter Matthews with Jesse Smith, Timothy Lassiter with Wm. Lassiter and _____ (Blank in original book) with James Minyard.

Wednesday. Present: Christopher Riddick, James Gregory and Jethro Ballard, Justices.

William Harris appointed Guardian to William Pugh Jameson Orphan of Samuel Heath Jameson decd. He to give Bond of 1000 pds. Jethro Ballard and Richard Mitchell Securitys.

Thomas Hunter, Joseph Riddick, Simon Stallings and James Baker who were appointed to make a Division of the Estate of John Rountree decd. made report.

James Small appointed Overseer of the Road in the Room of John Small resigned.

Present: William Baker and Simon Stallings.

Francis Speight, Henry Speight, Philip Lewis and Isaac Pipkin junr. to Audit and Settle the accounts of Fereby Parker Extrx. of Francis Parker decd. with the Estate.

Francis Speight, Henry Spright, Philip Leiws and Isaac Pipkin junr. to make a Division of the Estate of Francis Parker decd. agreeable to the Will.

Jethro Ballard, Kedar Ballard and Benjamin Gordon appointed to Audit and Settle the accounts of James Small Extr. of Joshua Small decd.

A Noncupative Will was Exhibited by Jethro Sumner Admr. of Edwin Sumner decd. and was proved by the oaths of Jethro Sumner and Ebenezer Graham Witnesses thereto. Jethro Sumner quallified as

Admr. of Edwin Sumner decd. He to give Bond of 6000 pds. Jethro Ballard and William Harris Securitys.

Agreeable to an Order of the Supr. Court of Law of the District of Edenton where Josiah Collins made application for Administration on the Estate of Samuel Heath Jameson decd., the said Collins gave Bond of 1000 pds. with John Hamilton and Jacob Blount his Securitys.

Grand Jurors for Novr. Term 1793, viz. Sam'l. Smith, Foreman, Henry Smith, William Hurdle, Isaac Costen, James Costen, Noah Harrell, Asa Harrell, James Small, Isaac Langston, Micajah Riddick, James Outlaw, Simeon Brinkley, Abel Cross and Richard Barnes.

Thursday. Present: Thomas Hunter, William Baker, William Goodman and Henry Goodman, Justices.

Deed of Land - Jonathan Rogers to James Gatling proved by the oath of Patrick Hegerty.

The Sheriff of this County to Summons the following persons to serve as Petit and Grand Jurors at the Court at next setting (to wit) John Lang, John Hoffler, Francis Speight, William Hurdle, David Cross, Demsey Trotman, Luten Lewis, Joseph Taylor, Jonathan Rogers, Moses Hill, Elisha Cross, John B. Walton, Noah Felton, Benjamin Gordon, Lewis Walters, Moses Briggs, Jonathan Williams, Abraham Green, William Cleaves, William Pierce, John Parker Gatling, Nathaniel Riddick, Charles Eure, Jacob Eason, James B. Sumner, Jonathan Lassiter, Elijah Harrell, Timothy Walton, William Warren junr. and Demsey Langston.

James Gatling granted Administration on the Estate of John Gatling decd. He to give Bond of 6000 pds. William Harriss and Mills Lewis Securitys.

Inventory of the Goods & etc. of the Estate of John Gatling decd. was exhibited by James Gatling.

The Guardian of Elizabeth King orphan of Henry King decd. to sell ___ of the young Negros belonging to the said orphan to pay a debt for raising and maintaining her other Negros.

James Gatling Admr. of the Estate of John Gatling decd. to sell all the perishable part of the Estate of the decd.

Court Adjourned.

INDEX

Allen 101
Alphin 30,44
Anderson 17
Arline 3,27,49,62,63,64,67,68,75,78,85,86,97
Arnold 1,5,11,14,15,19,20,26,35,36,38,44,51,53,64,65,84,85,90,98,103
Atkinson 28
Babb 97
Bagley 9,16,32,52,71,89,90,99
Baker 1,2,4,5,6,8,9,10,11,12,13,14,15,18,21,22,24,25,26,28,29,30,32,35,36,37,38,39,41,43,45,46,47,48,49,50,51,53,54,56,57,58,59,60,61,62,63,64,65,67,68,69,70,71,72,75,77,78,79,81,82,83,84,85,86,88,90,92,94,95,96,97,98,99,102,103,104
Ballard 8,12,13,17,21,22,24,25,26,28,29,35,36,39,44,46,47,48,50,51,55,57,58,62,63,65,66,67,69,70,73,76,78,81,83,84,90,91,94,96,98,103,104
Barnes/Barns 5,6,10,11,12,13,19,21,28,29,30,33,35,40,41,46,47,48,53,58,60,62,65,66,67,70,72,75,76,79,81,82,84,85,86,95,99,100,104
Barr 26,68,73
Beasly 48,103
Beeman 10,28,32,35,44,45,46,48,62,76,85,86,89,90,94
Bennett/Bennit 28,36,55,57,61,64,68
Benton/Binton 4,5,6,8,10,11,12,21,22,26,27,29,30,32,35,36,38,40,41,43,44,45,48,50,51,54,56,57,58,59,60,61,63,64,65,68,70,71,73,76,77,78,81,82,86,91,95,97,98,99,101

Berryman/Berriman 13,37,49,55,60,61,94
Bethey 9,10,20,21,29,35,58,77,78,79,83,95,98
Bird 93
Blair 65
Blanshard 6,7,12,15,19,30,34,39,41,43,44,52,55,59,60,69,73,74,76,80,81,85,88,90,92,93,94,95,97,100,102
Blount 104
Bond 3,7,11,15,19,21,22,24,25,29,30,34,38,39,44,53,54,59,61,65,67,73,77,80,81,86,87,88,91,93,102
Boon 35
Booth 5,6,14,15,19,30,36,39,40,44,48,53,59,69,81,82,97,103
Bowen 37
Bowing 8
Boyce 11,19,23,24,28,33,34,35,44,47,56,60,64,65,67,68,72,78,80,93
Brady/Braddy 31,32,40,45,46,49,55,66
Brayshar 2
Brickell 8,12,13,14,15,17,23,70,102
Brickett 92
Briggs/Brigs 4,35,38,47,48,57,59,76,78,79,85,104
Brinkley 4,8,27,37,38,39,40,41,53,60,74,79,92,100,102,104
Bristow/Brisco 10,13,19,28,32,34,38,39,40,46,56,72,87,92
Brooks 10,13,26,27,30,40,48,53,62,65,68,79,80,82,85,89,95,96
Browne/Brown 5,7,12,15,16,18,19,21,26,28,30,31,32,40,41,47,49,54,59,60,68,75,76,79,81,82,83,85,86,89,91,92,97,102,103
Burket 46
Carter 1,12,18,20,28,32,42,46,52,62,63,65,67,75,76,78,85,87,95
Chaney 13
Cleaves 11,14,19,30,33,34,35,40,44,45,48,57,79,85,104
Clozel 42,100
Coffield 82
Cole 36
Collins/Collings/Cullins 9,26,29,48,56,58,62,64,67,77,104
Copeland 1,3,7,15,17,24,30,31,32,36,39,41,47,49,62,74,95,101
Costen/Costin 4,6,11,18,26,30,44,47,53,54,59,62,65,70,71,72,76,77,82,88,91,99,100,104
Cowpers/Cowper 27,66,76,85,91
Crafford/Crawford 2,6,14,26,30,35,40,42,45,61,65,66,82,84,85,95,96
Cross 10,12,13,16,19,21,25,26,27,28,29,30,32,33,35,40,41,44,45,46,48,49,50,53,56,57,58,60,61,62,63,64,65,66,67,70,72,73,75,78,79,81,82,84,85,86,91,96,97,100,101,104

Crutchlow 81,82
Cuff 28,30
Cumming/Cummings 2,9,68
Curle 47,48,57,62,82,100,103
Darden 14,15,29,36,37,46,49,
  61,62,71,79,89,90,95
Daughtee/Daughtie/Daughty/
Doughtee/Doughtie 5,11,14,19,
  21,26,35,37,39,40,44,49,
  54,56,57,63,65,71,75,79,
  85,87,97,99,101
Davidson 1,2,7,10,28,33,57,73
Davis 1,2,5,17,26,38,44,50,56,
  60,64,81,87
Delaney 100
Dewpres (?) 8
Dilday/Delday 3,9,26,27,31,47,
  49,52,76,90
Douglas 59
Drake 3,27
Draper 1
Drury 21,23,38
Dudley 23
Duke 12,32
Dunn 76,77,81,82,83
Dure 69,70,72,81,82,87,91,100
Dwire/Dwyre 67,71
Eason 1,2,3,4,5,6,7,8,9,10,12,
  15,17,18,19,21,22,23,24,
  25,26,28,29,30,34,35,36,
  37,38,42,44,47,49,50,51,
  53,56,58,60,61,63,65,66,
  70,71,73,74,76,79,80,82,
  83,84,85,86,88,89,90,95,
  104
Edwards 16,19,20,25
Ellis 1,2,5,7,8,12,14,19,20,
  21,25,26,27,29,31,35,37,
  41,42,43,44,46,47,48,50,
  54,55,57,58,68,70,72,77,
  79,86,99,102
Eure 1,2,5,6,7,8,10,11,12,14,
  15,18,19,22,26,27,29,31,
  35,40,42,44,45,46,48,53,
  54,55,58,59,62,67,68,70,
  72,76,77,78,79,82,91,93,
  94,95,98,104
Evans 84
Farrow 48
Faulk 27,49
Felton 1,14,19,34,36,37,43,
  45,54,60,64,67,68,70,90,
  104
Figg 30,33,40,57
Finney 8,18,22,41,53
Fitt 88

Forrest/Forrist/Forest 5,14,29,
  30,33,37,38,44,45,46,48,
  56,57,58,60,64,66,68,70,
  79,82,103
Foster 7,10,74
Fountain 27
Freeman 3,4,5,10,12,14,15,16,
  21,23,25,29,30,31,32,33,
  38,38,41,43,44,48,49,53,
  54,55,56,57,59,66,70,71,
  76,77,78,79,81,87,91,92,
  94,100
Fryer 28
Fullington 14,17,22
Garlock 59
Garrett 5,18,41,54,75,91
Garvey 2,88
Gatling 3,9,10,15,16,18,20,21,
  23,28,30,31,35,39,41,42,
  44,46,47,48,51,52,54,56,
  58,59,60,70,71,72,75,76,
  84,85,86,88,90,91,92,96,
  98,102,104
Gibson 16,25
Glover 83
Gooden 50
Goodman 1,3,5,6,8,9,10,11,12,
  17,18,19,20,21,22,24,25,
  27,28,29,31,33,35,36,38,
  39,41,42,43,44,45,46,47,
  48,49,50,51,52,53,54,57,
  58,59,62,63,64,65,55,57,
  68,69,70,71,72,73,74,75,
  76,77,78,79,80,81,82,83,
  84,85,86,87,88,89,91,95,
  96,97,98,99,100,101,102,
  104
Gootie 16
Gordon 3,5,6,12,13,14,17,22,
  23,24,25,29,30,33,37,38,
  39,41,43,45,46,47,50,54,
  65,70,71,73,74,82,84,85,
  86,87,88,90,91,94,98,100,
  103,104
Graham 89,103
Granbery 1,2,6,7,10,15,21,22,
  24,26,27,29,33,37,46,47,
  56,58,62,64,67,70,71,85,
  95
Green 6,7,12,16,23,27,28,36,
  38,43,48,67,68,76,77,79,
  84,92,98,104
Gregory 3,8,9,10,13,17,19,20,
  22,23,24,25,26,27,29,32,
  33,36,38,39,40,42,44,46,
  47,49,53,55,58,61,62,63,
  65,67,68,70,72,73,74,77,
  78,80,81,82,83,84,85,86,
  87,88,89,90,91,92,93,94,
  97,99,103

Griffin 21,24,44,51,59,
    64
Griggs 86
Gwinn/Gwin 18,25,32,50,
    73,91,94,103
Hall 35,55,68
Hamilton/Hamelton 18,74,
    75,76,80,104
Hare 4,5,6,15,19,23,25,
    38,41,48,51,54,57,
    58,60,61,66,68,75,
    76,82,89,91,93,94,
    95,102
Hargrove/Hargroves 14,23
Harrell 1,2,3,6,7,10,11,
    13,14,17,19,21,23,
    24,25,26,28,30,31,
    33,34,35,36,37,38,
    40,41,42,43,44,45,
    47,48,51,53,54,55,
    57,58,60,61,62,63,
    65,67,68,70,72,73,
    74,75,76,78,79,80,
    81,82,84,85,87,91,
    92,93,95,96,100,
    101,102,103,104
Harriss/Harris/Harress
    5,9,10,12,14,16,21,
    22,25,29,30,33,34,
    35,37,40,41,44,45,
    47,48,52,53,54,58,
    59,61,62,64,69,78,
    81,82,83,84,90,91,
    93,95,100,103,104
Harvey/Harvy 45,48
Haslett/Haslet 25,66,67,
    78,85
Hawes 13
Hayes/Hase/Hays 16,29,
    56,67,68,95,99
Hegerty/Hagerty 17,34,
    40,41,44,45,46,50,
    57,58,62,64,69,75,
    82,83,89,95,97,99,
    102,104
Henderson 100
Hiatt 9,28,79,103
Hill 4,7,10,11,13,15,16,
    17,21,22,26,28,29,
    30,31,32,34,35,38,
    39,40,41,42,44,47,
    51,52,53,54,56,61,
    64,65,67,68,69,70,
    71,73,74,75,76,78,
    84,85,87,89,90,91,
    93,96,98,99,100,
    102,104
Hilton 53

Hines 13,44,61
Hinton 5,9,19,24,25,27,30,36,37,38,
    39,40,41,44,46,48,54,56,59,60,
    61,65,66,69,70,74,76,79,82,85,
    87,88,89,90,91,94,95,96
Hobbs 1,3,11,14,16,17,20,31,35,43,
    44,47,51,53,60,64,65,72,74,79,
    82,87,89,90,91,93,95,100
Hocton 39
Hodges 2,17,38,50,53,75
Hoffler/Jofler 4,10,11,12,26,28,41,
    42,43,65,66,70,79,82,85,95,104
Holland 84
Howard 13,27,59,72,88,93,98
Howell 9,16
Hudgins 5,10,12,14,26,30,34,37,40,43,
    44,45,47,54,57,59,61,69,70,74,75,
    79,87,89,90,91,94
Hughes/Hewes/Hughs 29,55,65,67,93
Hunter 3,4,6,7,8,9,10,11,12,13,14,15,
    16,17,18,20,21,22,23,24,25,26,27,
    28,29,30,31,32,33,34,35,36,37,38,
    39,40,42,43,44,46,47,49,51,52,53,
    54,56,57,58,59,60,63,64,69,70,72,
    73,74,76,78,79,80,81,82,84,87,88,
    90,91,92,94,95,98,99,102,103,104
Hurdle 4,8,9,10,11,12,14,23,24,26,29,
    34,35,37,38,43,47,48,49,53,55,56,
    57,58,60,61,64,68,73,74,76,78,79,
    83,84,85,86,87,88,89,90,91,92,93,
    95,97,98,99,100,104
Iredell 15,27,47,65,75
Jameson/Jamison 69,81,83,90,103,104
Jernagan/Jarnigan 81,82
Jones 1,3,4,6,7,8,18,24,25,27,30,31,
    38,39,40,41,44,47,48,50,51,53,
    57,59,60,65,70,73,76,80,83,84,
    88,90,91,92,95,97,99,100,102
Jordon 16,70
Kelly 27,43,52,58
King 11,14,20,28,33,35,37,46,56,65,67,
    68,71,76,79,80,81,82,83,84,85,88,
    91,92,96,98,99,102,104
Kittrell 3,13,14,15,18,32,33,38,45,57,
    62,63,64,68,77,80,81,83,85,86,95
Knight 6,11,14,25,26,68,79,91,98
Landing 2,10,19,28,30,33,35,40,61,72,
    85,86,101
Lang 21,24,66,67,71,77,83,97,101,104
Langston 1,7,30,37,39,40,41,43,47,48,
    53,56,65,85,91,98,100,101,104
Lassiter/Lasseter 5,6,10,14,18,21,26,
    27,29,30,33,34,35,36,38,39,43,44,
    45,48,52,54,55,60,61,64,65,69,70,
    71,72,73,74,78,80,81,82,85,86,88,
    92,93,96,99,100,102,103,104
Lawrence/Laurence 10,23,48,59,62,71,
    80,95

Lee 9,10,13,19,21,23,29,37,38,
     46,48,60,76,79,82,85,92,
     96
Lewis 5,7,12,13,16,20,23,30,
     32,36,40,43,44,45,46,48,
     52,53,54,56,58,59,60,62,
     63,65,68,70,73,75,76,81,
     82,83,84,89,91,92,100,
     101,102,103,104
Lilly 38
Lodsom 102
McCoy 28
McCullgh (?) 21
McCullok/McCullock/McColloh
     25,30,33,39,44,50
McDonald 2
Manion 28
March 9
Marshall/Marshal 13,15,26,29,
     35,36,44,47,48,52,54,58,
     59,60,63,90,95,97,103
Matthews 7,14,22,27,30,33,37,
     40,43,45,64,68,95,103
Matthias 35,60,81,85
Meltear 6,7,22,26,39,49,50,
     60,61,64,66,68,87,88,94
Menshew/Menchew/Minshew/Minchew
     11,22,30,34,39,48,53,61,
     64,67,70,73,77,79,82,85
Menyard/Minyard 6,103
Meredith 1
Miller 1,9,26,30,33,35,37,40,
     45,47,53,64,67,68,74,93
Mironey/Meroney 18,28,93
Mitchell/Mitchall 2,9,12,21,
     27,35,53,60,79,91,100,
     103
Moore/Moor/More 18,27,49,52,
     67,70,83,100
Morgan 14,26,38,53,57,61,64,
     85,89,97
Morris/Morriss 1,7,29,46,48,
     56,66,79,90
Napper 49
Nichols 70,71
Nixon 49,51
Norfleet 4,11,12,19,23,29,30,
     35,36,37,39,41,42,44,48,
     49,50,51,56,57,62,63,66,
     68,82,89,91,94,98,103
Norris/Nouris 48,88
Odom 5,11,13,15,16,18,19,23,
     24,25,27,28,29,32,35,36,
     37,40,44,45,46,47,48,49,
     50,52,53,58,60,62,64,68,
     69,70,72,73,75,76,79,81,
     85,86,87,88,89,94,95,98,
     99

Ostin/Osten 48,84,101
Outlaw 4,5,10,13,16,18,21,23,
     26,31,35,43,49,60,64,65,
     66,71,74,76,80,87,91,92,
     100,104
Owens 46
Packer 91
Parker 5,9,10,11,12,14,15,16,
     17,19,20,21,23,26,27,28,
     29,30,32,34,36,37,39,40,
     44,45,46,47,48,49,51,52,
     53,56,57,59,60,61,63,64,
     66,67,68,70,71,74,75,76,
     77,79,81,82,83,85,86,89,
     90,91,92,93,97,98,99,100,
     101,102,103
Parnell 31,92,100,102
Pentell 86
Perry/Parry/Perrey 2,13,19,26,
     43,56,58,66,71,79,84,85,
     86,100
Phelps/Filps 8,18,28,46,56,66,
     68,71,84,95,102
Phillips 27
Pierce 61,66,71,79,104
Piland/Pyland 8,16,20,21,25,26,
     28,30,33,35,37,40,42,48,55,
     56,62,63,67,68,70,76,84,85,
     87,95,103
Pipkin/Pipken/Pepkin 3,8,10,11,
     15,16,17,18,20,23,33,34,39,
     40,44,45,46,52,55,58,66,72,
     73,92,96,103
Polson 55,67,81
Powell 2,5,13,21,26,28,29,30,35,
     37,40,41,42,43,44,53,55,58,
     59,60,61,65,76,78,81,82,87,
     88,90,91,98,99,102,103
Pruden 1,5,14,26,29,53,68,70,85,
     90
Pugh 89
Purvis 76
Raby/Rabey 25,55,67,71
Ransom 66,99
Rawls/Rawles 49,53,59,69,81,82,
     97,103
Reed/Reid 51,77,78,79,83,89,90
Rice 4,5,6,7,8,9,10,11,13,14,15,
     17,18,22,26,27,28,29,30,32,
     36,38,39,40,41,42,43,44,46,
     47,48,49,51,53,54,55,58,59,
     60,62,63,65,66,69,70,72,76,
     78,82,83,84,85,86,88,90,91,
     92,94,95,96,97,98,99,100,102

Riddick/Reddick 1,3,4,5,
6,7,8,9,10,11,12,13,
14,15,17,18,19,20,21,
22,23,24,25,26,27,28,
29,30,31,32,33,34,35,
36,37,38,39,40,41,42,
43,44,45,46,47,48,49,
51,52,53,54,55,57,58,
59,60,61,62,63,64,65,
66,67,68,70,71,72,73,
74,75,76,77,78,79,80,
82,83,84,85,86,88,89,
90,91,92,93,94,95,96,
97,98,99,100,102,103,
104
Ritter 46,48,62,76
Roberts 7,9,10,12,19,21,
22,30,35,36,37,39,
40,44,48,51,52,54,
56,58,59,60,63,64,
66,70,73,74,78,79,
85,86,88,95,97,98,
103
Robertson 42,46,63,89
Robins/Robbins 23,28,29,
30,34,36,52,54,58,
59,70,76,92
Rochell/Rochel 36,39
Rogers 3,10,12,14,16,17,
19,20,24,26,27,29,
48,50,51,57,63,64,
65,66,67,68,69,71,
72,73,75,77,79,82,
83,86,88,90,96,97,
100,101,103,104
Rogerson 1,54,84
Rooks 8,13,14,27,42,66,
100
Ross 90
Rountree/Roundtree 2,3,
4,5,7,9,11,12,15,
18,20,29,33,34,35,
37,42,43,44,51,58,
60,65,70,73,74,76,
82,85,87,88,89,90,
91,92,93,94,95,98,
100,102,103
Russell/Russel 19,49,50,
66
Saunders 6,12,13,16,17,
21,23,29,36,37,49,
67,71,72,76,80,82,
99
Savage 77
Scott 4,6,27,63,69,70,
76,77,78,80,81,82,
83,91,92,93,94
Sears 9,31,40,49,55,64,
65,95
Sharp 52

Shepherd 19,79
Simors 84
Skinner 16,27,30,42
Skito 8
Slavin 21,103
Small 1,2,11,15,19,24,32,36,40,42,43,
44,46,50,51,53,55,59,68,73,77,
79,94,98,100,103,104
Smith 5,7,8,10,19,20,25,26,30,32,33,
35,43,44,48,52,60,64,65,68,69,70,
73,76,77,78,79,80,82,85,87,90,91,
95,100,101,103,104
Sparkman 6,8,13,23,30,31,45,46,48,49,
62,67,68,75,78,79,92,101
Sparling 31
Speight/Spight 4,5,6,7,10,11,15,16,18,
19,21,25,27,29,30,34,35,38,40,44,
45,46,47,52,53,54,56,57,58,61,64,
66,67,69,70,71,72,73,75,76,77,79,
81,82,85,88,89,90,91,95,96,97,98,
99,100,103,104
Spivey 2,7,11,12,13,16,17,19,21,27,29,
30,31,32,33,34,36,39,49,51,52,59,
72,73,74,76,78,79,80,81,89,92,93,
94,96,98,102
Stallings 4,7,11,13,14,17,20,21,26,27,
29,31,34,40,42,43,44,47,48,52,53,
58,59,60,61,63,65,65,68,69,70,74,
75,78,80,81,84,88,89,90,91,93,95,
96,97,98,100,103
Stott 31,47
Stroud 86
Sumner 4,5,6,7,8,10,12,15,16,17,18,19,
21,22,23,24,26,27,29,33,34,35,36,
37,38,39,40,41,42,43,44,45,46,47,
48,49,51,53,54,55,57,58,59,60,61,
63,64,65,66,67,68,69,70,71,72,73,
74,75,76,77,78,79,81,82,84,89,90,
91,92,95,97,98,99,101,102,103,104
Taylor 9,12,14,16,19,23,25,26,28,45,
48,56,60,63,65,66,72,77,78,79,89,
102,104
Thomas 6,13,27,30,80,95
Thorburn 31
Travis 16,70
Trevathan 80
Trotman 3,4,5,7,8,10,11,12,14,15,16,
17,19,20,21,22,24,27,28,29,31,32,
34,40,41,42,43,47,52,53,55,59,62,
63,65,66,68,69,71,72,75,77,80,82,
84,85,88,89,90,91,92,93,94,95,96,
99,104
Tugwell 72,82
Turner 51,62,89
Twine 85
Umfleet 28,46
Vallentine/Vollentine/Volentine/Volintine
11,46,52,62,67,69,71,74,76,77,
78,79,89,91,94

Vann/Van 3,8,10,12,13,19,20,
    21,23,29,30,32,36,40,45,
    46,47,53,54,58,60,61,64,
    66,69,70,73,75,76,80,81,
    82,84,91,95,100,101
Varden 32
Walker 48
Wallis/Wallus 23,49,50,80,96,
    99,101
Walters 5,9,10,14,22,26,29,35,
    37,40,41,45,47,54,57,60,
    61,62,64,68,71,75,81,95,
    96,97,101,104
Walton 1,3,5,7,9,10,11,12,13,
    14,15,18,21,23,24,25,28,
    29,33,34,35,39,40,41,42,
    43,44,47,51,52,53,54,59,
    60,63,65,68,69,70,73,74,
    76,78,81,84,85,86,87,88,
    90,91,95,96,98,100,104
Ward 39
Warren 13,19,24,29,32,40,44,
    46,48,52,53,56,65,70,75,
    83,91,95,100,101
Washington 76
Watson 14,23,24,28,48,103
Weatherly 14,35,46
Weaver 97
Webb 19,20,25,26,30,32,41
White 2,16,27,31,42,49,72,74,
    76,81,92,100
Wiggins 11,21,34
Wilder 9
Wilkinson/Wilkenson 15,17,20,
    25,28,29,39
Willey/Willy 12,40,48,55,57,
    64,65,67,69,70,75,79,82,
    91,94,100
Williams 5,8,10,11,13,14,18,
    19,20,26,30,31,32,35,44,
    50,53,55,56,57,60,62,63,
    64,65,67,68,69,70,74,75,
    77,82,83,88,90,93,94,95,
    97,100,102,104
Wills 36,39,66,69,91,100
Winborn 101
Wood 27
Wright 1,65
Wynns 69,70,72,81
Young 36

www.ingramcontent.com/pod-product-compliance
Lightning Source LLC
Chambersburg PA
CBHW020058020526
44112CB00031B/283